Economic Analysis

Economic
Analysis

C. E. FERGUSON
Professor of Economics

and

S. CHARLES MAURICE
Assistant Professor of Economics

Both of Texas A&M University

1970 **RICHARD D. IRWIN, INC.**
Homewood, Illinois
IRWIN-DORSEY LIMITED
Georgetown, Ontario

Library of Congress Catalog Card No. 71–105533
Printed in the United States of America

Preface

This textbook is concerned with the microeconomic theory of value and distribution. In this respect it does not differ from most available intermediate textbooks in price theory. To create a market or to encroach upon the existing one, however, the product must be differentiated and, for any given level of difficulty, improved. We hope we have done this.

Since the senior author of this book has written another Irwin text, *Microeconomic Theory*, it seems appropriate for us to detail the ways in which the two books differ. To do so also furnishes a fair description of the level and emphasis of *Economic Analysis*. First there are some visually apparent differences. *Microeconomic Theory* is longer, contains mathematical footnotes and extensive journal references, and it contains the Appendix for graduate students. Second, as implied by its greater length, *Microeconomic Theory* contains discussions of some theories or aspects of theories that are not included in *Economic Analysis;* as examples, General Equilibrium, Welfare Economics, and Linear Programming. One of the chief objects of *Economic Analysis* is to present basic theory that can readily be covered in a one-semester course while still giving the student time for intense practice in analysis. In short, *Economic Analysis* is directed toward the professor who prefers to concentrate upon fundamentals or who must use all of his available time in doing so.

The final basic difference is the most critical one, and it is the characteristic that we hope differentiates our product from all others. *Microeconomic Theory* is aptly titled because it is concentrated exclusively upon theory; economic analysis enters only in the questions at the end of the chapters and in Professor Machlup's admirable Appendix. We hope *Economic Analysis* is also aptly titled. Economic theory is discussed and explained; but the emphasis is placed on using this theory to analyze prototypes of real-world situations. This emphasis is maintained throughout and is highlighted at the end of each chapter.

Many people have contributed substantially to the final product before you. They are too numerous to list. What is good in the book may well be attributable to them; unfortunately, what is bad must be attributed to us.

College Station, Texas   C. E. F. and S. C. M.
February, 1970

Contents

vii

Effects for a Normal Good. Inferior Goods. Giffen's Paradox. Alternative Approach. Conclusion. Analytical Exercise.

5. Theory of Production   101

Introduction. Production Functions: *Fixed and Variable Inputs, the Short and Long Runs. Fixed or Variable Proportions.* Production with One Variable Input: *Total Output or Product. Average and Marginal Products. Law of Diminishing Marginal Physical Returns. Three Stages of Production.* Production with Two Variable Inputs: *Product Curves for Different Amounts of Fixed Input. Production Isoquants. Diminishing Marginal Rate of Technical Substitution. Economic Region of Production.* Optimal Combination of Resources: *Input Prices and Isocosts. Production of a Given Output at Minimum Cost.* Conclusion. Analytical Exercise.

6. Theory of Cost   127

Introduction: *Social Cost of Production. Private Cost of Production.* Planning Horizon: *Beginning the Firm. Shape of Long-Run Total Cost Curves. Long-Run Average and Long-Run Marginal Costs. Economies of Scale. Diseconomies of Scale. Summary.* Theory of Cost in the Short Run: *Short-Run Total Cost. Average and Marginal Costs.* Relations between Short- and Long-Run Average and Marginal Costs. Conclusion. Analytical Exercise.

7. Theory of Price in Perfectly Competitive Markets   158

Introduction: *Free Markets. Profit Maximization.* Perfect Competition: *Small Size, Large Numbers. Homogeneous Product. Free Mobility of Resources. Perfect Knowledge. Conclusion.* Planning the Firm: *Demand of a Firm in Perfect Competition. Total Revenue, Total Cost, and Profit. Alternative Approach to Long-Run Planning. Zero and Negative Profit Solutions.* Short-Run Equilibrium of a Firm: *Short-Run Profit Maximization. Profit, Loss, and the Firm's Short-Run Supply Curve. Short-Run Industry Supply Curve. Summary of the Short Run.* Long-Run Equilibrium in a Perfectly Competitive Market: *Long-Run Adjustment of an Established Firm. Long-Run Adjustment of the Industry. Long-Run Equilibrium in a Perfectly Competitive Firm.* Constant and Increasing Cost Industries: *Constant Cost Industries. Increasing Cost Industries.* Conclusion. Analytical Exercise.

8. Theory of Price under Pure Monopoly   188

Introduction. Demand and Marginal Revenue under Monopoly: *Calculation of Marginal Revenue. Graphical Derivation of Marginal Revenue from Linear Demand. Graphical Derivation of MR when Demand Is Nonlinear. Marginal Revenue, Demand, and Elasticity.* Short-Run Equilibrium under Monopoly: *Cost under Monopoly. Short-Run Equilibrium.* Long-Run

chapter 1

Scope and Methodology of Economics

1.1 SCOPE OF ECONOMICS

Over the past hundred years or more, economics has become a well-defined member of the social sciences. While several disciplines are concerned with social action dominated by a means-end relation, the particular relation unique to economics can be stated with some precision. As most *Principles* texts avow, economics is a study of the proper method of allocating scarce physical and human means (resources) among competing ends—an allocation that achieves some stipulated *optimizing* or *maximizing* objective. The area of study is circumscribed by the stipulation that the means consist of human, natural, and manmade resources and that the ends be economic goods or economic objectives.

1.1.a—Ends and Goals

It is helpful to distinguish ends and goals. The combined process of production and exchange is one in which a collection of resources distributed among individuals is transformed into a collection of goods, which are distributed among those responsible for production. The two distributions are, of course, not necessarily the same. Let us define economic goods themselves as "ends." Then the word "goal" may be used to describe the fundamental motivations of the various economic agents. For example, economists frequently assume that consumers attempt to maximize satisfaction and that entrepreneurs attempt to maximize profit. So defined, the goals of economic agents provide the economist with a frame of reference that permits systematic analysis of individual economic behavior. In general, every economic agent competes with every other agent in the sense that each tries to obtain "as much" as possible,

1

and total possibilities are limited by the resource base. But in a broader view, it is the mutual cooperation of agents with conflicting goals that is ultimately responsible for the production of economic goods and services.

When the principles of microeconomic behavior have been discovered, our attention can be focused on a macroeconomic problem that has beset economics since its inception as a science. Indeed, one might say it was the attempt to resolve this problem that caused economics to become a science. The problem may be stated as a question: Will the independent maximizing behavior of each economic agent eventually result in a social organization that, in a *normative* sense, maximizes the well-being of society as a whole? Adam Smith suggested an answer to this when he presented his doctrine of the "invisible hand." According to Smith, each individual, bent on pursuing his own best interest, is inevitably led, as if by an unseen hand, to pursue a course of action that benefits society as a whole. This is a happy and optimistic doctrine. It has, however, been increasingly questioned as the social and industrial milieu has undergone great change. If all economic agents are atomistic in size relative to the total economic society, either Smith's "invisible hand" or an IBM machine will seek out an optimal organization of economic activity. But if all agents are not atomistic, one must ask if this optimum will be reached. Or will the very large agents "play" an economic game in which they achieve gains at the expense of counterbalancing losses on the part of smaller units? The answers to these questions are not at all clear. But they are very important, both from the standpoint of theory and from that of policy. Some tentative answers are suggested in the concluding chapter of this book.

1.1.b—Norms and Policy

The discussion of ends and goals, especially in the last paragraph above, leads to a further discussion of *welfare norms* and economic policy (*positive* economics). Economists, in their role as economists, cannot establish normative objectives for a society. For example, an economist cannot say that free public education is desirable or that some minimum level of income should be received by each family unit. Of course, as a citizen he can vote for school bond issues and for legislators who favor income redistribution; but an economist *as an economist* cannot determine social goals.

The business of an economist is a positive, not a normative, one. That is, given a social objective, the economist can analyze the problem and suggest the most efficient means by which to attain the desired end. This book is accordingly devoted to the positive aspects of economic analysis, not to the normative decisions that a society must make.

1.1.c—Relation of Economics to Other Social Disciplines[1]

Broadly conceived, social science is the study of the totality of man's social behavior. However, this totality is so extensive in scope that no individual can confidently hope to gain knowledge of every aspect of social behavior. As Adam Smith long ago pointed out, the division of labor tends to augment total physical production; similarly, the division of academic labor tends to enhance our total understanding of man's social action. But the division of a social totality into compartments is not so easily accomplished as the division of jobs along an assembly line; nor do the division lines tend to stay put once they are drawn. The various areas of study are interrelated, and it is only by somewhat arbitrary decisions that the subject matter of social science is divided among the various specialties.

In this light, Spengler says that "since the several segments of social studies are mutually interrelated, a specialist's mastery of the behavior-forms allotted to his social science is governed by his understanding of related behavior-forms treated by other social sciences."[2] Yet this understanding is, to some extent, made more difficult by the very process of specialization itself. In the first place, "important modes of collective behavior have escaped significant analysis because no unseen hand has been present to coordinate the activities of diverse specialists and insure analysis of *all* significant forms of interpersonal behavior." Second, "developments within fields of specialization frequently have weakened and sometimes have nearly destroyed interfield communication. The comparatively homogeneous tongue of what passed for social science in the past seemingly has given place to a Babel of symbol-ridden jargons."[3]

Accordingly, to promote a wider general understanding of social behavior, there is need for interdisciplinary cooperation in the study of certain problems that transcend any one special field and, furthermore, for the development of a comparatively uniform language base. Through foundation grants and certain university-sponsored interdisciplinary projects, some advances have been made in the direction of greater cooperation among specialists. This, in turn, has been facilitated by the recent introduction of a new language that permits specialists to communicate with one another with precision and clarity. Specifically, the utilization

---

[1] For a thorough discussion, see J. J. Spengler, "Generalists versus Specialists in Social Science: An Economist's View," *American Political Science Review*, Vol. XLIV (1950), pp. 358–79.

[2] *Ibid.*, p. 359.

[3] *Ibid.*, p. 360.

of mathematics, its language and its logic, has stimulated, perhaps more than ever before, interdisciplinary understanding and cooperation.[4]

1.2 METHODOLOGY

A person observing the real world of economic phenomena is confronted with a mass of data that is, at least superficially, meaningless. To discover order in this morass of facts and to arrange them in a meaningful way, it is necessary to develop theories to explain various aspects of human behavior, and thus to explain the otherwise meaningless data. By abstracting from the real world, it is possible to achieve a level of simplicity at which human action may be analyzed. But in the process of abstraction, the analyst must be careful to preserve the essential features of the real world problem with which he is concerned. That is to say, simplification is necessary; but at the same time a theory must capture the essence of the fundamental economic problem it is designed to solve.

1.2.a—Model Analysis

Since this text is entirely concerned with economic models and their use in analyzing real world economic problems, it is important to give attention to the use of model analysis in general before undertaking a study of specific economic models. It is convenient to do this schematically with the aid of the diagram in Figure 1.2.1.[5]

The real world usually serves, at least tentatively, as the starting point. A particular problem, or merely a desire to understand, motivates one to move from the complicated world of reality into the domain of logical simplicity. By means of theoretical abstraction, one reduces the complexities of the real world to manageable proportions. The result is a logical model presumably suited to explain the phenomena observed. By logical argument (i.e., deduction) one then arrives at logical or model conclusions. However, these must be transformed, by means of theoretical interpretation, into conclusions about the real world.

Let us summarize to this point. The economist, having begun with a portion of the real world, proceeds, through the use of completely theoretical means, to arrive at conclusions about the real world. His first step entails abstraction from the real world into a simplified logical model. His second step requires the use of logical argument to arrive at

---

[4] As examples, see Paul Lazerfeld (ed.), *Mathematical Thinking in the Social Sciences* (Glencoe: Free Press, 1954); and Herbert Simon, *Mathematical Models of Man* (New York: John Wiley & Sons, Inc., 1957).

[5] Adapted from a diagram appearing in C. H. Coombs, Howard Raiffa, and R. M. Thrall (eds.), "Mathematical Models and Measurement Theory," *Decision Processes* (New York: John Wiley & Sons, Inc., 1954), p. 22.

an abstract conclusion. His final step consists of a return to the real world by means of an interpretation that yields conclusions in terms of the concrete, sensible world of physical reality.

Another approach provides a different method of achieving the same goal. Let us call it the "statistical method" to distinguish it from the "deductive method" previously discussed. Again starting from the real world, we may, by means of experimental abstraction, arrive at an experimental design. That is, we may, by a process of simplification, design a statistical model that is useful in analyzing the real world. In this instance, however, we obtain observations by experimentation, rather than

FIGURE 1.2.1

Model Analysis

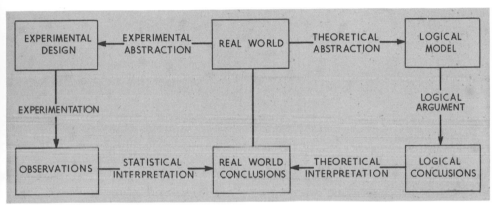

theorems by logical deduction. These observations, given proper statistical interpretation, yield conclusions concerning the real world.

Although there is some disagreement over the relative merit of the two methods, the tenor of present thinking is that they are complementary. That is to say, deductive and statistical methods are mutually reinforcing, rather than completely alternative, instruments of analysis. However, since professional opinion regarding methodology is not uniform, this chapter contains a brief discussion of three positions commonly held.[6]

1.2.b—Extreme Apriorism

One group embraces theorists who feel that *only* the right-hand portion of our diagram is applicable. This group, prominent since the time of

---

[6] The remainder of this section is based on Fritz Machlup, "The Problem of Verification in Economics," *Southern Economic Journal*, Vol. XXII (1955), pp. 1–21.

John Stuart Mill, has such modern advocates as Mises,[7] Robbins,[8] and Knight,[9] all of whom presumably believe that economic theory is not amenable to verification or refutation on purely empirical grounds. Instead, they think that "economic science is a system of a priori truths, a product of pure reason . . . , a system of pure deduction from a series of postulates. . . ."[10]

One of the clearest explanations of the position held by these writers is found in Mises' definition of a praxeologist, or what Machlup calls an extreme apriorist. According to Mises, a praxeologist is one who believes (a) that the fundamental premises and axioms of economics are absolutely true; (b) that the theorems and conclusions deduced from these axioms by the laws of logic are, therefore, absolutely true; (c) that, consequently, there is no need for empirical testing of either the axioms or the theorems; and (d) that the deduced theorems could not be tested, even if it were desirable to do so. Thus the extreme apriorist relies upon introspection and logic to develop the whole body of economic principles.

1.2.c—Ultraempiricism

At the opposite extreme is a group, led by T. W. Hutchinson,[11] whose members Machlup calls ultraempiricists. Fundamentally, these economists "refuse to recognize the legitimacy of employing at any level of analysis propositions not independently verifiable."[12] Instead of beginning with a system of axioms, the ultraempiricists presumably prefer to start with a body of what they call facts. Starting with facts of course entails sacrificing the very simplicity that is sought. One's approach immediately involves all the complexities of the real world; and he is deprived of the use of the single tool—model analysis—that enables him to escape the morass of meaningless facts and to reach conclusions of some generality.

1.2.d—Logical Positivism

The final methodological position is labeled "logical positivism." It has been clearly stated by Bridgman[13] and various "operational philos-

---

[7] Ludwig von Mises, *Human Action* (New Haven, Conn.: Yale University Press, 1959).

[8] Lionel Robbins, *An Essay on the Nature and Significance of Economic Science* (2d ed.; London: Macmillan & Co., Ltd., 1935).

[9] Frank H. Knight, "The Limitations of Scientific Method in Economics," in R. G. Tugwell (ed.), *The Trend of Economics* (New York: Crofts, 1930). Reprinted in *The Ethics of Competition* (New York: Harper, 1935).

[10] Machlup, *op. cit.*, p. 5.

[11] T. W. Hutchinson, *The Significance and Basic Postulates of Economic Theory* (London: Macmillan & Co., Ltd., 1938).

[12] Machlup, *op. cit.*, p. 7.

[13] P. W. Bridgman, *The Logic of Modern Physics* (New York: The Macmillan Co., 1927).

ophers,"[14] and it finds wide acceptance among modern economists.[15] The positive economists agree that the basic axioms or assumptions of theory are not subject to independent empirical verification. At the same time, they consider it both possible and desirable to test the deduced hypotheses, and thereby to test indirectly the system of axioms underlying economic theory.

In sum, the apriorists believe that no aspect of economic theory is susceptible of empirical test, whereas the empiricists think that every facet of theory can and must be proved empirically at each step in a chain of analysis. The positive economists take a middle position. They assert that the conclusions (or theorems) of a model should be tested. If these conclusions are found to be in sufficiently close correspondence with reality, the basic assumptions underlying the model are deemed acceptable. Accordingly, positive economics puts primary emphasis upon the predictive powers of a model: if the predictions derived from one model prove "better" than the corresponding predictions drawn from another model, the former is tentatively selected as preferable. If subsequently a theory is advanced that explains more of the relevant facts or, in a probabilistic sense, conforms more closely to reality, this new theory is deemed superior to the one previously accepted. In every case the test is a pragmatic one: that theory is preferred which best explains the observable phenomena of economic life.

1.3 EQUILIBRIUM AND COMPARATIVE STATICS

Methodologically, we side with the logical positivists. Theory comes first, and then an empirical or statistical investigation to determine whether the results of that theory correspond to the real world. In this course, however, we are concerned only with economic theory and economic analysis—the right-hand side of Figure 1.2.1. Empirical testing is left to the specialized field called econometrics.

To reemphasize, this course is concerned first with developing well-established microeconomic theories and second with analyzing real world problems by means of these theories. To elucidate more, and perhaps to give some warning to the student, we quote what Donald Dewey said of one of his own books, but which applies equally well to this one: "this book employs the method of austere, sustained, and, I regret, largely humorless abstraction that has served economics so well in the past. Given the excruciating complexity of so many of the problems . . . , I

---

[14] See, for example, Anatol Rapoport, *Operational Philosophy* (New York: Harper, 1954).

[15] For example, P. A. Samuelson, *Foundations of Economic Analysis* (Cambridge, Mass.: Harvard University Press, 1947); Milton Friedman, "The Methodology of Positive Economics," *Essays in Positive Economics* (Chicago: University of Chicago Press, 1953), pp. 3–43; and Machlup, *op. cit.*

cannot see that any other method will allow us to cut through to first principles and deal with these problems according to their importance. Either we simplify drastically . . . , or we wander forever in the wilderness. . . ."[16]

1.3.a—Equilibrium

Most of economic theory can conveniently be divided into "equilibrium statics," "comparative statics," and "equilibrium dynamics." This text concerns only the first two, which contain by far the larger part of economic theory. The word "statics" denotes that our attention is focused on one moment in time and, in particular, that we do not allow time to enter our analysis in such a way as to affect the results. Thus we cannot analyze speculation in commodity markets, nor can we decide when to cut a tree or to stop maturing wine; but we can analyze a very wide variety of economic problems.

"Equilibrium" means balance; more specific to our needs, it means *balancing of forces.* This is something that it will be well to remember, because throughout the rest of the book we determine equilibrium by balancing opposing forces. For example, in the theory of consumer behavior we balance what a consumer would *like* to do with what he is *able* to do with his limited money income. In the theory of the firm, we balance the demand for a producer's output with the technical and market forces that determine supply.

These examples could be multiplied many times over. In the remainder of this chapter we simply explain the meaning of equilibrium and comparative statics by means of the simplest and most important model in economic theory—the model of demand and supply. This model is analyzed in detail in Chapter 2; and most of the rest of the book is concerned with the determinants of demand and supply. At present, but not subsequently, we assume that the student has a rudimentary familiarity with the demand-supply model.

Consider Figure 1.3.1. The negatively sloped DD' curve shows, let us say, the weekly demand for apples in a certain city. The positively sloped SS' curve shows the supply. The negative and positive slopes simply indicate that buyers are willing to take more and sellers to offer less the lower is price. Our object is to prove that point E (with price $O\bar{P}$ and quantity $O\bar{Q}$) is the market equilibrium, the point where the two opposing forces are in balance. To get the proof, we show that at any price other than $O\bar{P}$, there will be forces that push the price in the direction of $O\bar{P}$.

---

[16] Donald J. Dewey, *Modern Capital Theory* (New York: Columbia University Press, 1965), p. vii.

FIGURE 1.3.1

Demand and Supply

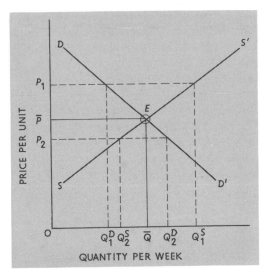

QUANTITY PER WEEK

First, suppose price is *anywhere* above $O\bar{P}$, say OP_1. At this price grocers wish to sell OQ_1^s apples per week. They place their orders and stock their shelves accordingly. But at the price OP_1, buyers are only willing to purchase OQ_1^D apples per week. As a result, sellers accumulate costly and unwanted inventories of apples. The grocers have a clear incentive to reduce the price of apples so as to get rid of their undesired inventories.

Further, this is not only true of the price OP_1 but of *any* price above $O\bar{P}$. At any price above $O\bar{P}$, the quantity sellers wish to offer exceeds the quantity buyers are willing to purchase. Thus at any point above $O\bar{P}$, price must be reduced in the direction of $O\bar{P}$ to clear out undesired accumulations of stock.

Let us now look at the other side. When price is "too low," buyers take the initiative. Suppose price is anywhere below $O\bar{P}$, say OP_2. Buyers wish to purchase OQ_2^D apples per week; but at this price grocers are only willing to supply OQ_2^s per week. All who wish to buy apples at the price OP_2 cannot do so. Some of the dissatisfied buyers therefore bid slightly more for apples in the hope of getting them away from others. In part they are successful because some people are only willing to buy apples at the price OP_2 or less. But others are willing to pay more than OP_2; and until the price is bid up to $O\bar{P}$, there will be dissatisfied buyers in the market who will offer more for apples.

Here we have two opposing forces: buyers who are willing to purchase larger quantities at lower prices, and sellers who are only willing to offer larger quantities at higher prices. The two forces are in balance at E, the point of equilibrium where both buyers and sellers are satisfied.

The above account may seem to be somewhat unrealistic in that consumers seldom make price bids (except in the stock market). Prices are set by sellers and are not changed *immediately* to establish an equilibrium. However, sellers are sensitive to sales and will not hesitate to raise price in order to ration existing quantities. If they do not, a second market—called a black market—will develop; and in this market, consumers truly make price bids.

1.3.b—Comparative Statics

When our equilibrium position is determined, as in Figure 1.3.1, we can say that the price of apples will be $O\bar{P}$ and that $O\bar{Q}$ apples will be sold per week. This analysis is based upon the *given* demand and supply curves. But demand and/or supply can change; and we should like to be able to say what will happen to equilibrium price and quantity. This is the object of comparative statics.

Briefly, comparative statics involves the comparison of two static equilibria for the purpose of determining what happens to the variables when there is a shift from one equilibrium to another. Now consider Figure 1.3.2. D_1D_1' and SS' are again the demand and supply of apples per week in a certain city. Our equilibrium analysis shows us that market price is OP_1 and quantity demanded and supplied is OQ_1.

FIGURE 1.3.2

Comparative Statics

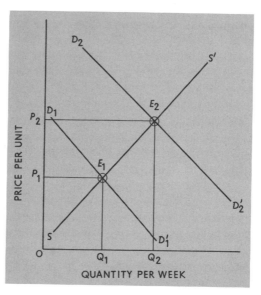

The demand for apples depends upon several things, especially taste, money income, and the prices of related commodities such as oranges. Let us suppose there is a severe freeze in Florida that kills a large portion of the orange crop. As a result the *rationing price*[17] of oranges goes up, and the demand for apples increases from D_1D_1' to D_2D_2'. Our equilibrium moves from E_1 to E_2; price rises from OP_1 to OP_2, and quantity increases from OQ_1 to OQ_2.

This is the method of comparative statics. We postulate a basic change in one of the functional relations in the model and then inquire how this affects the equilibrium values of the variables. From this example we can say that an increase in demand, supply remaining constant, will cause an increase in both equilibrium price and quantity.

1.4   EQUILIBRIUM: PARTIAL AND GENERAL

As we have seen, our study of microeconomic theory is to be the analysis of equilibrium and the comparative static analysis of changes between equilibria. But even then there are two fundamental approaches to static and comparative static analysis—called the "general equilibrium method" and the "partial equilibrium method." Curiously enough, both methods had their basic development at about the same time, in the late 19th century.

There is no doubt that all facets of an economy are interrelated. If pressed far enough, the price of beef depends not only on the price of pork but upon the prices of buttons, color television sets, and tickets to the Masters golf tournament. The wages of unskilled labor depend not only on the wages of semiskilled labor but on the charges of neurosurgeons as well. Everything is related to everything else; and a *complete* treatment of economic theory must take this into account. This was the approach of Walras in his pathbreaking *Elements of Pure Economics*. He analyzed—mathematically, to be sure—the *general equilibrium* of the entire economic system when all interdependencies are recognized.

The resulting system of equations, theorems, and proofs—and it should be emphasized that general equilibrium theory is *essentially* mathematical —is a delight to mathematicians and mathematical economists alike. Indeed, the work of John von Neumann and others on general equilibrium theory has contributed significantly to the development of pure mathematics.

But if the equilibrium system of general equilibrium economics is beautiful, the comparative static system is indescribably messy. Except for very restrictive and specialized cases, one simply cannot say what will

---

[17] If this term is not obvious, it is explained in Chapter 2.

happen when there is some change in the economy. Yet surely economists and intelligent laymen must be able to do so. What will happen if minimum prices are set for agricultural products or labor? when an excise tax is imposed on beer, color television sets, and perfume? when there is a freeze in Florida?

There are thousands of questions of this type that are important both to individuals and to governments; and they can be given answers that are *approximately* correct. To get these comparative static answers we must sacrifice the beauty of general equilibrium models for the practicality of partial equilibrium models.

The development of partial equilibrium theory is the most significant contribution Marshall made in his *Principles of Economics*. Everything depends upon everything else; but most things depend in an essential way upon only a *few other things*. Basically, Marshall suggested that we ignore the general interdependence of everything and concentrate only upon the *close interdependence* of a few variables.

The demand for beef obviously depends upon the prices of other meats and fowl. On the other hand, as a first approximation we can ignore the price of automobiles, airplane fares, and so forth. According to Marshall and his many followers, we can temporarily hold *other things constant*—impound them in a *ceteris paribus* assumption, in the jargon of economics—and concentrate our attention on a few closely related variables.

Thus in the previous section we were able to say that when the supply of oranges decreased and the price of oranges increased, the demand for apples and the price and quantity of apples sold increased. We could not have done this—and certainly we could not have done it graphically—if we had to consider the remote and tedious relations that run through thousands of markets.

In this text—as, for that matter, in all intermediate theory texts—we adopt the approach of Marshall. We assume that *most*, but not *all*, of the economic interrelations can be ignored. We analyze our problems and realize that our answers are first approximations. But now return to Figure 1.2.1 We build our model on the basis of real world conditions, and then we go through purely logical analysis. Before we make any definite statements or predictions about the real world, we must go through the "interpretation" stage. Here it is necessary to realize that we have held many "other things" constant. Thus we must conclude that a decrease in the supply of oranges will *tend* to cause an increase in the price of apples. If our partial equilibrium theory is sound, as it is in the oranges-apples example, our answers—even though first approximations —will be qualitatively correct. This is about all one can demand of economic theory. Quantitative results are up to the econometricians.

1.5 ANALYTICAL EXERCISE

Consider Figure 1.5.1. First, explain the basic changes in the functional relations that give rise to the points labeled 1–9. Second, explain the comparative static shifts in price and quantity that take place in each of the nine cases. In the graph, DD' and SS' are the initial demand and supply curves. D_1D_1' and S_1S_1' indicate increases in demand and supply respectively, while D_2D_2' and S_2S_2' reflect decreases.

FIGURE 1.5.1

Shifts in Demand and Supply

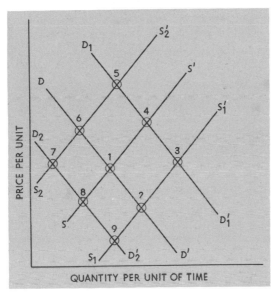

chapter 2

Demand and Supply

2.1 INTRODUCTION

In Chapter 1 we mentioned that economics is concerned with the problem of scarcity. Because goods are scarce, they have a price. Therefore, one of the fundamental tasks of economics is to analyze the factors that determine the prices and purchases of all commodities. The more important determinants are usually separated into two categories: those affecting the demand for a good and those affecting supply. The purpose of this chapter is to explain what demand and supply are and to show how they determine price and quantity in the market.

Thomas Carlyle, a Scottish historian of some repute, was fond of criticizing economists. It was he who referred to Malthus and Ricardo as the "respectable professors of the Dismal Science," and thereby gave economics a name it has never quite overcome—possibly, as Galbraith said, because it has never quite deserved to. But more to the point, Carlyle said that "it is easy to train an economist; teach a parrot to say Demand and Supply." This is another epigram that has survived because it is humorous and contains a large measure of truth.

To be sure, one cannot simply say "demand and supply" and solve all economic problems, but a fundamental understanding of this simple economic model enables one to analyze *rationally* many, if not all, real world problems. It is to this that we now direct our attention.

2.2 MARKET DEMAND SCHEDULES

Suppose a very large group of people gather in a market to buy their week's supply of some commodity, say X. Suppose also that an auctioneer in the market has everyone turn in a list indicating the amount of X he is willing and able to purchase that day at each price, $1, $2, $3, $4, $5, $6, and so forth. When the auctioneer adds up the amounts that each person is willing and able to buy at each of the prices, he obtains the figures shown in Table 2.2.1. The table shows a list of prices and of quantities that consumers are willing and able to buy per period of time at each price in the list. This list of quantities and prices is called a *demand schedule.*

As you would probably expect, consumers are willing to buy more at lower prices. This result follows from the *law of demand.* Since a considerable portion of Chapters 3 and 4 are devoted to analyzing the law of demand, we now assume that the following is correct: people are willing and able to buy more at lower prices than at higher prices. If the student doubts this assumption, he should try to think of a specific item he would buy in larger amount the greater its price.

TABLE 2.2.1
Market Demand Schedule

Quantity Demanded (Units of x)	Price per Unit (Dollars)
2,000	$6
3,000	5
4,000	4
5,000	3
5,500	2
6,000	1

Principles: A demand schedule is a list of prices and of the corresponding quantities that consumers are willing and able to buy at each price in the list per unit of time. The market demand schedule is the sum of the quantities that all individual consumers in the market demand at each price. Consumers are willing and able to buy more of an item the lower its price. That is, *quantity demanded varies inversely with price.*

2.2.a—Graphing Demand Schedules

Quite often it is more convenient to work with the graph of a demand schedule, called a *demand curve*, rather than with the schedule itself. Figure 2.2.1 is the graph of the schedule in Table 2.2.1. Each price-quantity combination ($6–2,000, $5–3,000, and so on) is plotted; then the six points are connected by the curve labeled DD'. This curve indicates the quantity of X consumers are willing and able to buy per unit of time at *every* price from $6 to $1. Since consumers demand more at lower prices, the curve slopes downward.

Note that when deriving a demand curve from a set of price-quantity data given by a demand schedule, one assumes that price and quantity

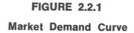

FIGURE 2.2.1

Market Demand Curve

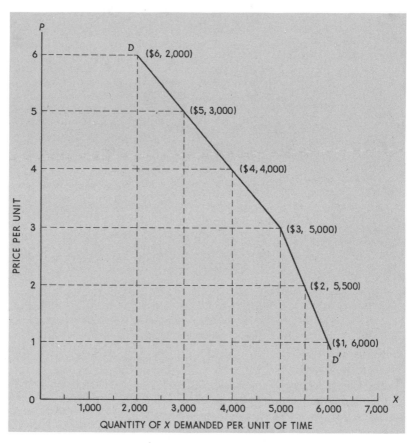

are infinitely divisible. Price can be *any* number between $6 and $1; quantity demanded can also be any number. This assumption is not too unrealistic when we consider that the quantity is *per unit of time*. In any case the sacrifice in realism is more than counterbalanced by the gain in analytical convenience.

2.2.b—Factors Influencing Demand

Why is the demand schedule in Table 2.2.1 what it is? That is, why do consumers demand 2,000 units rather than 3,000 units at $6 per unit? Or why do they not demand more at every price in the list? Let us consider the factors that could, in fact, cause people to be willing and able to purchase either more or less at each price.

First, the consumers' incomes can change, and this affects demand. For some commodities an increase in income causes consumers to demand more of the good at each price; for others an increase causes them to demand less. Since the effect of income on demand is analyzed in Chapter 4, we do not discuss it here. We need only note that when income changes, demand changes.

Second, changes in consumers' tastes can change demand. If people read that scientists have discovered that eating rutabagas makes women more beautiful, women consumers would probably be willing and able to buy more rutabagas than before at the prevailing price. In other words, their *tastes* change and affect the demand for rutabagas.

Third, the prices of *other* goods affect the demand for a given good. More specifically, when the price of a closely related good changes, the demand for the good in question is affected. For example, suppose both beef and pork sell for $1 per pound; now let the price of beef fall to $.50 a pound. Consumers will buy less pork at $1 than they did before the price of beef fell.

Finally, people's expectations affect demand. When people think the price of a good is going to rise, they have an incentive to increase their rates of purchase before price rises. On the other hand, expecting price to fall causes some purchases to be postponed.

Therefore, when economists draw up a demand curve such as that in Figure 2.2.1, they do so under the assumption that *other things remain the same.* The other things are (1) consumers' incomes (and the income distribution among consumers), (2) tastes, (3) the prices of other goods, and (4) expectations. It is not that economists think price is the sole determinant of the quantity of a good consumers demand. They realize many other things affect quantity, but they are interested in *isolating* the effect of price changes.[1]

2.2.c—Changes in Demand

When price falls (rises) and consumers purchase more (less) of a good, other things remaining the same, we say that *quantity demanded* increases (decreases). We do not say that *demand* increases or decreases when price changes. Demand increases or decreases only when one or more of the factors held constant in deriving demand change. For example if consumers' incomes change, causing them to demand more of a good at each price than they previously did, the demand for that good in-

---

[1] At times economists also examine the effect upon quantity demanded of changes in one of the "other things," for example income or prices of other goods. We will see examples of this in Chapter 4. This is a problem in comparative statics, as discussed in Chapter 1.

creases. Demand decreases if the income change causes them to demand less than before at each price.

Figure 2.2.2 illustrates changes in demand. The demand curve for X is at first D_0D_0'; at the price Op, consumers buy Ox_0 units per period of time. Tastes change and demand decreases (shifts to the left) to D_1D_1'. Now consumers buy only Ox_1 units per period at the price Op. In fact it is easy to see that at every price consumers buy less X after the shift than before. Now perhaps the price of some closely related good changes,

FIGURE 2.2.2

Shifts in Demand

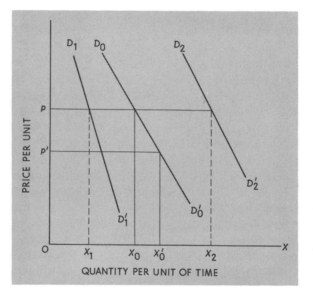

causing demand to increase (shift to the right) to D_2D_2'. At Op consumers purchase Ox_2 units per period; and at every other relevant price they buy more than before. If, however, demand is $D_0D'_0$ and price falls from Op to Op', other things remaining the same, we say that *quantity demanded* changes from Ox_0 to Ox_0'. These relations may be summarized as follows:

Relations: When price falls (rises), other things remaining the same, quantity demanded rises (falls). When something held constant in deriving the demand curve changes, demand increases or decreases. An increase in demand indicates consumers are willing and able to buy more at each price in the list. A decrease in demand indicates they are willing and able to buy less at each price. Thus changes in demand are represented by shifts in the demand curve; changes in quantity demanded are shown by movements along the original demand curve.

2.3. DEMAND ELASTICITY

We have noted without full explanation that quantity demanded varies inversely with price along a demand curve. Frequently economists are interested not only in the direction in which quantity varies when price changes but also in the *responsiveness* of quantity demanded to changes in price. The measure of responsiveness along a given demand curve is called the *elasticity of demand.*

2.3.a—Responsiveness of Quantity Demanded to Price

For some products, a small change in price over a certain range of the demand curve results in a significant change in quantity demanded. In this case, quantity demanded is very responsive to changes in price. For other products, or perhaps for the same product over a different range of the demand curve, a relatively large change in price leads to a correspondingly smaller change in quantity demanded. That is, quantity demanded is not particularly responsive to price changes.

Economists classify demand as *elastic* or *inelastic* on the basis of the relative responsiveness of quantity demanded to changes in price. More specifically, demand is said to be elastic if the proportional change in quantity demanded exceeds the proportional change in price, whereas it is inelastic if the proportional change in quantity demanded is less than the proportional change in price. In fact it is possible to give a precise measure to relative responsiveness or elasticity. Before turning to specifics, however, it is instructive to examine the relation between elasticity and the total expenditure on a commodity (i.e., the total revenue received by the sellers of the commodity).

2.3.b—Elasticity and Total Expenditure

The total expenditure on a commodity is product price multiplied by the quantity bought. Along a particular demand curve, quantity rises when price falls, and vice versa; thus three things can possibly happen to total expenditure when there is a change in price. First, suppose the price change "outweighs" the quantity change—that is, quantity demanded is not particularly responsive to price. Then total expenditure falls when price falls and rises when price rises. In this case, demand is inelastic. If, on the other hand, a price rise leads to a decrease in total expenditure —or a price decline to an increase in total expenditure—demand is

TABLE 2.3.1
Relations between Price Elasticity
and Total Expenditure

	Elastic Demand	*Unitary Elasticity*	*Inelastic Demand*
Price rises............	*TE* falls	No change	*TE* rises
Price falls............	*TE* rises	No change	*TE* falls

elastic. In this case quantity demanded is very responsive to price changes. Demand has *unitary elasticity* if a change in price and the corresponding quantity change cause no change in total expenditure. These relations are summarized in Table 2.3.1.

We should now emphasize that it is not accurate to say that a given demand curve is elastic or inelastic. In almost all cases, demand curves have both an inelastic and an elastic range, along with a point or range of unitary elasticity. We can only speak of demand as being elastic or inelastic over a particular range of price or quantity magnitudes.

2.3.c—Computation of Elasticity

As noted above, the elasticity of demand refers to the relative responsiveness of quantity demanded to changes in price. It is useful at times to have a specific measure of relative responsiveness rather than merely to speak of demand as being elastic or inelastic. For example, we might wish to determine, over a certain range of prices, which of two demand curves is the more elastic. For this we need a measuring device. That device is the coefficient of price elasticity (η):

$$\eta = -\%\Delta Q / \%\Delta P = -\frac{\Delta Q/Q}{\Delta P/P} = -\frac{\Delta Q}{\Delta P}\frac{P}{Q},$$

where Δ is "the change in," and P and Q denote price and quantity demanded.

Since price and quantity vary inversely, a minus sign is used in the formula to make the coefficient positive. From the formula we see that the relative responsiveness of quantity demanded to changes in price measures the ratio of the proportional change in quantity demanded relative to that of price. If η is less than one, demand is inelastic; $\%\Delta Q < \%\Delta P$. If η is greater than one, demand is elastic; $\%\Delta Q > \%\Delta P$. If $\eta = 1$, demand has unitary elasticity; $\%\Delta Q = \%\Delta P$.

The process of deriving the coefficient of elasticity between two price-quantity relations involves a simple computation; certain problems, however, are involved in selecting the proper base. As an example, let us

TABLE 2.3.2
Demand and Elasticity

Price	Quantity Demanded	Total Expenditure	Elasticity
$1.00	100,000	$100,000	ELASTIC
.50	300,000	150,000	UNITARY
.25	600,000	150,000	INELASTIC
.10	1,000,000	100,000	

consider the demand schedule given in Table 2.3.2. Suppose price falls from $1 to $0.50; quantity demanded rises from 100,000 to 300,000 and $P \times Q$ or TE rises to $150,000. By the analysis of subsection 2.3.b, demand is elastic since total expenditure increases.

Let us now compute η:

$$\eta = -\frac{\Delta Q/Q}{\Delta P/P} = -\frac{(100,000 - 300,000) \div 100,000}{(\$1 - \$0.50) \div \$1} = -\frac{-2}{1/2} = 4.$$

As expected, the coefficient is greater than one. But some caution must be exercised. ΔQ and ΔP are definitely known from Table 2.3.2; but we really do not know whether to use the value $Q = 100,000$ or $Q = 300,000$ and the value $P = \$1$ or $P = \$0.50$. Try the computation with the "other" values of P and Q:

$$\eta = -\frac{(300,000 - 100,000) \div 300,000}{(\$0.50 - \$1) \div \$0.50} = \frac{2}{3}!$$

It actually looks as though demand is inelastic, despite the fact that we know it is elastic from the total expenditure calculation.

The difficulty lies in the fact that elasticity has been computed over a wide arc of the demand curve but evaluated at a specific point. We can get a much better approximation by using the *average* values of P and Q over the arc. That is, for large changes such as this, we should compute η as

$$\eta = -\frac{Q_1 - Q_0}{Q_1 + Q_0} \div \frac{P_1 - P_0}{P_1 + P_0},$$

where subscripts 1 and 0 refer to new and to initial prices and quantities demanded. Using this formula, we obtain

$$\eta = -\frac{(100,000 - 300,000) \div (100,000 + 300,000)}{(\$1 - \$0.50) \div (\$1 + \$0.50)} = \frac{3}{2}.$$

Demand is indeed elastic when allowance is made for the very discrete or finite change in price and quantity demanded.

Exercise: Compute η for a change in price from $0.25 to $0.10.

Summary: Demand is said to be elastic, of unitary elasticity, or inelastic according to the value of η. If $\eta > 1$, demand is elastic; a given percentage change in price results in a greater percentage change in quantity demanded. Thus small price changes result in more significant changes in quantity demanded. When $\eta = 1$ demand has unit elasticity, meaning that the percentage changes in price and quantity demanded are precisely the same. Finally, if $\eta < 1$, demand is inelastic. A given percentage change in price results in a smaller percentage change in quantity demanded.

2.3.d—Graphical Computation of Elasticity

The formulas developed in Section 2.3.c are relevant for arc elasticity, the price elasticity for movements between two discrete points on a

FIGURE 2.3.1

Computation of Point Elasticity

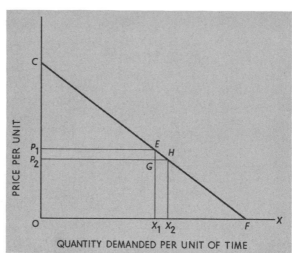

demand curve. At times, however, we are interested in elasticity at a specific point or the elasticity for very small changes in price and quantity. Understanding the method of graphical computation of point elasticity permits one to estimate price elasticity by a visual inspection of the demand curve.

In Figure 2.3.1 the line CF is a linear demand curve for commodity X. The problem is to measure price elasticity at point E, where price is

Op_1 and quantity demanded is Ox_1. First let price fall very slightly from Op_1 to Op_2, so quantity demanded increases from Ox_1 to Ox_2; that is, p_2 and x_2 are very near p_1 and x_1.

Next consider the formula for point elasticity:

$$\eta = -\Delta Q / Q \div \Delta P / P.$$

From the figure, $\Delta Q = x_1 x_2$ and $Q = Ox_1$ at E. Similarly $\Delta P = p_1 p_2$ and $P = Op_1$ at E. Thus,

$$\eta = -\frac{x_1 x_2 / Ox_1}{p_1 p_2 / Op_1} = \frac{x_1 x_2}{p_1 p_2} \cdot \frac{Op_1}{Ox_1}.$$

Since $x_1 x_2 = GH$ and $p_1 p_2 = EG$,

$$\frac{x_1 x_2}{p_1 p_2} = \frac{GH}{EG}.$$

Furthermore EGH and $Ex_1 F$ are similar right triangles inasmuch as each corresponding angle is equal. Thus

$$\frac{GH}{EG} = \frac{x_1 F}{Ex_1} = \frac{x_1 F}{Op_1},$$

since $Ex_1 = Op_1$. Hence

$$\eta = \frac{GH}{EG} \cdot \frac{Op_1}{Ox_1} = \frac{x_1 F}{Op_1} \cdot \frac{Op_1}{Ox_1} = \frac{x_1 F}{Ox_1}.$$

But $x_1 F / Ox_1 = Op_1 / p_1 C = EF / EC$. Thus graphically the coefficient of price elasticity at the point E is

$$\eta = \frac{EF}{EC}.$$

Utilizing this formula, it is easy to determine the ranges of demand elasticity for a linear demand curve. First note the following relations in Figure 2.3.1. When $EF = EC$, $EF/EC = 1$; hence, at that point the demand curve has unit elasticity. Second, when $EF > EC$, $EF/EC > 1$ and demand is elastic. Finally, when $EF < EC$, $EF/EC < 1$ and demand is inelastic.

Thus we can locate a point on DD', the linear demand curve in Figure 2.3.2, such that $DP = PD'$; at this point, demand has unitary price elasticity, or $\eta = 1$. Next consider any point to the left of P, such as P_1. At P_1, $\eta = (P_1 D'/DP_1) > 1$. Thus for a linear demand curve the coefficient of price elasticity is greater than unity at any point to the left of the midpoint on the demand curve. Demand is elastic in this region. Finally, at any point to the right of P, say P_2, the coefficient of price elasticity is $\eta = (P_2 D'/DP_2) < 1$. Over this range, demand is inelastic.

FIGURE 2.3.2

**Ranges of Demand Elasticity
for Linear Demand Curve**

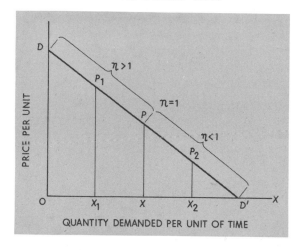

When demand is not linear, such as DD' in Figure 2.3.3, one can easily approximate point elasticity in the following manner. Suppose we want to compute the elasticity of DD' at point E. First draw the straight line AB tangent to DD' at E. Note that if AB were actually the demand

FIGURE 2.3.3

**Computation of Point Elasticity
for Nonlinear Demand Curve**

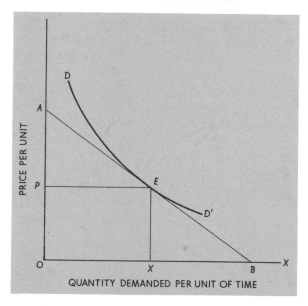

curve, EB/AE would be its elasticity at point E. Note also that for very small movements away from E along DD', the slope of AB is a relatively good estimate of the slope of DD'. Now the elasticity formula may also be written as

$$\eta = \frac{1}{\Delta P/\Delta Q} \cdot \frac{P}{Q}.$$

Since the slopes of DD' and AB (which are tangent at E) are approximately equal in the neighborhood of E, $\Delta P/\Delta Q$ is the same for each curve. Therefore, the elasticity of AB at E is approximately equal to the elasticity of DD' at E. The point elasticity of DD' at E is approximately EB/AE.

These results may be summarized as follows:

Relation: given any point E on a demand curve, construct the straight line tangent to the curve at E. Call this line AEB. The coefficient of price elasticity is approximately EB/AE. If the demand curve is linear this measure is precise. Furthermore, for a linear demand curve: (a) demand is elastic at higher prices, (b) has unit elasticity at the midpoint of the demand curve, and (c) is inelastic at lower prices. Thus in case of linear demand elasticity declines as one moves downward along the curve.

2.3.e—Factors Affecting Price Elasticity

Whether demand is elastic or inelastic is an important consideration, especially for government policy in individual commodity markets. For example, suppose the demand for wheat is elastic. An increase in the price of wheat would accordingly result in a proportionately greater reduction in quantity demanded. Farmers would thus obtain a smaller total revenue from the sale of wheat. Now suppose the government establishes a minimum wheat price above the market equilibrium price. Wheat sales would be reduced, and so too would farmers' incomes, unless the price support were accompanied by a minimum sales guarantee. On the other hand, if the demand for wheat is inelastic, a minimum price above the equilibrium price would increase farmers' total revenue.

Price elasticities range quite widely. Two basic factors determine elasticity: availability of substitute goods and the number of uses to which a good may be put. These factors go a long way toward explaining variations in elasticities.

The more and better the substitutes for a specific good, the greater its price elasticity will be. Goods with few and poor substitutes—wheat and salt, for example—will always tend to have low price elasticities. Goods with many substitutes—wool, for which cotton and manmade fibers may be substituted, for instance—will have higher elasticities.

Similarly, the greater the number of uses a commodity has, the greater its price elasticity will be. Thus a commodity such as wool—which can be used in producing clothing, carpeting, upholstery, draperies and tapestries, and so on—will tend to have a higher price elasticity than a commodity with only one or a very few uses—butter, for example.

2.3.f—Other Elasticities

At times, economists are concerned with the relative responsiveness of quantity demanded to changes in either income or the price of some related good. To measure this responsiveness we use the coefficients of income elasticity and cross-elasticity.

As you will recall, when deriving a demand curve for a good X, we held constant such things as income and the prices of related goods. The price of X determines the point on the demand curve the consumer selects; income and the prices of related goods, among other things, determine the *position* of the demand curve, i.e., how far from or close to the axes the curve stands.

The responsiveness of quantity demanded to income changes, other things remaining the same, is measured by the coefficient of income elasticity (η_M). Specifically, the income elasticity of demand is the ratio of the percentage change in quantity demanded to the percentage change in money income. Symbolically

$$\eta_M = \frac{\Delta Q/Q}{\Delta M/M} = \frac{\Delta Q}{\Delta M} \cdot \frac{M}{Q}.$$

Note that we do not put a minus sign in the equation. As we shall show in Chapter 4, quantity demanded can vary either directly or inversely with income; that is, $\Delta Q/\Delta M$ can be either positive or negative. Therefore, η_M can be either positive or negative.

Similarly, it is possible to measure the responsiveness of quantity demanded to changes in the price of some related good. This is called price cross elasticity of demand. Hold everything constant except the price of some related good Y. The cross elasticity is the ratio of the percentage change in quantity demanded to the percentage change in the price of Y. More specifically,

$$\eta_{xy} = \frac{\Delta x/x}{\Delta p_y/p_y} = \frac{\Delta x}{\Delta p_y} \cdot \frac{p_y}{x}.$$

As in the case of income elasticity, one can make no general statement about the sign of η_{xy}. At a given price of X, quantity demanded may vary directly with the price of some related good, i.e., $\Delta x/\Delta p_y$ is positive. For example, the quantity of Fords demanded at a particular price will increase if the price of Chevrolets rises and decrease if the price of Chevrolets falls. Goods such as these are called substitutes; η_{xy} is positive. On the other hand, if the price of gasoline rises and the quantity of Fords demanded decreases at a particular price, η_{xy} would be negative. Fords and gasoline, and similarly related pairs of goods, are called complements. It should be emphasized that in these examples, *demand* shifts; we are not considering changes in quality demanded along a stationary demand curve.

2.3.g—Summary

Demand is price inelastic, elastic, or unitary according as $-\%\Delta Q/\%\Delta P$ is less than, greater than, or equal to one. A decrease in price occasions a decrease, an increase, or no change in total expenditure respectively. The elasticity of a good is influenced primarily by the availability of substitute goods and by the number of uses to which a good may be put. Economists also use income elasticity to measure the effect of income changes upon quantity demanded and cross elasticity to measure the effect of changes in the prices of related goods upon quantity demanded of the good in question. We shall subsequently see that these are important concepts in economic analysis.

2.4   SUPPLY SCHEDULE

To get at an understanding of supply, assume that a large number of farmers sell cabbage in the same market. One particular farmer is willing to grow and sell 1,000 cabbages per season if the price per unit of cabbage is $0.25. If the price of cabbage were $0.35, he would be willing to grow more, say 2,000. The higher price induces the farmer to take land out of cultivation of other crops and put it into the cultivation of the now relatively more lucrative cabbage. A still higher price, $0.50 perhaps, would be required to induce him to market 3,000 cabbages, and so on. That is, the farmer allocates his time and land so as to make as much money as possible. Higher and higher prices are required to induce him to re allocate more and more of his time and land to cabbage production.

A portion of the farmer's cabbage supply schedule might therefore be as follows:

Price	Quantity Supplied
$0.25	1,000
.35	2,000
.50	3,000
.75	4,000
1.25	5,000

This schedule shows the *minimum price* that induces the farmer to supply each amount in the list. Note that in contrast to demand analysis, price and quantity supplied are directly related. We must postpone the explanation of why price and quantity vary directly until Chapter 7, after we have analyzed cost and production. For the present we assume that the supply schedule shows the minimum price necessary to induce producers voluntarily to offer each possible quantity for sale. We also assume that an increase in price is required to induce an increase in quantity supplied.

2.4.a—Graphing Supply Schedules

First, consider the supply schedule in Table 2.4.1. This table shows the minimum price necessary to induce firms to supply, per unit of time, each of the six quantities listed. In order to induce greater quantities, price must rise; or in other words, if price increases from $4 to $5, firms will increase quantity supplied from 6,000 units to 6,500 units. Remember that

TABLE 2.4.1
Market Supply Schedule

Quantity Supplied (Units of X)	Prices (Dollars)
7,000	$6
6,500	5
6,000	4
5,000	3
4,000	2
3,000	1

we are assuming a large number of noncolluding firms; in case of a single firm supplying the entire market, a different principle applies (as shown in Chapter 8). Figure 2.4.1 shows a graph of the schedule in Table 2.4.1. This supply curve is drawn under the assumption that price and quantity are directly related, so the curve is positively sloped.

2.4.b—Factors Influencing Supply

As in the case of demand, we might ask why the supply schedule in Table 2.4.1 is what it is. Why, for example, does a price of $5 induce a quantity supplied of 6,500 rather than a price of $4? Or why is not a lower quantity supplied at each price in the list. A much more thorough discussion of supply is undertaken in Chapter 7. For now, we will only briefly mention four factors that affect supply. These are the factors generally held constant when drawing a supply curve.

First, technology is assumed constant. If a more efficient method of production is discovered, firms generally change the amounts they are willing to supply at each price. Second, the prices of factors of production

FIGURE 2.4.1

Market Supply Curve

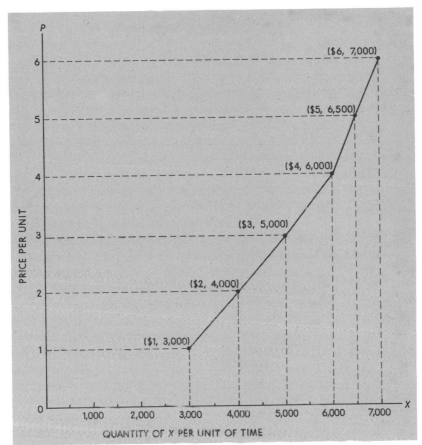

QUANTITY OF X PER UNIT OF TIME

are usually held constant. For example, a change in wage rates or in the prices of raw materials will change the supply curve. Third, the prices of related goods (in production) are held constant. If the price of corn rises while the price of wheat remains the same, some farmers will switch from growing wheat to growing corn, and less wheat will be supplied. Fourth, the expectations of producers are assumed not to change.

2.4.c—Changes in Supply

When price rises and firms are induced to offer a greater quantity of a good for sale, we say *quantity supplied* increases. When one or more of the factors mentioned in Section 2.4.b change, firms are induced to offer more or less at each price in the schedule; in this case we say supply changes. Consider Figure 2.4.2 in which S_0S_0' is the initial supply curve. If price falls from $O\bar{p}$ to Op', the quantity of X supplied decreases from Ox_0 to Ox_0', other things remaining the same. If technology changes and supply consequently changes from S_0S_0' to S_2S_2', we say supply increases. Firms now wish to offer Ox_2 at price $O\bar{p}$, and they wish to offer more units for sale at each price in the entire range of prices. A movement from

FIGURE 2.4.2

Shifts in Supply

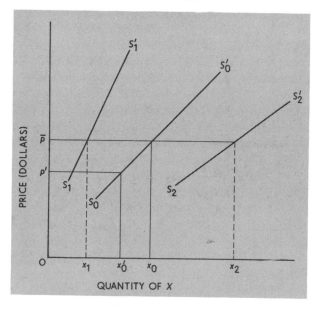

S_0S_0' to S_1S_1' is a decrease in supply. Firms then wish to offer less for sale at each price in the range.

These relations may be summarized as follows:

Relations: When price rises (falls), other things remaining the same, quantity supplied rises (falls). When something held constant in deriving supply changes, for example technology, supply increases or decreases. If firms are induced to offer more (less) at each price, supply has increased (decreased).

2.5 SUPPLY ELASTICITY

As is the case for demand, the coefficient of supply elasticity measures the relative responsiveness of quantity supplied to changes in price *along a given supply schedule.* The computation technique is essentially the same as that used for demand elasticity.

2.5.a—Computation

The coefficient of supply elasticity is defined as

$$\eta_s = \frac{\Delta Q/Q}{\Delta P/P} = \frac{\Delta Q}{\Delta P} \cdot \frac{P}{Q},$$

where ΔQ is change in quantity supplied, ΔP is the change in price, and P and Q are price and quantity supplied. Since Q and P are assumed to change in the same direction, the coefficient is positive. One can use an averaging technique like that discussed for demand when the changes are discrete, i.e., when differences in the bases used affect η_s.

If the percentage change in quantity supplied exceeds the percentage change in price, supply is elastic and $\eta_s > 1$. If the two percentages are equal, supply has unitary elasticity and $\eta_s = 1$. If the percentage change in price exceeds the percentage change in quantity, supply is inelastic and $\eta_s < 1$. Therefore, the more elastic is supply, the more responsive is quantity supplied to price changes.[2] Note, however, that in contrast to demand we cannot relate supply elasticity to positive or negative changes in total dollar value supplied, i.e., changes in price times quantity supplied at that price. Since price and quantity vary directly, an increase in price increases quantity supplied, and hence increases the dollar value of quantity supplied whether supply is elastic or inelastic. A fall in price likewise decreases the dollar value of quantity supplied.

2.5.b—Determinants of Supply Elasticity

The responsiveness of quantity supplied to increases in price depends in large measure upon the time period of adjustment and upon how easily resources can be adapted to the production of the good in question. Suppose the price of a particular good increases. If the resources used to produce that good are readily accessible without increasing their prices, and if production can physically be increased easily, supply is more elastic than if the opposite holds true. That is, supply would be *less* elastic if the

---

[2] Estimating supply elasticity at a point on a supply curve is quite simple. First, draw a tangent to the curve at the point where elasticity is to be calculated. Extend the tangent toward the left until it reaches the origin, the vertical axis, or the horizontal axis. If the tangent crosses the vertical axis, supply is elastic at the point; if it crosses the horizontal axis it is inelastic; if it passes through the origin, supply has unitary elasticity. For a straight line supply, merely check which axis supply crosses and make the same estimation as described for a tangent line.

additional resources are obtainable only at rapidly increasing prices.[3] For a price decrease, elasticity depends upon how rapidly resources can be released from the production of the good.

Economists sometimes speak of momentary, short-run, and long-run supply and supply elasticity. As an example, let us consider the supply of people in a particular profession, say lawyers. Three supply curves for lawyers are shown in Figure 2.5.1. $L_M L_M'$ is the momentary supply of lawyers. At a moment of time there are OL_M lawyers, and this number cannot be instantaneously changed. Suppose the average income of law-

FIGURE 2.5.1

**Effect of Time of Adjustment
on Supply Elasticity**

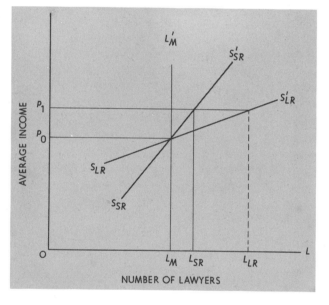

yers rises from Op_0 to Op_1; at that moment or over a very short period of time, the number of lawyers cannot be increased. Since quantity does not respond at all, the vertical supply curve $L_M L_M'$ is infinitely inelastic.

Within a reasonably short period of time, however, the rise in the average income of lawyers will induce an increase in the number of lawyers, perhaps from OL_M to OL_{SR}. The increase in income will induce some retired lawyers to begin practice again; some businessmen with law degrees will be induced to leave their companies and enter practice. The resulting short-run supply curve is $S_{SR} S_{SR}'$, the supply curve when a

---

[3] Chapter 7 contains a much more extensive discussion of the relations between supply and the availability of additional resources.

reasonably short period of adjustment is permitted. This curve is more elastic than $L_M L_M'$ because when some adjustment time is permitted, quantity supplied is more responsive to price changes.

The long-run supply curve is $S_{LR} S_{LR}'$, which allows sufficient time for *all* adjustments to be made (we shall define short run and long run more precisely in Chapter 6). In our example, higher average incomes will induce more college graduates to enter law school, and the period of adjustment is long enough to permit them to begin practicing law. Alternatively, if average income declines relative to other professions requiring similar periods of training, the number of lawyers will decline appreciably. Thus the long-run supply curve $S_{LR} S_{LR}'$ is more elastic than $S_{SR} S_{SR}'$ because quantity is more responsive to price when sufficient adjustment time is permitted.

2.6 MARKET DETERMINATION OF PRICE AND QUANTITY

The purpose of studying supply and demand is to prepare us to analyze their interaction, which determines market price and quantity. A primary reason for separating them is to isolate the factors that determine each so that we can analyze the market effects of changing these factors. Before further analyzing the underlying forces behind the two schedules (in later chapters), we will first examine the interaction of supply and demand in the market.

2.6.a—Equilibrium

Suppose that in the market for X demanders and suppliers have the schedules set forth in Tables 2.2.1 and 2.4.1 respectively. These schedules are combined in Table 2.6.1. Suppose also that an auctioneer, who does not know the schedules, is assigned the task of finding a price that clears the market; that is, a price at which quantity demanded equals quantity supplied. The auctioneer does not know the market-clearing price, since the schedules change from time to time. Therefore, he begins by picking

TABLE 2.6.1
Market Demand and Supply

Price (Dollars)	*Quantity Supplied* (Units of X)	*Quantity Demanded* (Units of X)	*Excess Supply* (+) *or Demand* (-) (Units of X)
$6...........	7,000	2,000	+5,000
5..........	6,500	3,000	+3,500
4...........	6,000	4,000	+2,000
3...........	5,000	5,000	0
2...........	4,000	5,500	−1,500
1...........	3,000	6,000	−3,000

some price at random and announcing this price to the demanders and suppliers, who then tell him the amounts they wish to purchase or sell at that price. The first price chosen may or may not clear the market. If it does, exchange takes place; if not the auctioneer must choose another price. This time, however, he need not proceed purely at random.

The auctioneer knows from long experience that if quantity demanded exceeds quantity supplied (excess demand), he can raise the price and cause quantity demanded to decrease and quantity supplied to increase. That is, excess demand will decrease when price rises. He knows also that if quantity supplied exceeds quantity demanded (excess supply), he can reduce price and cause a reduction in quantity supplied and an increase in quantity demanded. That is, a price reduction reduces excess supply.

Suppose the first price chosen is $5; 3,000 units are demanded but 6,500 units are offered for sale. There is an excess supply of 3,500 units at that price. To reduce excess supply the auctioneer reduces price, say to $1. Now since consumers demand 6,000 but producers are willing to supply only 3,000, excess demand is 3,000. The auctioneer raises price to $4 and quantity supplied exceeds quantity demanded by 2,000. He therefore reduces price to $3. Quantity demanded equals quantity supplied and the market is cleared. The equilibrium price and quantity are $3 and 5,000 units.

We can also express the equilibrium solution graphically. In Figure 2.6.1, DD' and SS' are the market demand and supply curves (these are not graphs of the schedules in Table 2.6.1). It is clear that Op_e and Ox_e are the market-clearing or equilibrium price and quantity. Only at Op_e does quantity demanded equal quantity supplied. In this model we need not make our assumption about the auctioneer. Consumers and producers themselves bid the price up or down if the market is not in equilibrium.

Suppose price happens to be $O\bar{p}$, greater than Op_e. At $O\bar{p}$ producers supply $O\bar{x}_s$ but only $O\bar{x}_d$ is demanded. An excess supply of $\bar{x}_d\bar{x}_s$ developes. This surplus accumulates for the producer. When this happens producers are induced to lower price in order to keep from accumulating unwanted surpluses. (This is the same thing our auctioneer would have done.) Note that at any price above Op_e there is an excess supply, and producers will lower price. On the other hand, suppose price is $O\hat{p}$. Demanders are willing and able to purchase $O\hat{x}_d$, while suppliers are only willing to offer $O\hat{x}_s$ units for sale. Some consumers are not satisfied; there is an excess demand of $\hat{x}_s\hat{x}_d$ in the market. Since their demands are not satisfied, consumers bid the price up (See Chapter 1). Again this is what our auctioneer would have done if a shortage existed. As consumers continue to bid up the price, quantity demanded decreases and quantity supplied increases until price reaches Op_e and quantity is Ox_e. Any price below Op_e causes a shortage, and the shortage causes consumers to bid

FIGURE 2.6.1

Market Equilibrium

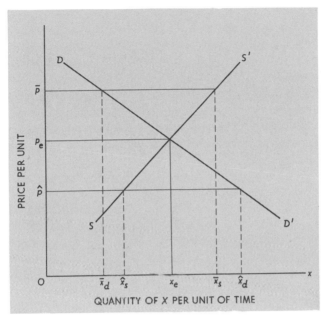

QUANTITY OF X PER UNIT OF TIME

up the price. Given no outside influences that prevent price from being bid up or down, an equilibrium price and quantity is attained. This equilibrium price is the price that clears the market; both excess demand and excess supply are zero in equilibrium. Equilibrium is attained in the market because of the following:

Principles: When price is above the equilibrium price, quantity supplied exceeds quantity demanded. The resulting excess supply induces sellers to reduce price in order to sell the surplus. If price is below equilibrium, quantity demanded exceeds quantity supplied. The resulting excess demand causes the unsatisfied consumers to bid up price. Since prices below equilibrium are bid up by consumers and prices above equilibrium are lowered by producers, the market will converge to the equilibrium price-quantity combination.

2.6.b—Demand and Supply Shifts

So long as the determinants of demand and supply do not change, the price-quantity equilibrium described above will not change. Before finishing our study of the market, however, we must see how this equilibrium is disturbed when there are changes in one or more of the factors held constant in deriving demand and supply.

A bit of intuitive reasoning may ease the transition to the graphical analysis that follows. Consider the career you plan after graduation. Let us suppose you plan to be an electrical engineer. If granted the wish, would you prefer a large or small number of engineers to be graduated at the time you are? Obviously you should wish for a small number because the larger the number of new engineers entering the market, the smaller will the starting salary be.

Consider another example. Does a cotton farmer bringing his crop to market want a large or small amount of cotton marketed at the same time? Again, obviously, a small amount because the larger the amount of cotton available, the lower the price of cotton will be. It should thus be

FIGURE 2.6.2

Changes in Equilibrium Prices and Quantities

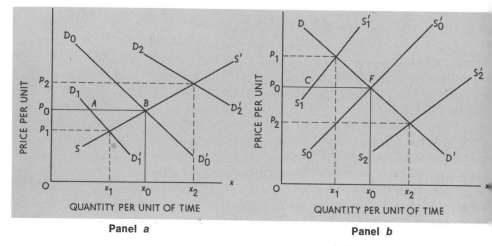

| Panel *a* | Panel *b* |

intuitively clear that the greater the supply, the greater will be the quantity sold but the lower the price will be. In like manner, the greater the demand—for engineers, cotton, or anything else—the greater both *quantity* and *price* will be. These relations are intuitively clear; but they can be refined by graphical analysis, to which we now turn.

In panel *a*, Figure 2.6.2, Op_0 and Ox_0 are the equilibrium price and quantity when demand and supply are D_0D_0' and SS'. Suppose income falls; thus demand decreases to D_1D_1'. At Op_0 quantity supplied exceeds the new quantity demanded by AB, i.e., excess supply at Op_0 is AB. Faced with this surplus sellers reduce price until the new equilibrium is reached at Op_1 and Ox_1. Now suppose the price of some substitute good increases so that demand increases to D_2D_2'. At price Op_1 quantity demanded far exceeds quantity supplied, and hence a shortage occurs. The excess demand causes consumers to bid the price up until the new equilibrium at Op_2 and Ox_2 is reached. We can see that if supply remains fixed and demand decreases, quantity and price both fall; if demand increases, price and quantity both rise. This direct relation between price and quantity would be expected when we consider that the movements take place *along* the supply curve, which is positively sloped.

Panel *b*, Figure 2.6.2, shows what happens to price and quantity when demand remains constant and supply shifts. Let demand be DD' and supply S_0S_0'. The original equilibrium thus occurs at price Op_0 and quantity Ox_0. Now let input prices rise so that supply decreases to S_1S_1'. The shortage of CF at Op_0 causes consumers to bid up price until equilibrium is reached at Op_1 and Ox_1. Now let technology improve so that supply increases to S_2S_2'. The surplus at Op_1 causes producers to lower price. Equilibrium occurs at Op_2 and Ox_2. Thus we see that if demand remains constant and supply decreases, price rises and quantity falls; if supply increases, price falls and quantity increases. This inverse relation is expected since the movement is *along* a negatively sloped demand curve.

The direction of change is not always immediately apparent when both supply and demand change simultaneously. In panel *a*, Figure 2.6.3, D_0D_0' and S_0S_0' are the initial demand and supply curves. Their intersection determines the equilibrium price and quantity, Op_0 and Ox_0. Now suppose supply increases to S_1S_1' and demand increases to D_1D_1'; price rises to Op_1 and quantity rises to Ox_1. While quantity always increases when both demand and supply increase, price may either increase, decrease, or even remain the same. Suppose supply shifts to S_1S_1' but demand shifts only to the position indicated by the dashed demand curve crossing S_1S_1' at A. With this shift quantity still rises (although by a lesser amount), but price falls to Op_2. Furthermore, by constructing the change in supply or demand still differently, we can cause price to remain at Op_0 while quantity increases.

To see the effect of a decrease in both supply and demand, consider D_1D_1' and S_1S_1' in panel *a* as the original schedules. Next, let them both decrease to D_0D_0' and S_0S_0'. Quantity and price decrease from Ox_1 and Op_1 to Ox_0 and Op_0. While quantity always decreases when both curves decrease, price need not fall.

Exercise: In order to see the point just made, manipulate supply or demand so that price rises above Op_1 as both curves decrease.

Panel *b*, Figure 2.6.3, shows the effect of an increase in one curve accompanied by a decrease in the other. Let supply *increase* from S_0S_0' to S_1S_1', and let demand *decrease* from D_0D_0' to D_1D_1'. Price falls from Op_0 to Op_1 and quantity rises from Ox_0 to Ox_1. While price *must* fall when supply increases and demand decreases, quantity need not increase.

FIGURE 2.6.3

Effects of Supply and Demand Shifts

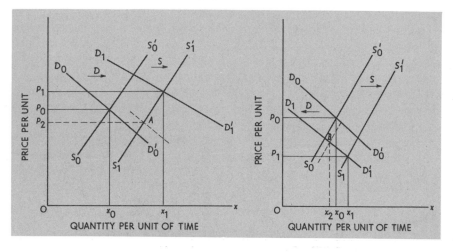

Panel *a*   Panel *b*

Suppose that while demand went to D_1D_1', supply increased only to the position indicated by the dashed line crossing D_1D_1' at B. The new equilibrium entails a price reduction (although not so large as before), but now quantity decreases to Ox_2 rather than rising to Ox_1. To see the effect of a decrease in supply accompanied by an increase in demand, simply assume that demand shifts from D_1D_1' to D_0D_0' and supply from S_1S_1' to S_0S_0'. Price must rise. In this illustration quantity decreases; but quantity may change in either direction.

Exercise: Prove this last point for yourself.

Principles: (1) When demand increases (decreases), supply remaining constant, both price and quantity increase (decrease). (2) When supply increases (decreases), demand remaining constant, price falls (rises) and quantity rises (falls). (3) When both demand and supply increase (decrease) quantity increases (decreases), but price can either increase or decrease, depending upon the relative magnitude of the shifts. (4) When supply and demand shift in opposite directions the change in quantity is indeterminant; but price always changes in the same direction as demand.

2.7 SUPPLY AND DEMAND IN REAL MARKETS

By this time some students may question the relevance of demand and supply analysis to real world problems. What if sellers do not know the demand or the supply schedules? In fact, do they even know what demand and supply are? It may therefore be profitable to show how demand and supply determine price and allocate output in the absence of perfect knowledge about the schedules.

Suppose one day the newspapers all print a scientific report stating that rhubarb (not rutabagas) makes women more beautiful. Now we know, having gone through the first part of this chapter, that the demand for rhubarb probably increases. But perhaps the grocers, some of whom have not read this chapter, do not know this. How can the market allocate under these conditions?

First, consider what happens to the rhubarb on the grocers' shelves. Assuming that demand in fact increases, grocers find that what had

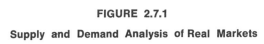

FIGURE 2.7.1

Supply and Demand Analysis of Real Markets

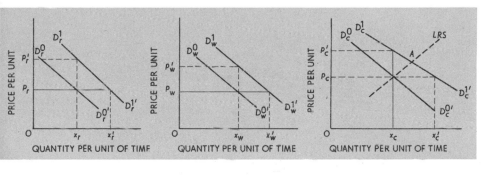

| Panel a | Panel b | Panel c |
| Retail Market | Wholesale Market | Commodity Market |

previously been a week's supply of rhubarb at the established price now lasts only until Thursday morning. Customers complain that they cannot get rhubarb. We can use demand analysis to examine the situation *even though buyers and sellers are completely unaware of demand and supply analysis.*

Panel a, Figure 2.7.1, shows what happens in the retail market. Price is Op_r, and Ox_r per week is the rate of sales when demand is $D_r{}^0 D_r{}^0{}'$. Demand increases to $D_r{}^1 D_r{}^1{}'$. At Op_r consumers now want Ox_r' units per week. Grocery stores consequently run out of rhubarb before the week is over. The profitable thing for grocers is to order more rhubarb from wholesalers. When they do, the wholesalers sell more rhubarb and their stocks begin to run low. This is shown in panel b. The original demand is $D_w{}^0 D_w{}^0{}'$; that is, this is the demand by grocers for wholesale rhubarb. When demand at retail increases, demand at wholesale increases also.

Before the shift in demand, retail grocers wanted Ox_w at a wholesale price of Op_w; they now want Ox_w'.

As their inventories run low, wholesalers instruct their buyers in the commodity market to buy more rhubarb. At any one time, however, there is a limit to the amount of rhubarb available. Therefore, as the buyers try to increase their purchases, they bid against one another and force price up. Panel c indicates what happens in the commodity market. The old demand of wholesalers for rhubarb was $D_c{}^0D_c{}^{0\prime}$; price was Op_c. Suppose the quantity available is Ox_c (the momentary supply). When wholesalers' demand rises to $D_c{}^1D_c{}^{1\prime}$, a shortage of x_cx_c' develops at price Op_c. Price rises to Op_c' to ration the available rhubarb among the competing buyers. (It might be well to note that the scales of the graphs in Figure 2.7.1 are different.)

Wholesalers now pay a higher price in the commodity market and consequently raise their price to grocers, to Op_w' perhaps. As they tell the grocers, their costs have risen and they are forced to raise prices. The grocers now pay the wholesale price of Op_w', so they raise the retail price to Op_r'. As they tell their complaining customers, costs have risen so they are forced to raise prices. Costs to the grocers and to the wholesalers have, of course, risen; but ultimately it was the increased demand that caused the price rise. And this price must rise until it rations the available rhubarb to those prospective buyers who are both willing and able to pay the price.

Everything that occurs in the transition period occurs not because we draw some curves but because of individual action in the market. We use demand and supply curves only to analyze more clearly what takes place in the market.

We can take the analysis a few steps further. Suppose the higher price in the commodity market induces farmers to increase their rhubarb crop or induces farmers growing other crops to switch to rhubarb. Remember Ox_c and Op_c make up only one point on the long-run supply curve. Assume that there is an upward sloping long-run supply (LRS) passing through point A in panel c. In the commodity market price falls and quantity increases after all adjustments are made (point A, panel c). The increased quantity supplied causes price to fall and quantity sold to rise in the wholesale and in the retail market.

To test his understanding of the analysis, the student should do the following:

Exercises: (1) Complete the graphs in panels *a, b,* and *c* to indicate the new price-quantity relations in the three markets and describe the reason for the changes. (2) Using the three supply curves, L_M, S_{SR}, and S_{LR} in Figure 2.5.1, first draw a demand for lawyers going through the point indicating a price of Op_o and a quantity of OL_M. Next draw an increased demand for lawyers. Determine the price and quantity resulting in each of the three periods, describing reasons why each position occurs even though no one actually *knows* the position of the curves. Finally, carry out the same analysis for a decrease in demand.

Exercise: Use the analytical reasoning of this subsection to answer the following problem. Suppose a frost kills a large portion of the orange crop, with a resulting higher price of oranges. It has been said that such an increase in price benefits no one since it cannot elicit a supply response, i.e., supply is fixed until the next harvest. The higher price, it is said, simply "lines the pockets of profiteers." Analyze this position (*hint:* be sure to focus on the rationing function of market price).

Exercise: Suppose that at a fixed price quantity demanded exceeds quantity supplied. Buyers queue up to buy the good, as it were. Is there an economic explanation, involving competitive forces, of *who* is first in the queue?

2.8 ANALYTICAL EXERCISES

For various reasons, the government sometimes interferes with the working of demand and supply in the market. Without evaluating the

FIGURE 2.8.1

Effect of Ceiling Price

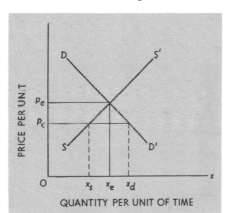

desirability of the interferences we can use demand and supply curves to analyze the economic effects of two types of interference, namely the setting of minimum and maximum prices.

If the government imposes a maximum or ceiling price on a good, the effect is to cause a shortage (and to create a black market that rations the quantity available). In Figure 2.8.1 a ceiling price of Op_c is set on good X. No one can legally sell X for more than Op_c per unit, which is below the equilibrium price Op_c. At the ceiling price Ox_s is the quantity supplied but Ox_d is demanded, causing a shortage of $x_s x_d$. Since quantity supplied is less than quantity demanded at the ceiling price, there must be some method of allocating the limited quantity among all those who are willing and able to buy a larger amount. The sellers may devise the method; perhaps consumers queue, with suppliers deciding who comes first in the queue on the basis of under-the-counter offers. On the other hand, the government may devise some system of rationing. But in this case, black markets will develop. In any case the market does the allocating. But when restricted by outside requirements, the allocation is either

FIGURE 2.8.2

Effect of Floor Price

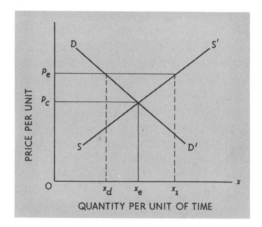

QUANTITY PER UNIT OF TIME

based upon nonmarket considerations or the market mechanism functions less effectively outside the law.

In contrast the government may feel that the suppliers of X are not earning as much income as they "deserve" and therefore set a minimum or floor price. We can see the results of such actions in Figure 2.8.2. Being dissatisfied with the equilibrium price and quantity, Op_e and Ox_e, the government sets a minimum price of Op_f. Since the law of demand could not concurrently be repealed, consumers demand less (Ox_d) and, at the higher price, producers wish to supply more (Ox_s). An excess supply of $x_d x_s$ develops. In order to maintain the price of Op_f, the government must agree to purchase whatever quantity the market does not take at the floor price Op_f. Thus the government purchases $x_d x_s$ units of the commodity. Alternatively, the government could simply restrict production to Ox_d. The vertical dotted line at that point then becomes the new supply. A price of Op_f now clears the market.

Exercise: We have already analyzed the "welfare distorting" effects of a ceiling price in detail. Do the same for a floor price. In this case, who has an incentive to cheat? How can an organization similar to black markets develop?

2.9 CONCLUSION

Economists every day use demand and supply analysis, often as simple as that discussed in this chapter, to solve complex problems and answer questions dealing with the real world. In fact, demand and supply are probably the most frequently used tools in the economist's bag.

Therefore much of the remainder of this book is devoted to demand and supply and to the factors that influence demand and supply. As we shall see, however, one must be able to decide *which* demand and *which* supply are relevant for the solution of a particular problem before he can use these tools fruitfully.

In all cases a fundamental concept to remember is that when the price of something falls, more is taken; when the price of something rises less is taken. In the next two chapters we turn to the theory of consumer behavior to see why this is so.

QUESTIONS AND PROBLEMS

1. Make up an inelastic demand schedule (i.e., table). Compute the coefficient of elasticity between two points. Graph the corresponding demand curve. Show what happens when the price of a competitive good falls. Show what happens when consumers' incomes increase. (What assumption must be made to answer the last part of the question?)

2. A decrease in supply raises price. But the higher price causes a decrease in demand, which in turn causes an (at least partially) offsetting fall in price. Comment.

3. The following statement is taken from the *Wall Street Journal*, March 30, 1966: "A retired Atlanta railroad conductor complains that he can no longer visit his neighborhood tavern six times a week. Since the price of his favorite beer went up to 30 cents a glass from 25 cents, he has been dropping in only five times a week." Assuming the man in question consumed the same amount of beer *per visit* before and after the price change, calculate the elasticity of his demand for tavern-dispensed beer.

4. Contrast an individual's "demands" with his "wants."

chapter 3

Theory of Consumer Behavior: Tools of Analysis

3.1 INTRODUCTION

In the discussion of demand and supply in Chapter 2 we postulated certain characteristics of demand curves without analyzing the specific behavioral patterns upon which they are based. Since demand itself is directly related to the way in which consumers are willing and able to act, it is necessary to understand consumer behavior in order to understand the determinants of demand. This chapter and the following describe the modern theory of consumer behavior and the relations between that theory and the theory of demand. First, the tools of analysis are developed; then these tools are used to analyze the way in which consumer behavior affects demand, with particular emphasis upon explaining why market demand curves are negatively sloped.

3.1.a—Utility

The simplest approach to the theory of consumer behavior is based upon a concept called *utility*, which is defined as the satisfaction a person obtains from the goods and services he consumes. Utility is, of course, a subjective phenomenon because each person's physiological and psychological makeup is different from every other's. Yet, if one sought a single criterion to distinguish modern microeconomic theory from its classical antecedents, he would probably find it to be the introduction of *subjective value theory* into economics. Historically, the process of development was a long and involved one. Our discussion of it, however, will be brief; only the most important steps are mentioned.

The earliest psychological approaches to the theory of demand were based upon the notion of subjective utility, as found in the works of

Gossen (1854), Jevons (1871), and Walras (1874). Just as modern theorists do, they assumed that any good or service consumed by a household provides utility. In contrast to most modern theorists, however, they also assumed that utility is cardinally measurable and additive and that the utility derived from one good is independent of the rate of consumption of any other good. We must digress briefly for a

Definition: Cardinal measurability implies that the *difference* between two numbers is itself numerically significant. For example, apples are cardinally measurable; and one may say that four apples are exactly twice as many as two apples. A measurement system is said to be *ordinal* if items can only be ranked as 1st, 2nd, 3rd, and so on. Note: Numerical significance cannot be attached to the difference between 1st and 2nd, 2nd and 3rd, and so on. Each measurement system ranks items. The difference is that in an ordinal system, one can say (for example) that x is greater than y; in a cardinal system, he can say by how much x exceeds y.

Now to return to our train of thought. The more of one good consumed, the greater the total utility associated with it. Each *additional* unit of the good consumed per unit of time adds to total utility, but each adds less than the previous unit. For example, one piece of candy per day might yield a measurable five units of utility. Two pieces per day might yield 9 units of utility; 3 pieces, 11 units; and so on. That is, the second piece of candy adds four units of utility; one less than the first. The third adds two units to the total, two less than the second. Since utility was assumed to be cardinally measurable and additive by these theorists, and since the consumption of one good was assumed to have no effect upon the utility derived from another, a person's total utility is simply the sum of the utilities provided by all the goods he consumes.

Later economists, such as Edgeworth (1881), Antonelli (1886), and Fisher (1892), objected to the additivity assumption. Instead, they assumed that while utility is cardinally measurable, it is not simply the sum of the independent utilities obtained from the consumption of each good. These theorists related the level of total utility to the rates of consumption of all goods simultaneously. In terms of the previous example, the extra or *marginal* utility added by each additional piece of candy depends, among other things, upon the amount of ice cream consumed. Likewise, the extra or marginal utility added by each additional serving of ice cream depends, among other things, upon the amount of pie consumed. Nonetheless, this newer form of the theory rests upon the questionable assumption of *cardinally* measurable utility.

Implicit in the paragraph above is an important

Definition: Marginal utility is the addition to total utility attributable to the addition of one unit of a good to the current rate of its consumption. According to the paragraph above, the marginal utility of good X depends not only upon its rate of consumption but upon the rates of consumption of other goods as well.

The last major step in the development of modern utility theory enabled economists to use the concept of utility without resorting to the assumption of cardinal measurability. This final step, which is essentially attributable to Pareto (1906), led to the use of *indifference curves* in analyzing consumer behavior. However, before we use indifference curves, it is essential to examine the assumptions underlying this concept.

3.1.b—Assumptions

First, we assume that each consumer has complete information on all matters pertaining to his consumption decisions. A consumer knows the full range of goods available in the market; he knows the technical capacity of each good to satisfy a want. Furthermore, he knows the exact price of each good, and he knows these prices will not be changed by his actions in the market. Finally, the consumer knows what his income will be during his planning period. Given all this information, we also assume that each consumer tries to maximize his satisfaction from consumption *given* his limited income.

Admittedly these assumptions are abstractions from reality. The consumer has only a fairly accurate notion of what his income will be for a reasonable planning period, not perfect knowledge. He only has a notion of the capacity of a good to satisfy a want, not precise knowledge of its capacity to satisfy. No consumer actually succeeds in the task of spending his limited income so as to maximize satisfaction. This failure is attributable to the lack of accurate information. Yet the more or less conscious effort to attain maximum satisfaction from a limited income determines an individual's demand for goods and services. The assumption of complete information does not distort the relevant aspects of the economic world.

Second, we assume that each consumer is able to rank all conceivable bundles of commodities. That is, when confronted with two or more bundles of goods, he is able to determine his order of preference among them. For example, assume that a person is confronted with two choices: (*a*) he can have five candy bars, six pints of ice cream, and one soft drink; or (*b*) he can have four candy bars, five pints of ice cream, and three soft drinks. The person can say one of three things: (*a*) he prefers the first bundle to the second; (*b*) he prefers the second to the first; or (*c*) he would be equally satisfied with either.

Therefore, when evaluating two bundles of goods, an individual either prefers one bundle of goods to the other, or he is indifferent between the two. Since we will use the concept of preference and indifference time and again, it is essential to understand this concept thoroughly now. If a consumer prefers one group of goods to another group, he obviously believes he will get a higher level of satisfaction from the preferred group. The less preferred bundle would, he believes, give less utility than the other. If a person is indifferent between two bundles, he would be perfectly willing to let someone else (or perhaps the flip of a coin) determine his choice. An economist would say that in the consumer's mind either bundle would yield him the same level of utility.

Much of what follows is based upon the consumer's ability to rank groups of commodities; it is important, however, to note what we *did not say* about consumer preference and indifference.

First, we did not say that the consumer estimates *how much* utility or *what level* of satisfaction he will attain from consuming a given bundle of goods. Only the ability to *rank* is fundamental; the ability to measure utility cardinally is not necessary.

Second, we did not imply that an individual can say by *how much* he prefers one bundle of goods to another. Admittedly, a consumer might be able to say he likes one group of goods a great deal more than another group, and perhaps just a little more than still another group. But "great deal" and "just a little" are imprecise; they are *ordinal* rankings; and their meanings differ from one person to another. Therefore, at this level of abstraction the theory of consumer behavior is not based upon the assumption that the consumer is able to state the amount by which he prefers one bundle to another.[1]

Third, we did not say *we think he should* choose one bundle over the other, or that we believe he will be better off if he did so. It is only necessary that the consumer be able to rank bundles according to the order of anticipated satisfaction.

Furthermore, we assume that the consumer's preference pattern possesses the following characteristics:

a) Given three bundles of goods (*A*, *B*, and *C*), if an individual prefers *A* to *B* and *B* to *C*, he must prefer *A* to *C*. Similarly, if an individual is indifferent between *A* and *B* and between *B* and *C*, he must be indifferent between *A* and *C*. Finally, if he is indifferent between *A* and *B* and prefers *B* to *C*, he must prefer *A* to *C*. This assumption obviously can be carried over to four or more different bundles.

b) It therefore follows that if an individual can rank *any pair* of bundles chosen at random from all conceivable bundles, he can rank *all conceivable bundles*.

c) If bundle *A* contains at least as many units of *each commodity* as

---

[1] It is not quite correct to say that it is impossible to measure the degree of preference. Advanced studies in price theory frequently deal to a greater or lesser extent with the application of probability theory to the problem of ranking budgets. Considerable controversy exists concerning the relevance of that approach.

bundle *B*, and *more* units of at least one commodity, *A* must be preferred to *B*.

Summarizing, the assumptions necessary to analyze consumer behavior can be set out in the following compact form.

Assumptions: (*a*) Each consumer has exact and full knowledge of all information relevant to his consumption decisions—knowledge of the goods and services available and of their technical capacity to satisfy his wants, of market prices, and of his money income.

(*b*) Each consumer has a preference pattern that (*i*) establishes a rank ordering among all bundles of goods; (*ii*) for pairwise comparisons, indicates that *A* is preferred to *B*, *B* preferred to *A*, or that they are indifferent; (*iii*) for three or more way comparisons, indicates that if *A* is preferred (indifferent) to *B* and *B* is preferred (indifferent) to *C*, *A* must be preferred (indifferent) to *C;* (*iv*) states that a greater bundle (in the sense of having at least as much of each good and more of at least one) is always preferred to a smaller one.

3.2 INDIFFERENCE CURVES

Using the assumptions set forth above, we can now analyze two concepts that are fundamental to the theory of consumer behavior.

Definition: An indifference curve is a locus of points—or particular bundles or combinations of goods—each of which yields the same level of total utility or satisfaction.

Definition: An indifference map is a graph that shows a set of indifference curves.

For analytical purposes let us consider a consumer who can use only two different goods, *X* and *Y*, each of which is continuously divisible or infinitesimally variable in quantity.[2] Figure 3.2.1 shows a portion of this consumer's indifference map consisting of four indifference curves labeled I–IV. Our consumer considers all combinations of *X* and *Y* on indifference curve I to be equivalent (for example, 20 *X* and 42 *Y*, and 60 *X* and 10 *Y*). That is, he believes these combinations will yield him the same satisfaction, and thus he is indifferent between them. Since he is indifferent between the two specified combinations, he is obviously willing to

---

[2] Admittedly, the possibility of continuous variation in quantity *is* perhaps less frequently encountered than "lumpiness," but this assumption permits a great gain in analytical precision at the sacrifice of very little realism. The assumption that bundles consist of no more than two separate goods enables us to analyze the problem of consumer behavior with two dimensional graphs. This assumption is made, therefore, purely for simplicity of exposition. With the use of the differential calculus, bundles of any number of different goods can be handled. But the analytical results based on two goods are exactly the same as those based upon more than two. Here again, the gain in simplicity outweighs the loss of realism.

FIGURE 3.2.1

Indifference Curves

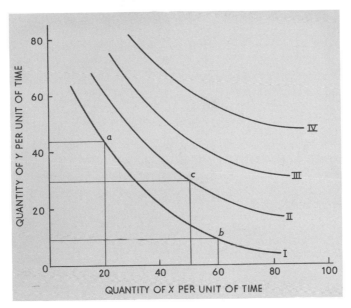

substitute X for Y in order to move from point a to point b. In other words, he is willing to give up 32 units of Y to obtain 40 additional units of X. Conversely, if he is presently situated at b he is willing to forego 40 units of X to obtain an additional 32 units of Y. Thus he is willing to substitute at the *average* rate of ⅘ units of Y per unit of X.

All combinations of goods on indifference curve II (say 30 Y and 50 X) are superior to *any* combinations of goods on I. Likewise, all combinations on III are superior to any combination on II. Each indifference curve that lies above a given indifference curve represents combinations of X and Y that are considered superior to, or capable of yielding more utility than, every combination on the given curve. At every utility level designated by a particular indifference curve, the consumer is willing to substitute X for Y or Y for X at some rate so as to leave him on the same curve (i.e., with the same satisfaction or *real* income) but consuming different combinations of goods.

Since X and Y are assumed to be continuously divisible, each indifference curve specifies an infinite number of combinations that yield the same amount of satisfaction. Further, it is important to note that the specific utility numbers attached to I, II, III, and IV are immaterial. The numbers might be 5, 7, 12, 32 or 96, 327, 450, 624 or any other set of numbers that *increase*. For the theory of consumer behavior, only the shape of the indifference curves matters. That is to say, only the ordinal ranking of commodity bundles is important. Since a precise measurement of utility is unnecessary, the theory of consumer behavior does not have to be based on the questionable concept of measurable utility. The indifference curves and the concept of preference are all that are required —all bundles of goods situated on the same indifference curve are equivalent; all combinations lying on a higher curve are preferred.

Relations: A consumer regards all bundles yielding the same level of utility as equivalent. The locus of such bundles is called an indifference curve because the consumer is indifferent as to the particular bundle he consumes. The higher, or further to the right, an indifference curve, the greater is the underlying level of utility. Therefore, the higher the indifference curve, the more preferred is each bundle situated on the curve.

To summarize, the essential difference between the older approaches mentioned above and the approach followed here lies in the nature of the measurement scale involved. In the older approaches, utility was assumed to be *cardinally measurable* in some sort of units. The indifference curve approach requires only *ordinal* (ordered or ranking) measurement. Thus the only requirement is that indifference curves rank bundles of goods according to preference. In Figure 3.2.1 all combinations on IV are most preferred; all combinations on III are preferred to those on II and are less desirable than those on IV, and so on.

3.3 CHARACTERISTICS OF INDIFFERENCE CURVES

Indifference curves have four characteristics that are important in our discussion of consumer behavior. The first property is an assumed one; the second and fourth are based upon our assumptions about consumer behavior; the third is a logical necessity.

For simplicity, assume once more that there are only two continuously divisible goods, X and Y. The X–Y plane is called *commodity space*. The first property results from the following assumption: each point in commodity space lies on one, and only one, indifference curve. This assumption is, of course, derived from the prior assumption that X and Y are continuously divisible. Each point in commodity space represents some specific combination of the two goods and hence some level of utility. As mentioned above, it is possible to take away Y and add X or take away X and add Y in an infinite number of ways and leave the consumer with the same level of satisfaction. Thus each point in commodity space lies on an indifference curve (and from the third property, each lies on only one indifference curve). However, for obvious reasons, when graphing an indifference map, only a relatively few curves are used to represent the entire map. But remember: an infinite number of indifference curves lie between any two indifference curves that are drawn.

Second, indifference curves are negatively sloped. This property is based on the assumption that a consumer prefers a greater bundle of goods to a smaller one. An upward sloping indifference curve would indicate that a consumer is indifferent between two combinations of goods, one of which contains more of *both* goods. The fact that a positive amount of one good must be added to the bundle to offset the loss of another good (if the consumer is to remain at the same level of satisfaction) implies negatively sloped indifference curves.

Third, indifference curves cannot intersect. This property is a logical necessity, as illustrated in Figure 3.3.1. In this graph I and II are in-

FIGURE 3.3.1

Indifference Curves Cannot Intersect

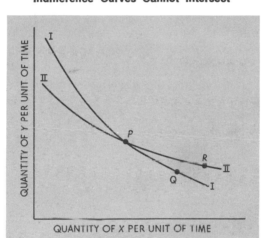

QUANTITY OF X PER UNIT OF TIME

difference curves, and the points *P*, *Q*, and *R* represent three different bundles (or combinations of *X* and *Y*). *R* must clearly be preferred to *Q* because it contains more of both goods. *R* and *P* are equivalent because they are situated on the same indifference curve. In like manner, the consumer is indifferent between *P* and *Q*. Indifference is a "transitive" relation—that is, if a consumer is indifferent between *A* and *B* and between *B* and *C*, he must be indifferent between *A* and *C*. In our case, *R* and *P* are equivalent, as are *P* and *Q*. Hence *R* must be equivalent to *Q*. But as previously mentioned, *R* is preferred to *Q* because it contains more of both goods. Hence intersecting indifference curves, such as those shown in Figure 3.3.1, are logically impossible.

The fourth property is that indifference curves are *concave from above* —that is, an indifference curve must lie above its tangent at each point, as illustrated in Figure 3.3.2. The reasoning behind this property is discussed in the next section dealing with the marginal rate of substitution.

Let us note that these four properties preclude certain patterns that indifference curves might otherwise take. Figure 3.3.3 shows four of these excluded relations.

Panel *a* indicates that goods *X* and *Y* are perfect substitutes, and thus we would simply consider *X* and *Y* to be the same good. Panel *b* shows indifference curves concave from below; we will subsequently analyze this type of relation. Panel *c* shows that the consumer considers one of the commodities a "good" but the other a "bad." Since increasing *X* de-

FIGURE 3.3.2

Indifference Curves Are Concave from Above

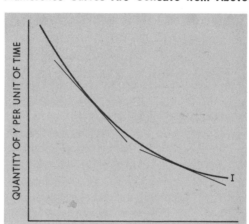

QUANTITY OF *Y* PER UNIT OF TIME

QUANTITY OF *X* PER UNIT OF TIME

creases his satisfaction for each level of *Y*, he prefers less *X* to more; *X* yields disutility to him and would thus never be purchased by a rational consumer. Finally, panel *d* shows that while the consumer does not consider *X* a nuisance (it does not give disutility), he does not gain utility from *X*. Again, no rational consumer would consider spending a part of his limited income on a commodity that does not contribute to his satisfaction.

The results of this section may be summarized in the following:

Relations: Indifference curves have the following properties: (*a*) some indifference curve passes through each point in commodity space; (*b*) indifference curves slope downward to the right; (*c*) indifference curves cannot intersect; and (*d*) indifference curves are concave from above. In particular, indifference curves whose qualitative properties resemble those in Figure 3.3.3 are precluded from analysis.

FIGURE 3.3.3

Excluded Types of Indifference Curves

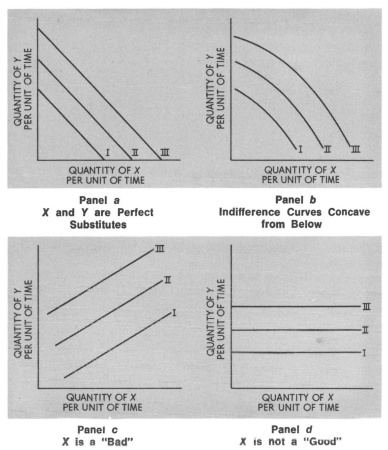

Panel *a*
X and Y are Perfect
Substitutes

Panel *b*
Indifference Curves Concave
from Below

Panel *c*
X is a "Bad"

Panel *d*
X is not a "Good"

3.4 MARGINAL RATE OF SUBSTITUTION

As previously emphasized, one essential feature of subjective value theory is that different combinations of commodities can give rise to the same level of utility. In other words, the consumer is indifferent as to the particular combination he obtains. Therefore, as market prices might dictate, one commodity can be substituted for another in the right amount so that the consumer remains just as well off as before. He will, in other words, remain on the same indifference curve. It is of considerable interest to know the rate at which a consumer is willing to substitute one commodity for another in his consumption.

The reason for analyzing this rate of substitution so carefully lies in the concept of utility maximization. As we shall see later in this chapter, a consumer attains maximum satisfaction from his limited money income when he chooses a combination of goods such that the rate at which he is *willing* to substitute goods is the same as the rate at which he is *permitted* to substitute by market prices. Therefore to understand utility maximization one must understand the rate of substitution in consumption.

3.4.a—Substitution in Consumption

Consider Figure 3.4.1. An indifference curve is represented by I. The consumer is indifferent between bundle R, containing 4 units of X and

FIGURE 3.4.1

The Marginal Rate of Substitution

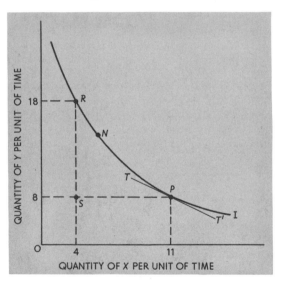

18 of Y, and bundle P, containing 11 units of X and 8 of Y. The consumer is willing to substitute 7 units of X for 10 of Y. The *rate* at which he is willing, on average, to substitute X for Y is therefore

$$\frac{\Delta Y}{\Delta X} = \frac{RS}{SP} = \frac{18 - 8}{4 - 11} = -\frac{10}{7},$$

where Δ means "the change in." This ratio measures the average number of units of Y the consumer is willing to forego in order to obtain one additional unit of X (over the range of consumption pairs under consideration).[3] Thus he is willing to give up $1\frac{3}{7}$ units of Y in order to gain one unit of X. Stated alternatively, the ratio measures the amount of Y that must be sacrificed ($1\frac{3}{7}$ units) per unit of X gained if the consumer is to remain at precisely the same level of satisfaction.

In our subsequent use, we would find it very cumbersome to have the minus sign on the right-hand side of the equation above. Thus we define the rate of substitution as

$$-\frac{\Delta Y}{\Delta X} = \frac{10}{7}.$$

The rate of substitution given by the ratio above is obviously the negative of the slope of a straight line joining points R and P. The ratio could be quite different between two alternative points, say N and P. But as the point R moves along I toward P, the ratio RS/SP approaches closer and closer to the slope of the tangent TT' at P. In the limit, for extremely small movements in the neighborhood of P, the negative of the slope of I, which is the negative of the slope of its tangent at P, is called the marginal rate of substitution of X for Y.

Definition: The marginal rate of substitution of X for Y measures the number of units of Y that must be sacrificed per unit of X gained so as to maintain a constant level of satisfaction. The marginal rate of substitution is given by the negative of the slope of an indifference curve at a point. It is defined only for movements along an indifference curve, never for movements among curves.

Note: Since we wish the marginal rate of substitution to be positive, and since $\Delta Y/\Delta X$ is necessarily negative, the *minus* sign must be attached.

As should be obvious, the term "margin" is again used (as it always is) to denote "the change in" when the change in question is very small.

Note: we shall hereafter use the mnemonic letters MRS to denote the marginal rate of substitution of X for Y in consumption or, more generally, the marginal rate of substitution of the variable plotted on the horizontal axis for the variable plotted on the vertical axis.

3.4.b—Interpretation of MRS

The meaning of MRS may be made clearer if we revert, for the moment, to the older marginal utility approach. First, recall that marginal utility is either (a) the increase in utility attributable to a small increase

---

[3] The ratio is, of course, negative since the change in Y associated with an increase in X is negative. This type of relation results directly from the postulate of negatively sloped indifference curves.

in the rate of consumption, or (b) the decrease in utility attributable to a small decrease in the rate of consumption.

Now refer to Figure 3.4.2. Suppose the consumer is initially at point P, purchasing OY_1 units of Y and OX_1 units of X. He accordingly attains the II level of satisfaction. Suppose his consumption of Y is reduced by a small amount, from OY_1 to OY_2. He moves to point Q on I and suffers a loss of utility represented by the difference between II and I, denoted II–I (for example, if II represents 100 units of utility and I represents 90, he loses 10 units of utility).

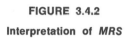

FIGURE 3.4.2

Interpretation of MRS

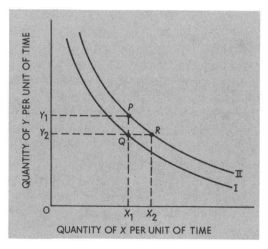

The marginal utility of this small reduction in Y consumption is thus the decrease in utility divided by the decrease in Y consumed. If we denote marginal utility by MU, we may represent this change by

$$MU_Y = \frac{II - I}{Y_1 Y_2}.$$

Now let the consumer return to the II level of utility by holding Y consumption at OY_2 and increasing X consumption from OX_1 to OX_2. The marginal utility of X, by our argument above, is

$$MU_X = \frac{II - I}{X_1 X_2}.$$

Taking the ratio of the two marginal utilities, one obtains

$$\frac{MU_X}{MU_Y} = \frac{II - I}{X_1 X_2} \div \frac{II - I}{Y_1 Y_2} = \frac{Y_1 Y_2}{X_1 X_2}.$$

But by the figure,

$$\frac{MU_X}{MU_Y} = \frac{Y_1Y_2}{X_1X_2} = \frac{PQ}{QR} = \text{rate of substitution.}$$

Thus for small movements in the neighborhood of R, the MRS of X for Y is the ratio of the marginal utility of X to the marginal utility of Y. We may thus formulate an alternative

Definition: the MRS of X for Y is equal to the ratio of the marginal utility of X to the marginal utility of Y. In symbols,

$$MRS_{X \text{ for } Y} = \frac{MU_X}{MU_Y}.$$

3.5 DIMINISHING MRS

The requirement that indifference curves be concave from above implies that the MRS of X for Y diminishes as X is substituted for Y along an indifference curve. This is illustrated in Figure 3.5.1.

FIGURE 3.5.1

Diminishing Marginal Rate of Substitution

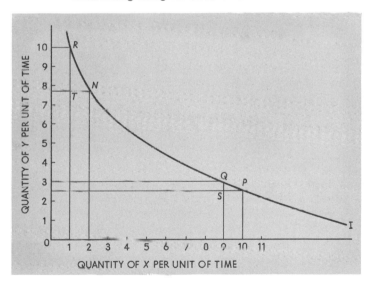

I is an indifference curve; R, N, Q, and P are four bundles situated on this curve. Consider a movement from R to N. In order to maintain the same level of utility, the consumer is willing to sacrifice slightly more than two units of Y to gain one unit of X. Now consider the consumer situated at Q. To move to P and gain one unit of X, the consumer now is willing to give up approximately ½ unit of Y.

This result follows logically from our assumptions. The more of a good one consumes, the more of that good he would probably be willing to trade for some other good. For example, if a person at a football game has ten hot dogs and one soft drink, he might be willing to trade three hot dogs for a soft drink. On the other hand, if the same person had only five hot dogs, but three soft drinks, he would perhaps be willing to trade only one hot dog for an additional soft drink.

A marginal utility interpretation of this example might help. First remember that the marginal utility of any commodity is smaller the greater the rate of its consumption. Now picture a graph (or construct one for yourself) in which the number of hot dogs is plotted on the vertical axis, the number of soft drinks on the horizontal.

When the number of hot dogs is great, the marginal utility of hot dogs is relatively low. Similarly, when the number of soft drinks is low, their marginal utility is relatively high. Thus the *MRS*, which is the ratio of the marginal utility of soft drinks to that of hot dogs, is relatively high. Now let the football fan substitute soft drinks for hot dogs (X for Y, in the previous notation). Increasing the rate of consumption of soft drinks decreases their marginal utility, while reducing the rate of consumption of hot dogs increases theirs. Thus the substitution of soft drinks for hot dogs must lead to a decrease in the *MRS* of soft drinks for hot dogs.

Diminishing *MRS* is further illustrated in Figure 3.5.2. I is an indifference curve, and P, Q, and R are three bundles situated on this curve. The horizontal axis is measured so that $OX_1 = X_1X_2 = X_2X_3$. Consider

FIGURE 3.5.2

Diminishing *MRS*

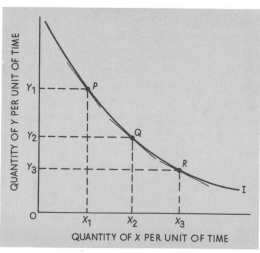

QUANTITY OF X PER UNIT OF TIME

first the movement from P to Q. If P is very close to Q, or the amount X_1X_2 is very small, the MRS at Q is

$$\frac{OY_1 - OY_2}{OX_2 - OX_1} = \frac{Y_1Y_2}{X_1X_2}.$$

Similarly, for a movement from Q to R, the MRS at R is

$$\frac{OY_2 - OY_3}{OX_3 - OX_2} = \frac{Y_2Y_3}{X_2X_3}.$$

By construction $X_1X_2 = X_2X_3$; but very obviously, $Y_1Y_2 > Y_2Y_3$. Hence the MRS is less at R than at Q. This is also shown by the absolutely decreasing slopes of the tangents at P, Q, and R.

3.6 THE BUDGET LINE

In Chapter 2 we emphasized that demand indicates what the consumer is willing and able to do. Thus far in this chapter we have concentrated upon what the consumer is *willing* to do; we must now discuss what the consumer is *able* to do.

3.6.a—Limited Money Income

If all consumers had an unlimited money income—in other words, if there were an unlimited pool of resources—there would be no problem of "economizing," nor would there be "economics." But since this utopian state does not exist, even for the richest members of our society, people are compelled to determine their behavior in light of limited financial resources. For the theory of consumer behavior, this means that each consumer has a maximum amount he can spend per period of time. The consumer's problem is to spend this amount in the way that yields him maximum satisfaction.

Continue to assume that there are only two goods, X and Y, bought in quantities x and y. Each individual consumer is confronted with market-determined prices p_x and p_y of X and Y respectively. Finally, the consumer in question has a known and fixed money income (M) for the period under consideration M is the maximum amount the consumer can spend, and we assume that he spends all of this on X and Y [4] Thus the

---

[4] In more advanced models, saving may be considered as one of the many goods and services available to the consumer. Graphical treatment limits us to two dimensions; thus we ignore saving. This does not mean that the theory of consumer behavior precludes saving—depending upon his preference ordering, a consumer may save much, little, or nothing. Similarly, spending may in fact exceed income in any given period as a result of borrowing or from using assets acquired in the past. The M in question for any period is the total amount of money to be spent during the period.

amount spent on X (xp_x) plus the amount spent on Y (yp_y) is equal to the stipulated money income. Algebraically,

$$M = xp_x + yp_y .$$ (3.6.1)

This is the equation of a straight line. Solving for y—since y is plotted on the vertical axis—one obtains

$$y = \frac{1}{p_y} M - \frac{p_x}{p_y} x .$$ (3.6.2)

Equation (3.6.2) is plotted in Figure 3.6.1. The first term on the right-

FIGURE 3.6.1

Budget Line

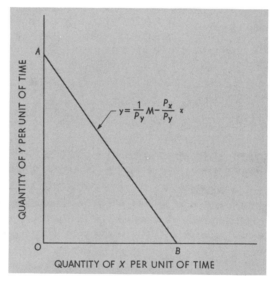

hand side of equation (3.6.2), $\frac{1}{p_y} M$, shows the amount of Y that can be purchased if no X is purchased at all. This amount is represented by the distance OA in Figure 3.6.1; thus $\frac{1}{p_y} M$ (or point A) is the ordinate intercept of the equation.

In equation (3.6.2) $- \frac{p_x}{p_y}$ is the slope of the line. Consequently, the slope of the budget constraint is the negative of the price ratio. To see this, consider the quantity of X that can be purchased if Y is not bought. This amount is $\frac{1}{p_x} M$, shown by the distance OB in Figure 3.6.1. Since the line obviously has a negative slope, its slope is given by

$$-\frac{OA}{OB} = -\frac{\dfrac{1}{p_y}M}{\dfrac{1}{p_x}M} = -\frac{p_x}{p_y}.$$

The line in Figure 3.6.1 is called the budget line.

Definition: The budget line is the locus of combinations or bundles of goods that can be purchased if the entire money income is spent. Its slope is the negative of the price ratio.

Note again our assumption that the consumer spends all his money income on X and Y. This implies that the bundle purchased must lie on the budget line.

3.6.b—Shifting the Budget Line

In much of the analysis that follows, we are interested in comparative static changes in quantities purchased resulting from changes in price and money income, both of which are represented graphically by shifts in the budget line.

In Figure 3.6.2, X is a specific good, the quantity of which is measured along the horizontal axis. In contrast, to the preceding discussion, how-

FIGURE 3.6.2

Budget Lines for Changing Income

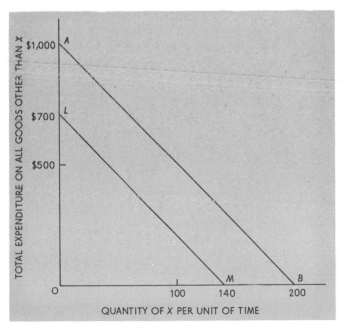

ever, Y does not represent another specific good. Let us now call Y "total expenditures on all goods other than X" and measure this amount along the vertical axis. Naturally, the unit of measurement along the horizontal axis is units of X per period of time, and the unit of measurement along the vertical is dollars. We assume that the prices of all goods other than X are fixed.

At the outset, let the price of X be $5 per unit and the consumer's income be $1,000. His budget line (in Figure 3.6.2) is represented by AB, a line from $1,000 on the vertical axis to 200 on the horizontal. At a price of $5, the consumer can purchase 200 units of X if he spends nothing on other goods (point B), he can spend $1,000 on other goods if he buys no X (point A), or he can consume any other combination represented by a point on AB.

As before, the slope of the budget line is the negative of the ratio of the prices. But the price of an additional dollar of expenditure on other goods is obviously one dollar. The negative of the price ratio is, therefore, $-p_x/1 = -p_x$, so the slope of AB is -5. To increase his consumption of X by one unit, the consumer must give up $5 in expenditures on other goods.

Now let the consumer suffer a $300 decrease in income while all other prices, including the price of X, remain the same. The new budget line is LM. The consumer can spend $700 (his new income) on other goods, buying no X; he can spend the entire $700 on X, purchasing 140 units; or he can consume at any other point on the line. The slope of the new budget line LM is the same (-5) since the price ratio has not changed. Thus a decrease in money income, prices unchanged, is represented by a parallel shift of the budget line, downward and to the left. It should be easy to see that an *increase* in money income, prices unchanged, is represented by a parallel shift in the other direction.

Figure 3.6.3 shows what happens to the budget line when the price of X increases, money income remaining the same. The axes in this figure are the same as those in Figure 3.6.2. Assume once again that the original money income is $1,000 and the original price of X is $5 per unit. The budget line AB is the same as in Figure 3.6.2. Now assume that the price of X increases to $10. As before the consumer can spend $1,000 on other goods if he purchases no X; the intercept of the budget line on the vertical axis thus remains the same. However, if the consumer spends all his income on X, at the new price of $10 he can buy only 100 units of X with his $1,000 income. The budget line intercepts the horizontal axis at B'. Note that the slope of the budget line (the negative of the price of X) becomes steeper, from -5 to -10. AB' represents the new budget line. An increase in the price of X thus rotates the budget line to the left around point A, the intercept on the vertical axis. It should be easy to see

FIGURE 3.6.3

Budget Lines for Changing Price of X

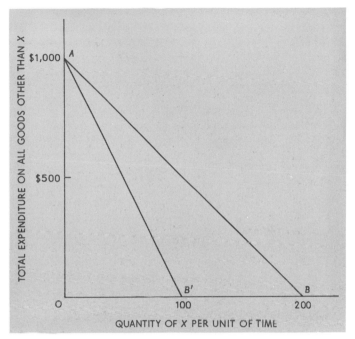

that a decrease in price causes the budget line to rotate to the right.

Let us now take an alternative approach and assume that both X and Y are specific goods. First consider an increase in money income from M to $M^* > M$, commodity prices remaining unchanged. The consumer can now purchase more—more of Y, more of X, or more of both. The maximum purchase of Y increases from $\frac{1}{p_y} M$ to $\frac{1}{p_y} M^*$, or from OA to OA' in Figure 3.6.4. Similarly, the maximum purchase of X increases from $\frac{1}{p_x} M$ to $\frac{1}{p_x} M^*$, or from OB to OB'. Since prices remain constant the slope of the budget line does not change. Thus an increase in money income, prices remaining constant, is shown graphically by shifting the budget line upward to the right. Since the slope does not change, the movement might be called a "parallel" shift. It readily follows that a decrease in money income is shown by a parallel shift of the budget line in the direction of the origin.

Figure 3.6.5 shows what happens to the budget line when the price of X increases, the money price of Y and money income remaining constant. Let the price of X increase from p_x to p_x^*. Since p_y and M are un-

FIGURE 3.6.4

Changing Money Income

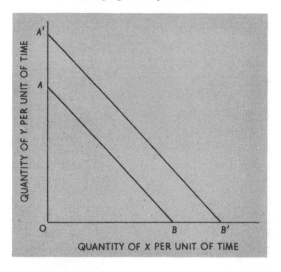

changed, the ordinate intercept does not change—it is OA in each case. But the slope of the line, the negative of the price ratio, changes from $-p_x/p_y$ to $-p_x^*/p_y$. Since $p_x^* > p_x$, $-p_x^*/p_y < -p_x/p_y$. In other words, the slope of the budget line becomes steeper.

FIGURE 3.6.5

Changing the Price of X

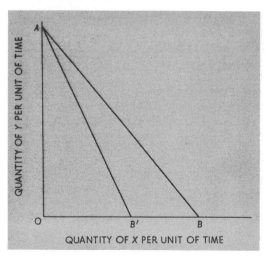

Alternatively, the price change can be explained as follows. At the original price p_x, the maximum purchase of X is $\frac{1}{p_x} M$, or the distance OB. When the price changes to $p_x{}^*$, the maximum purchase of X is $\frac{1}{p_x{}^*} M$, or the distance OB'. Thus an increase in the price of X is shown by rotating the budget line clockwise around the ordinate intercept. A decrease in the price of X is represented by a counterclockwise movement.

Relations: (a) An increase in money income, prices unchanged, is shown by a parallel shift of the budget line—outward and to the right for an increase in money income, and in the direction of the origin for a decrease in money income. (b) A change in the price of X, the price of Y and money income constant, is shown by rotating the budget line around the ordinate intercept—to the left for a price increase and to the right for a decrease in price.

3.7 CONSUMER EQUILIBRIUM

All bundles of goods (combinations of X and Y) designated by the budget line are available to the consumer in the sense that his income allows him to purchase them if he wishes. This line is established by his fixed money income and the given prices of the commodities available. The consumer's indifference map shows his rank ordering of all conceivable bundles of X and Y. The principal assumption upon which the theory of consumer behavior is built is that *a consumer attempts to allocate his limited money income among available goods and services so as to maximize his satisfaction or utility.* Given that assumption and the concepts developed in this chapter, it is a relatively simple matter to determine the way in which a consumer will allocate his income, i.e., select the most preferred bundle of goods available to him.

3.7.a—Maximizing Satisfaction Subject to a Limited Money Income

Graphically, the consumer's problem is depicted by Figure 3.7.1. A portion of his indifference map, represented by the four indifference curves drawn in that figure, indicates his preferences among different combinations of goods. Similarly, his budget line, LM, specifies the different combinations he can purchase with his limited income, assuming he spends all of his income on X and Y. Thus his choice of combinations is limited by his limited income.

Clearly, the consumer cannot purchase any bundle lying above and to the right of budget line LM, and hence he cannot consume any combination lying on indifference curve IV. He can attain some points on curves I, II, and III. Moreover, as already observed, an infinite number of in-

FIGURE 3.7.1

Consumer Equilibrium

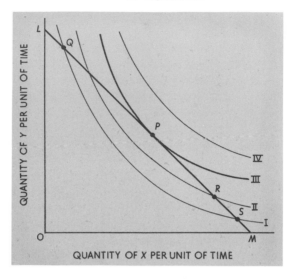

QUANTITY OF X PER UNIT OF TIME

difference curves lie between curves I and III. Therefore, all points on the budget line between Q and S are touched by some indifference curve (and, if we extend the map to include curves below I, all points above Q and below S are touched by some curve). Thus each point on the budget line yields some specific level of utility. Four of the infinite number of attainable combinations on LM are represented by points Q, P, R, and S.

Suppose the consumer is located at Q. Without experimenting, he cannot know for certain whether Q represents a maximum position or not. Thus let him experimentally move to combinations just to the left and right of Q. Moving to the left lowers his level of satisfaction to some indifference curve below I. But moving to the right brings him to a higher indifference curve; and continued experimentation will lead him to move at least as far as P, because each successive movement to the right brings the consumer to a higher indifference curve. If he continued to experiment, however, by moving to the right of P, the consumer would find himself upon a lower indifference curve with its lower level of satisfaction. He would accordingly return to the point P.

Similarly, if a consumer were situated at R, experimentation would lead him to substitute Y for X, thereby moving in the direction of P. He would not stop short of P because each successive substitution of Y for X brings the consumer to a higher indifference curve. Hence the position of maximum satisfaction—*or the point of consumer equilibrium*—is attained at P, where an indifference curve is just tangent to the budget line.

As you will recall, the slope of the budget line is the negative of the price ratio, the ratio of the price of X to the price of Y. As you will also recall, the slope of an indifference curve at any point is called the *MRS* of X for Y. Hence the point of consumer equilibrium is defined by the condition that the *MRS* must equal the price ratio.

The interpretation of this proposition is very straightforward. The *MRS* shows the rate at which the consumer *is willing to substitute* X for Y. The price ratio shows the rate at which he *can substitute* X for Y. Unless these two are equal, it is possible to change the combination of X and Y purchased so as to attain a higher level of satisfaction. For example, suppose the *MRS* is two—meaning the consumer is willing to give up two units of Y in order to obtain one unit of X. Let the price ratio be unity, meaning that one unit of Y can be exchanged for one unit of X. Clearly, the consumer will benefit by trading Y for X, since he is willing to give two Y for one X but only has to give one Y for one X in the market. Generalizing, unless the *MRS* and the price ratio are equal, some exchange can be made so as to push the consumer to a higher level of satisfaction.

Principle: The point of consumer equilibrium—or the maximization of satisfaction subject to a limited money Income—is defined by the condition that the *MRS* of X for Y must equal the ratio of the price of X to the price of Y.

3.7.b—Marginal Utility Interpretation

Let us write the condition for consumer equilibrium symbolically:

$$MRS_{x \text{ for } y} = \frac{p_x}{p_y} .$$

Now in section 3.4.b we found that

$$MRS_{x \text{ for } y} = \frac{MU_x}{MU_y} .$$

Thus we may write

$$\frac{MU_x}{MU_y} = \frac{p_x}{p_y} ,$$

or

$$\frac{MU_x}{p_x} = \frac{MU_y}{p_y} .$$

The relation just above provides an alternative view of the condition for consumer equilibrium. Dividing the marginal utility of a commodity by its price gives the marginal utility per dollar's worth of the commodity bought. In this light we can restate the condition for consumer equilibrium as the following

Principle: To attain equilibrium, a consumer must allocate his money income so that the marginal utility per dollar spent on each commodity is the same for all commodities purchased.

This principle is certainly plausible; and explaining why it is plausible illustrates a method of analysis that is used pervasively in economic theory. Suppose at the current allocation of income, the marginal dollar spent on X yields a greater marginal utility than the marginal dollar spent on Y. That is, suppose

$$\frac{MU_x}{p_x} > \frac{MU_y}{p_y}.$$

Reallocating one dollar of expenditure from Y to X will therefore increase total utility; and it must do so until the marginal utility per dollar's worth is the same for both commodities.

Exercise: Carry out the same line of reasoning for the case in which

$$\frac{MU_x}{p_x} < \frac{MU_y}{p_y}.$$

3.7.c—Corner Solutions

To this point, the discussion implies that in equilibrium the consumer will choose to consume some positive amount of both X and Y, regardless of relative prices. This circumstance obviously need not be the case. A consumer might choose to spend all of his income on one good and purchase none of the other. More particularly, in the next chapter we frequently analyze consumer behavior when X is one good and Y is taken to represent expenditure on all goods other than X. In this case, it would certainly not be uncommon for a consumer to purchase no X, especially if its relative price is high.

One set of theoretical circumstances under which a consumer would choose to spend all of his income on (say) good Y and none on X is depicted in Figure 3.7.2, panel *a*. Given the budget line LM and the indifference map represented by curves I, II, III, and IV, the highest level of satisfaction attainable from the given money income lies at point L on indifference curve III. The consumer chooses to purchase OL units of Y and no X. This point need not be a point of tangency at which the MRS equals the price ratio (although it could be such a point). Note than an equilibrium situation exists even though there is no point (at both nonnegative X and nonnegative Y) where the MRS equals the price ratio.

FIGURE 3.7.2

Corner Solutions

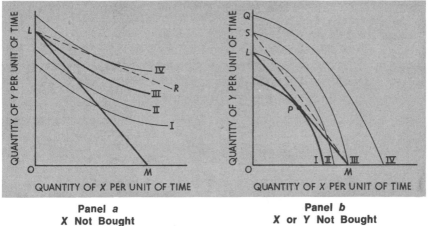

Panel *a*
***X* Not Bought**

Panel *b*
***X* or *Y* Not Bought**

Economists call such a situation a *corner solution*. Note also, however, that for a sufficiently substantial decrease in the price of X relative to the price of Y (say to a price ratio depicted by budget line *LR*), the budget line could become tangent to some indifference curve above III (curve IV) at a point where both X and Y are bought. Hence the consumer will purchase some positive amount of X if its relative price decreases sufficiently.

Consider now the case of a consumer whose indifference map is not made up of indifference curves concave from above but of the previously rejected curves that are concave from below. Panel *b*, Figure 3.7.2, depicts such a situation. Here the point at which the original budget line *LM* is tangent to an indifference curve, point *P*, lies not on the highest indifference curve attainable but on the *lowest*. The highest level of satisfaction that can be achieved, given the budget line *LM*, lies at point *M* on indifference curve III. The consumer purchases *OM* units of X and no Y. Furthermore, there is no price ratio that would induce him to consume at a noncorner or interior point. Suppose the price of Y declines so that the budget line is *SM*. Now the consumer is indifferent between spending all of his money on Y or all on X; but any other combination would give less satisfaction. A further decrease in the price of Y, say a budget line drawn from *Q* to *M*, would cause the consumer to choose *OQ* units of Y and no X. Now you probably see better why we originally rejected such indifference maps (with increasing *MRS*'s). They either result in "all or nothing" solutions or in unstable points of consumer equilibrium.

3.8 CONCLUSION

Now we are prepared to examine some of the more interesting aspects of consumer behavior—how the consumer behaves when confronted with changes in his income and in the price ratio. We also have the tools to analyze certain economic problems, for example, the relation between an indifference map and demand and the choice between leisure and work.

3.9 ANALYTICAL EXERCISE

A college student is cramming for final examinations. He has only six hours of study time remaining, and his goal is to get as high an *average* grade as possible in three subjects: economics, mathematics, and statistics (i.e., his goal is to maximize the sum of the test scores in the three subjects). He must decide how to allocate his time among the subjects.

According to the best estimates he can make, his grade in each subject will depend upon the time allocated to it according to the following schedule:

Economics		*Mathematics*		*Statistics*	
Hours of Study	*Grade*	*Hours of Study*	*Grade*	*Hours of Study*	*Grade*
0	20	0	40	0	80
1	45	1	52	1	90
2	65	2	62	2	95
3	75	3	71	3	97
4	83	4	78	4	98
5	90	5	83	5	99
6	92	6	86	6	99

The solution to this time allocation problem is obtained by a straight-forward application of the *MRS* = price ratio rule for consumer equilibrium. In this case, the *MRS* = price ratio must hold for all three pairs, i.e., economics-mathematics, economics-statistics, and mathematics-statistics. Further, as shown in section 3.4.b, any one of the *MRS*'s is given by the ratio of the "marginal return per additional hour of study" between any pair of subjects. The price of studying one subject for an additional hour is the hour sacrificed in studying for either of the other subjects. The price of studying one subject for an additional hour is, therefore, *one hour;* the price ratio is accordingly unity between any pair of subjects. Thus the student should allocate his time so that the three *MRS*'s are unity.

Let us now prepare a table showing the marginal return per additional hour spent on each subject. The way the table is prepared is as follows: if one additional hour is spent studying economics, i.e., the student goes from zero to one hour, his grade increases by 25 points; a second additional hour of study in economics increases his grade by 20 points, and so forth. Following this procedure, we obtain the table below.

Economics		*Mathematics*		*Statistics*	
Additional Hours	*Marginal Increase*	*Additional Hours*	*Marginal Increase*	*Additional Hours*	*Marginal Increase*
1.........25		1.........12		1.........10	
2.........20		2.........10		2......... 5	
3.........10		3......... 9		3......... 2	
4......... 8		4......... 7		4......... 1	
5......... 7		5......... 5		5......... 1	
6......... 2		6......... 3		6......... 0	

Since the "price" ratio is unity in all cases, we must find the time allocation that will (*a*) precisely use up the six available hours and (*b*) make all three *MRS*'s equal unity. A simple inspection of the table shows that the only allocation in which all *MRS*'s are unity is the one where the marginal increase in grade per additional hour of study is 10. This occurs when three hours are devoted to economics, two to mathematics, and one to statistics. This time allocation exactly uses up the available hours; and by our marginal maximization calculations, it is the one that maximizes the average grade.

QUESTIONS AND PROBLEMS

1. One of the basic assumptions underlying the theory of consumer behavior states that increases in utility tend to diminish as the consumption of a good increases. (*a*) If you think this is true, show what role the assumption plays in the development of the theory and in its conclusions. (*b*) If you think it is false, demonstrate that the main results of the theory of consumer behavior can be obtained anyway.

2. Both the marginal utility approach and the indifference curve approach yield the same equilibrium position for a rational consumer. Compare these explanations of equilibrium and discuss the relative advantages of the two approaches.

3. Comment on the following pair of statements: (*a*) consumer preferences are measured by relative prices; (*b*) consumer preferences are independent of relative prices.

4. There are three commodities X, Y, and Z. The table contains a list of

bundles composed of different combinations of these three goods. Determine the rank order of the bundles (in this problem, there are no bundles among which the consumer is indifferent).

Bundle	Amount of X	Amount of Y	Amount of Z	Rank Order
A	86	88	77	
B	86	87	76	
C	100	90	80	
D	79	80	69	
E	85	87	76	
F	79	79	68	
G	95	89	79	
H	80	80	70	
I	79	79	69	
J	86	87	77	

4

Theory of Consumer Behavior: Comparative Statics

4.1 INTRODUCTION

Having examined the conditions that determine consumer equilibrium we are now prepared to analyze the more interesting problems concerning responses to changes in two variables, money income and price. The methods of analysis developed in these studies are then used to analyze certain other economic problems.

4.2 CHANGES IN MONEY INCOME

Changes in money income, prices remaining constant, affect the quantities of commodities bought. As explained in Chapter 3, Section 3.6, an increase in money income shifts the budget line upward and to the right; since nominal prices remain constant, the movement is a parallel shift. We now analyze the precise way in which a change in money income affects consumption. At the outset, it may be well to emphasize that throughout this section we assume that the prices of all goods remain constant. That is, our comparative static analysis is restricted to a change in money income only.

4.2.a—Income-Consumption Curve: Normal Goods

In Figure 4.2.1 the quantity of X, some specific good, is measured along the horizontal axis; "Expenditure on All Goods Other Than X" is measured in dollars along the vertical axis. Each indifference curve (I, II, III, and IV) indicates the various combinations of X and expenditures on other goods that yield the same level of utility. For example, the consumer

FIGURE 4.2.1

Indifference Curves

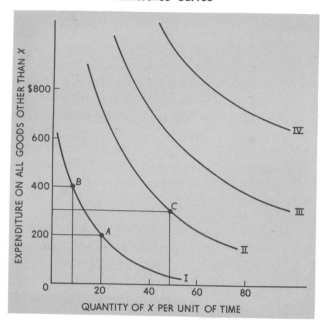

is indifferent between purchasing eight units of X and spending $400 on other goods (point B) and purchasing 20 units of X and spending $200 on other goods (point A). He considers C, 45 units of X and an expenditure of $300 on other goods, superior to either B or A. As always, all points on an indifference curve yield the same level of satisfaction; all combinations on higher indifference curves yield a greater level of satisfaction. In constructing indifference curves of this type (as of any other type), we do not need to know anything about the price of X; we need to know only that the prices of all other goods do not change. Note, however, that while the prices of all other goods do not change, the consumer is not restricted to purchasing a *proportionate* amount of each good other than X at every level of expenditure. For example, at point A the consumer spends $200 on other goods and at B, $400; but he does not necessarily double his consumption of *each* good in moving from A to B. He simply spends twice as much on all other goods taken together.

Now let us assume that the price of X is fixed at $10 per unit. Budget lines LM, L'M', L"M", and L'''M''' in Figure 4.2.2 indicate the various combinations of X and expenditures on other goods available to a consumer with incomes of $400, $700, $1,000, and $1,400 respectively. The method of derivation is exactly the same as that described in subsection

FIGURE 4.2.2

Income-Consumption Curve

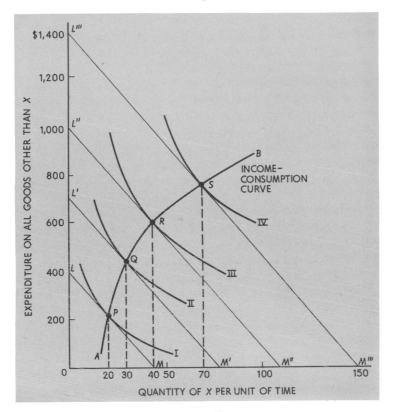

3.6.b. Indifference curves I–IV are qualitatively the same as those in Figure 4.2.1.

Using the analysis developed in Chapter 3, we can see that the equilibrium levels of consumption (points of tangency) are at points P, Q, R, and S. At an income of $400 the consumer buys 20 units of X at $10 each and spends the remainder, $200, on other goods; at an income of $700 he buys 30 units of X and spends $400 on other goods; and so forth. As income changes, the point of consumer equilibrium changes as well. The line connecting the successive equilibria is called the income-consumption curve. This curve shows the *equilibrium combinations* of X and expenditures on all goods other than X at various levels of money income, nominal prices remaining constant throughout. That is, it shows the various static equilibria corresponding to various income levels; it thus also

FIGURE 4.2.3

Engel Curve

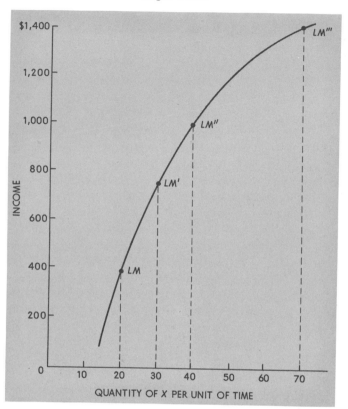

shows the comparative static effects of changes in money income at constant commodity prices.

This comparative static locus, labeled *AB* in Figure 4.2.2, is called the income-consumption curve.

Definition: The locus of points showing consumer equilibria at various levels of money income at constant prices is called the income-consumption curve.

The fact that the income-consumption curve does not bend backward indicates that good *X* is a *normal* good at all income levels. That is, more *X* is purchased as money income increases; the income-consumption curve is positively sloped in the case of a normal good.

Definition: A *normal* good is one whose consumption varies *directly* with money income at constant prices for *all* levels of money income.

4.2.b—Engel Curves

The income-consumption curve may be used to derive an Engel curve for a commodity.

Definition: An Engel curve is a locus of points relating equilibrium quantity to the level of money income. The name is taken from Christian Lorenz Ernst Engel, a 19th-century German statistician.

Engel curves are important for applied studies of economic welfare and for the analysis of family expenditure patterns.

An Engel curve derived from the income-consumption curve in Figure 4.2.2 is constructed in Figure 4.2.3. The four points LM, $L'M'$, $L''M''$, and $L'''M'''$ designate the amounts of good X consumed at each of the four similarly labeled budget lines in Figure 4.2.2. As we shall see, not all Engel curves have the same general slope as the one in Figure 4.2.3.

4.2.c—Alternative Approach

Consider Figure 4.2.4. Here X is a good and Y is some other good (not expenditure or all goods other than X). The scales on both axes are the number of units of X and Y. The price ratio is given by the negative of the slope of LM, the original budget line, and remains constant throughout.

With money income represented by LM, the consumer is in equilib-

FIGURE 4.2.4

Income-Consumption Curve

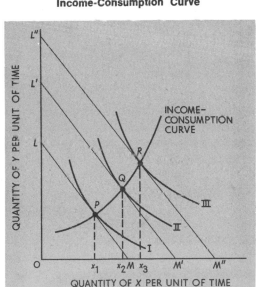

rium at point P on indifference curve I, consuming Ox_1 units of X. Now let money income rise to the level represented by $L'M'$. The consumer shifts to a new equilibrium point Q on indifference curve II. He has clearly gained. He also gains when money income shifts to the level corresponding to $L''M''$. The new equilibruim is at point R on indifference curve III. The income-consumption curve now shows the equilibrium combinations of X and Y purchased at various levels of money income, nominal prices remaining the same.

Engel curves relating the consumption of commodity X to income are constructed in Figure 4.2.5. Neither panel a nor panel b is directly based upon the particular income-consumption curve in Figure 4.2.4, but the process should be clear.

At the original equilibrium point P in Figure 4.2.4, money income is $p_x \cdot OM$ (or $p_y \cdot OL$). At income $p_x \cdot OM$, Ox_1 units of X are purchased. This income-consumption point can be plotted on a graph such as panel a, Figure 4.2.5. When the budget line shifts from LM to $L'M'$ (Figure 4.2.4), money income increases to $p_x \cdot OM'$ and consumption to Ox_2 units. This income-consumption pair constitutes another point on the Engel curve graph. Repeating this process for all levels of money income generates a series of points on a graph such as panel a, Figure 4.2.5. The Engel curve is formed by connecting these points by a line.

Two basically different types of Engel curves are shown in panels a and b, Figure 4.2.5. In panel a, the Engel curve slopes upward rather steeply, implying that changes in money income do not have a substantial effect upon the consumption of the good in question. An Engel curve with this property indicates that the good is bought when income is low,

FIGURE 4.2.5

Engel Curves

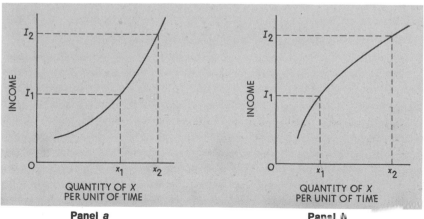

Panel a
Low Income Elasticity

Panel b
High Income Elasticity

but the quantity purchased does not expand rapidly as income increases. If "food" is treated as a single commodity, its Engel curve would look something like the curve in panel *a*, even though the curve for "steak" as a separate commodity probably would not. In summary, an Engel curve that is concave from above indicates a commodity whose income elasticity of demand is low (but positive).

On the other hand, steak and many other types of goods give rise to Engel curves more clearly represented by the curve in panel *b*. The relatively gentle upward slope indicates that the quantity bought changes markedly with income. Such a curve indicates a relatively high income elasticity of demand.

4.2.d—Inferior Goods

"Normal" goods are given that name because in most cases an increase in income causes an increase in the consumption of a good; this is the "normal" situation. In certain cases, however, an increase in income may cause a switch from margarine to butter, from dried to fresh vegetables. An increase in income may result in a decrease in the consumption of certain commodities. These commodities are called "inferior" goods.

Definition: An inferior good is one whose consumption varies inversely with money income (prices constant) over a certain range of income. It is thus a commodity whose income elasticity is negative over the range of income for which it is inferior.

Figure 4.2.6 shows an increase in income from the level given by the budget line LM to that given by $L'M'$. The two budget lines are parallel, so no change in relative price occurs; income increases from LM to $L'M'$ by an increase in money income, prices constant. In the change, the position of consumer equilibrium shifts from point P on indifference curve I to point Q on indifference curve II. As a result of the increase in real income at the constant relative prices, the quantity demanded of good X falls from Ox_1 to Ox_2. The income-consumption curve, over this range of real income values, rises backward from P to Q; and the entire income-consumption curve might resemble the curve $APQB$. Thus over the range PQ the Engel curve would be a negatively sloped line.

4.3 CHANGES IN PRICE

The reaction of quantity purchased to changes in price is perhaps even more important than the reaction to changes in money income. In this section we assume that money income and the nominal prices of all goods other than X remain constant while the nominal price of X changes. We are thus able to analyze the effect of price upon quantity purchased without simultaneously considering the effect of changes in money income.

FIGURE 4.2.6

Illustration of an Inferior Good

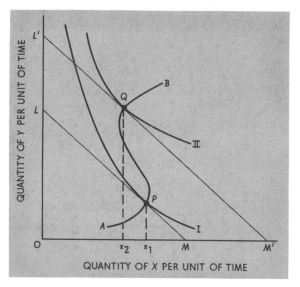

QUANTITY OF X PER UNIT OF TIME

4.3.a—Price-Consumption Curves

Figure 4.3.1 contains a portion of an indifference map for a consumer who can consume X (measured in units along the horizontal axis) and goods other than X (the total expenditures on which are measured in dollars along the vertical axis). The consumer has money income of $1,000. When X is priced at $25 per unit the consumer's budget line is LM. He can spend the entire $1,000 on other goods; he can spend the entire $1,000 on 40 units of X at $25 per unit; or he can purchase at some point along LM. By the analysis developed above he chooses to consume at point P, where LM is tangent to indifference curve I. He consumes 24 units of X, thereby spending $600 on this commodity. The remaining $400 is spent on other goods.

Assume that the price of X falls to $10. Now if the consumer wishes to spend all of his income on X, he can purchase 100 units. His budget line at the new price is LM', with a slope of −10 rather than −25. The new equilibrium point of tangency is designated by Q, at which he consumes 70 units of X at a total expense of $700 and spends the remaining $300 on other goods. If price falls to $8 per unit, other things remaining the same, his new budget line is LM'', with a slope of −8. At equilibrium point R he purchases 85 units of X. Note that he still spends $700 on X and $300 on all other goods. Finally the price of X falls to $5. The new budget line LM''' is tangent to indifference curve IV at point S. The

FIGURE 4.3.1

Price-Consumption Curve

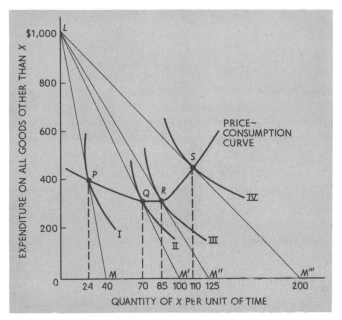

maximum utility level is attained by spending $550 on 110 units of X and $450 on goods other than X. Thus each price decrease causes the consumer to purchase more units of X. The line joining points P, Q, R, and S (and all other equilibria) is called the *price-consumption curve*. For a given money income it shows the amount of X consumed as its price changes, other prices remaining the same.

Definition: The price-consumption curve is a locus of equilibrium points relating the quantity of X purchased to its price, money income and all other prices remaining constant. In the case treated above, the price-consumption curve also shows how expenditure on all goods other than X changes as the price of X changes.

4.3.b—Demand Curves

The individual's demand curve for a commodity can be derived from the price-consumption curve, just as an Engel curve is derivable from the income-consumption curve. The price-quantity relations for good X at points P, Q, R, and S, and presumably for all other points on the price-consumption curve in Figure 4.3.1, are plotted in Figure 4.3.2. The horizontal axis is the same (units of X), but the vertical axis now shows the price of X. When the price of X is given by the slope of LM ($25), 24

FIGURE 4.3.2

Demand Curve

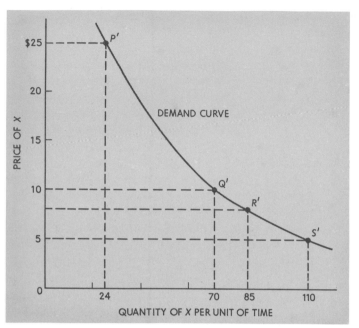

QUANTITY OF X PER UNIT OF TIME

units of X are purchased; this is indicated by point P' in Figure 4.3.2. If the price is \$10, 70 units are purchased (point Q'), and so forth. All other points on the curve are derived similarly. The locus of these points is called the demand curve for X.

Definition: The demand curve of an individual for a specific commodity relates equilibrium quantities bought to market price, money income and nominal prices of all other commodities held constant. The slope of the demand curve illustrates the law of demand: quantity demanded varies inversely with price, income and the prices of other commodities held constant.

Relation: As briefly mentioned in Chapter 2, market demand for a specific commodity is the horizontal sum of all individual demand curves.

4.3.c—Demand Elasticity

Recall from Chapter 2 that the elasticity of demand is the relative responsiveness of quantity demanded to changes in price. It may be determined from the changes in price and in the money income spent on the good.

At this point it may be helpful briefly to review the relation between price elasticity of demand and changes in the total expenditure upon the good in question. First, suppose the nominal price of good X declines by 1 percent. The demand for X is said to be price elastic, of unitary price elasticity, or price inelastic according as the quantity of X demanded expands by more than 1 percent, by exactly 1 percent, or by less than 1 percent.

Next recall that the total expenditure upon a good is the product of price per unit and the number of units purchased. Given an initial price and quantity bought, a unique initial total expenditure is determined. Now let price fall by 1 percent. If demand is price elastic, quantity demanded expands by more than 1 percent. Thus total expenditure must expand when price falls and demand is price elastic. By the same argument, one finds (a) that total expenditure remains constant when price falls and demand has unitary price elasticity and (b) that total expenditure declines when price falls and demand is price inelastic.

Let us now reexamine the relation between the price-consumption curve in Figure 4.3.1 and the demand curve in Figure 4.3.2. Note that when the price falls from $25 to $10 (from P to Q on the price-consumption curve), total expenditure on all goods other than X decreases from $400 to $300. If total expenditure on goods other than X declines, total expenditure on X must necessarily rise (from $600 to $700). Therefore demand is elastic between $25 and $10 inasmuch as an increase in total expenditure in response to a price decline implies elastic demand. When the price-consumption curve is negatively sloped between two points (P and Q in Figure 4.3.1), demand is elastic between those points (P' and Q' in Figure 4.3.2).

Consider now the price decline from $10 to $8 (from Q to R). Expenditure on other goods remains the same; with a fixed money income, expenditure on X therefore remains the same. The price-consumption curve neither declines nor rises and thus demand must be, on average, of unitary elasticity between Q' and R' on the demand curve. The student should now work out for himself that demand must be inelastic between R' and S' on the demand curve.

Relations: Demand has unitary price elasticity, is price elastic, or is price inelastic according as the price-consumption curve is horizontal, negatively sloped, or positively sloped. Thus the price-consumption curve in Figure 4.3.1 reflects commodity demand that is first (at higher prices) elastic, becomes unitary, and is inelastic thereafter. This relation holds for a price-consumption curve only when total expenditures on all other goods are plotted on the horizontal axis.

4.3.d—Demand and Price-Consumption Curves: Alternative Approach

As in the case of income-consumption curves, we can drop the assumption that the vertical axis denotes total expenditures on all goods other than X and assume an indifference map between two goods, X and Y.

FIGURE 4.3.3

Price-Consumption Curve

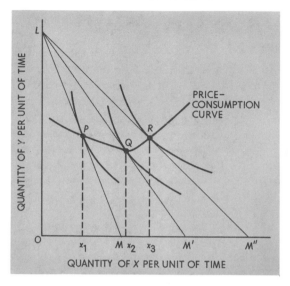

In Figure 4.3.3 a consumer's indifference map is represented by indifference curves I, II, and III. Given the price ratio designated by budget line LM, equilibrium is attained at point P. A fall in the price of X, the price of Y remaining the same, leads to the new budget line LM'.[1] At equilibrium point Q the consumer purchases more X and less Y. Finally when the price of X falls again, to the level indicated by LM'', the consumer buys more of both goods. The line connecting these points is, as before, the price-consumption curve.

The demand curve can be derived from the price-consumption curve just as before. When the price of X is given by the slope of LM in Figure 4.3.3, Ox_1 units of X are purchased. This price-consumption pair constitutes one point on the graph in Figure 4.3.4. Similarly, when the price of X falls to the level indicated by the slope of LM', quantity purchased increases to Ox_2. This price-consumption pair is another point that can be plotted on Figure 4.3.4. Plotting all points so obtained and connecting them with a line generates the consumer demand curve, as shown in Figure 4.3.4. Its shape indicates an important principle, called the Law of Demand.

---

[1] The student should realize that if the nominal price of Y and money income remain constant while the nominal price of X declines, the real price of Y increases, the real price of X decreases, and real money income increases. Our discussion refers almost exclusively to nominal prices and income. Note also that a proportional decrease in both prices would be equivalent to an increase in money income. The budget line would shift outward.

FIGURE 4.3.4

Demand Curve

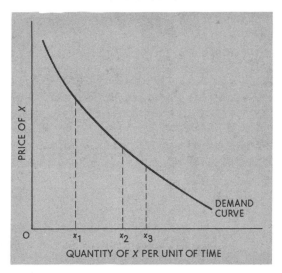

Principle: Quantity demanded varies inversely with price, money In-come and nominal prices of other commodities remaining constant.

4.4   SUBSTITUTION AND INCOME EFFECTS

A change in the nominal price of a commodity actually exerts two in-fluences on quantity demanded. In the first place, there is a change in relative price—a change in the terms at which a consumer can exchange one good for another. The change in relative price alone leads to a sub-stitution effect. Second, a change in the nominal price of a good (nominal income remaining constant) causes a change in real income, or in the size of the bundle of goods and services a consumer can buy. If the nomi-nal price of one good falls, all other nominal prices remaining constant, the consumer's real income rises because he can now buy more, either of the good whose price declined or of other goods. Thus the change in price leads to a change in real income and thus to an income effect upon quantity demanded.

4.4.a—Total Effect of a Price Decrease

When the price of one good changes, the prices of other goods and money income remaining constant, the consumer moves from one equilib-rium point to another. In normal circumstances, if the price of a good diminishes, more of it is bought; if its price increases, fewer units are taken. The overall change in quantity demanded from one equilibrium position to another is referred to as the total effect.

Definition: The total effect of a price change is the total change in quantity demanded as the consumer moves from one equilibrium position to another.

The total effect of a price change is illustrated in Figure 4.4.1. As before, units of X are plotted along the horizontal axis and total expendi-

FIGURE 4.4.1

Substitution and Income Effects for a Decrease in the Price of X

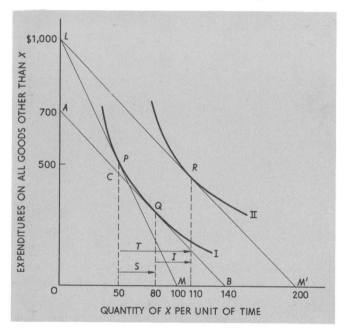

tures on all goods other than X are measured in dollars along the vertical axis. Assume again that the consumer originally has money income of $1,000 and that the original price of X is $10. Since the consumer can buy 100 units of X if he spends his entire income on X, the original budget line is given by LM. In equilibrium the consumer purchases 50 units of X, spending $500 on X and $500 on all other goods.

When the price of X falls to $5, the relevant budget line becomes LM'. Equilibrium consumption, designated by R, is now 110 units of X, $450 being spent on other goods and $550 on X. Since P is on indifference curve I and R is on II, and since II denotes a higher level of utility than I, the consumer is clearly at a higher level of satisfaction after the price decreases even though his money income has not changed. An economist would say that *real* income is greater. Put alternatively, at the new price of $5 the consumer could spend at the level indicated by *P* (that is, he could buy 50 units of *X* and spend $500 on other goods) and still have $250 left to spend on *X*, on other goods, or on both. The consumer is clearly better off.

The total effect of the decrease in the price of *X* is the 60-unit increase in the consumption of *X* (from 50 to 110 units, or the distance *T* in Figure 4.4.1). This total effect can be broken down into an income and a substitution effect. The substitution effect results from *X* being relatively cheaper than before the price decline. The consumer substitutes the cheaper good for relatively more expensive ones. The income effect results from the consumer's having more *real* income and hence being able to buy more of both *X* and of all other goods (even though nominal income is the same before and after the price change).

4.4.b—Income and Substitution Effects for a Normal Good

Assume that when the price of *X* decreases, the consumer is taxed exactly the amount of *money* that will cause his *real* income to remain constant. That is, he is taxed the amount that makes him continue to consume a bundle on the original indifference curve I. Since he is on the same indifference curve as before, he has the same *real* income. Thus after the price reduction he is taxed the amount *AL* in Figure 4.4.1.

The tax must be the amount that causes the consumer to attain equilibrium on indifference curve I at the *new* price ratio. The gain in real income (i.e., the increase in utility) is, therefore, taken away. Graphically, this is illustrated by constructing the fictitious budget line *AB*, which is tangent to indifference curve I but has a slope that represents the new price of *X*. Budget line *AB*, whose slope is −5 (the new price ratio), is tangent to I at point *Q*. Under these circumstances the consumer would purchase 80 units of *X* at a cost of $400 and spend $300 on other goods. The necessary tax is obviously $300, reflected by the distance from point *L* to point *A*. The consumer is no better off at *Q* than he was at *P*; but he substitutes 30 units of *X* (80 − 50) for $200 expenditure on other goods ($500 − $300). This change in the consumption of *X* is called the *substitution effect* (distance *S* in Figure 4.4.1). It is easy to see that given the price change and the fictitious reduction in real income, the consumer substitutes *X* for expenditures on other goods in order not to be made worse off. If he continued to consume 50 units of *X*, with the new budget line *AB* he would be at point *C*, where the level of satisfaction is clearly below that represented by indifference curve I. The consumer must substitute in order to remain as well off as he was before the price change.

Definition: The substitution effect is the change in quantity demanded resulting from a change in relative price holding *real income* constant. In other words, the substitution effect is the change in quantity demanded resulting from a change in price when the change is restricted to a movement along the original indifference curve.

The substitution effect involves a movement along the original indifference curve from P to the imaginary equilibrium Q. The remainder of the total effect, from Q to R or the distance I in Figure 4.4.1, results from the increase in real income; that is, from the shift from indifference curve I to curve II. Since AB and LM' are parallel, the movement does not involve a change in relative prices. It is a real income phenomenon.

Definition: The income effect is the change in quantity demanded resulting from the change in real income incident to the change in the price of X.

From the graph one may easily see that the total effect of the decrease in the price of X upon quantity demanded is the sum of the substitution effect and the income effect. In algebraic terms

Total Effect = Substitution Effect (utility constant) + Income
Effect (price ratio constant).

Or in our example:

60 units = 30 units + 30 units.

In this case the income effect reinforces the substitution effect in that both effects cause an increase in the consumption of X. The income effect is positive: an increase in real income leads to an increase in quantity demanded and vice versa.

Definition: A normal good is one for which the income effect is positive.

Principle: A positive income effect reinforces the negative substitution effect. Thus for a normal good, quantity demanded always varies inversely with price. The law of demand applies to all normal goods.

The result of this section may be summarized as follows.

Relations: The total effect of a price change may be decomposed into a substitution effect and an income effect. The substitution effect is the change in quantity demanded attributable exclusively to a change in the price ratio. The substitution effect is always negative. The income effect is the change in quantity demanded attributable exclusively to a change in real income. For normal goods, the income effect is positive. A positive income effect reinforces the negative substitution effect. Thus for normal goods, the demand curve always slopes downward to the right.

4.4.c—Inferior Goods

Our analysis of price changes has thus far been restricted to the case of a normal good. Returning the $300 imaginary tax (increasing real income) caused the consumption of X to increase. As we know from subsection 4.2.b, an increase in income need not occasion an increase in the consumption of a particular good. In the case of an inferior good the effect is the opposite.

FIGURE 4.4.2

Substitution and Income Effects for an Inferior Good

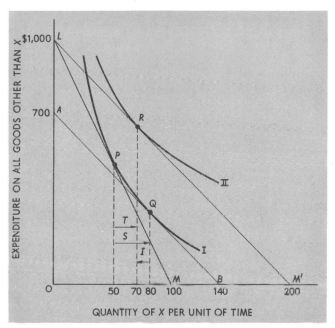

Consider Figure 4.4.2 in which X is now some other good. The consumer has money income of $1,000, the original price of X is $10 (budget line LM), and the original point of equilibrium is P (50 units of X and $500 expenditure on other goods). The price of X falls to $5, indicated by the budget line LM'; in equilibrium the consumer purchases 70 units of X and spends $650 on other goods (R). The total effect (the distance T) is an increase of 20 units.

Budget line AB indicates the imaginary tax of $300 that causes the consumer to choose point Q on the original indifference curve I. The substitution effect is therefore an increase in consumption by 30 units, or the distance S. Note that the substitution effect is *greater* than the total effect. Now we return the consumer's gain in real income and the consumer moves from Q to R. In this case the income effect (indicated by the distance I) is negative and to some extent *offsets* the substitution effect rather than reinforcing it. This offsetting effect is to be expected since good X is an inferior good.

Thus for all goods *the change in relative prices* (real income constant) that results from a decrease in price tends to cause an increase in consumption. But in the case of inferior goods, the *increase in real income* that results from the price decrease causes an offsetting decrease in consumption of the good. The law of demand, however, still holds in this case; the total effect of the decrease in price is an increase in quantity demanded.

4.4.d—Giffen's Paradox

In general, in fact almost always, the substitution effect is great enough to offset a negative income effect (if the good is inferior). But in one case, called *Giffen's Paradox*, the negative income effect is so strong that it more than offsets the substitution effect. Thus a decline in price leads to a decline in quantity demanded, a rise in price to a rise in quantity demanded.

Figure 4.4.3 illustrates Giffen's Paradox. The budget line *LM* indicates the consumption possibilities for a consumer with $1,000 income at a price of $10 per unit of X. Point P is the equilibrium (50 units of X and an expenditure of $500 on other goods). When the price of X decreases to $5 per unit, equilibrium is reached at point R on indifference curve II (40 units of X and $800 expenditure on other goods).

The consumer thus chooses to decrease his consumption of X by 10 units after a decrease in the price of X. The price-consumption curve between P and R obviously slopes backwards. Throughout a larger range it might look like curve *SPRT*. In the case of Giffen's Paradox the price-consumption curve is *backward rising* over a certain range.

We can analyze Giffen's Paradox more satisfactorily by separating the total effect into its component parts. In Figure 4.4.3 the line *AB* indicates the consumer's budget line at the new price of X after his gain in real income has been taken away. Under these conditions he would consume at Q (70 units of X). Following the analysis described above, the substitution effect causes him to *increase* his consumption of X after a decrease in the price of X (from 50 to 70 units). The substitution effect is, as always, negative. The income effect causes him to change his consumption from Q to R or from 70 to 40 units and is more than sufficient to offset the negative substitution effect. Adding the substitution and income

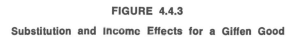

FIGURE 4.4.3

Substitution and Income Effects for a Giffen Good

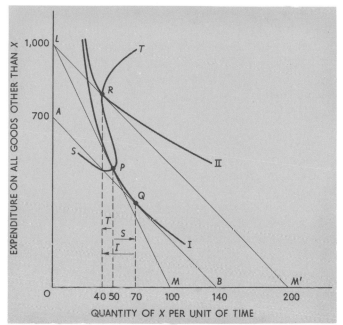

effects together, the total effect of the price decline is a decrease in quantity demanded from 50 units at $10 to 40 units at $5. For a commodity such as this, the law of demand is not valid over the specified range.[2]

Definition: Giffen's Paradox refers to a good whose quantity demanded varies directly with price. A good must be an inferior good to be in this category; but not all inferior goods conform to the conditions of Giffen's Paradox. The class of goods for which Giffen's Paradox holds constitutes the only exception to the law of demand.

Whether a commodity is an inferior good or not has nothing to do with the total effect of a price change. It is strictly an income phenome-

[2] In this text, and in almost all other usages, demand and the Law of Demand are defined in terms of constant money income. Thus real income changes as one moves along a demand curve; Giffen's Paradox can occur, and the law of demand is not universally valid. For certain uses, however, it is convenient to construct a demand curve based on constant real income (and, therefore, varying money income). Such demand curves are called income-compensated demand curves. The "income effect" is, in effect, subtracted out, leaving only the substitution effect. Such demand curves always slope downward to the right, irrespective of the type of good. For a thorough discussion of income-compensated demand curves, see Milton Friedman, "The Marshallian Demand Curve," *Journal of Political Economy*, Vol. LVII (1949), pp. 463–95.

non. Giffen's Paradox, on the other hand, relates only to certain inferior goods that violate the law of demand.

As an example, oleomargarine may be an inferior good, but it certainly does not belong in the Giffen's Paradox category. As we have seen in the past, a reduction in the price of oleomargarine leads to a substitution of margarine for butter. However, an increase in the real income of a family may cause a switch from margarine to butter. But in this case the income effect is not great enough to offset the substitution effect.

In all probability there are very few households in the United States or other industrial nations for which Giffen's Paradox obtains. A negative income effect is not all that is required—the good must also be very important in the entire family budget. The classic example is potatoes in 19th-century Ireland. The typical Irish peasant was so poor, it was said, that he spent almost all his cash income for the least expensive means of subsistence, potatoes.

Now suppose the price of potatoes falls. The same number of calories can now be bought for less expenditure on potatoes, so some money is available for green vegetables and perhaps meat. But these items also contain calories, so the consumption of potatoes can actually be reduced. Thus Giffen's Paradox is obtained—a reduction in price leads to a reduction in quantity demanded.

Giffen's Paradox is a bona fide exception to the law of demand. However, in the type of society with which we are presently concerned, Giffen's Paradox is a rare phenomenon. It occurs in few consumer units and, within these units, for very few commodities. Thus when all individual demand curves are aggregated to obtain market demand, it is safe to assume that market quantity demanded varies inversely with price for every commodity.

Exercise: Some people assert that there is another group of goods that violates the Law of Demand. These are goods that have "quality" or "snob" appeal, such as Dior dresses, Rolls Royce automobiles, breakfasts at Brennen's, and the like. It is sometimes argued that the greater the price of these goods, the greater the quantity demanded. Analyze the fallacy. (Hint: pose this question: if the argument is correct, why should not the prices of such goods be infinite?)

4.4.e—Alternative Approach

Just as we analyzed the price-consumption and the income-consumption curves by considering both X and Y as specific goods (rather than Y as expenditure on all goods other than X), so also can we isolate the income and substitution effects in this manner.

The effect of an *increase* in the price of X when X and Y are both goods is illustrated in Figure 4.4.4. The original price ratio is indicated by

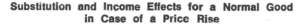

FIGURE 4.4.4

Substitution and Income Effects for a Normal Good in Case of a Price Rise

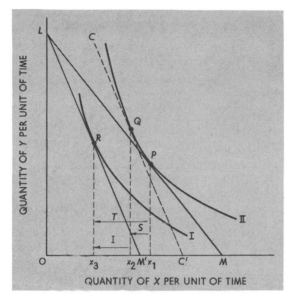

QUANTITY OF X PER UNIT OF TIME

the slope of LM. The consumer attains equilibrium at point P on indifference curve II, purchasing Ox_1 units of X. When the price of X rises, as indicated by shifting the budget line from LM to LM', the consumer moves to a new equilibrium position at R on indifference curve I. At this point he purchases Ox_3 units of X. The total effect of the price change is indicated by the movement from P to R, or by the reduction in quantity demanded from Ox_1 to Ox_3. In other words, the total effect is $Ox_1 - Ox_3 = x_1x_3$. This is a negative total effect because quantity demanded is reduced by x_1x_3 units.

When the price of X increases the consumer obviously suffers a decline in real income as indicated by the movement from indifference curve II to indifference curve I. Suppose that coincident with the price rise the consumer is given an amount of additional money just sufficient to compensate him for the loss in real income he would otherwise sustain. That is, he is given a compensatory payment just sufficient to make him choose to consume on indifference curve II under the new price regime. This new imaginary budget line is CC'; it is tangent to the original indifference curve II at point Q, but it reflects the new price ratio.

The substitution effect is shown by the movement from P to Q, or by the reduction in quantity demanded from Ox_1 to Ox_2. Now let the consumer's real income *fall* from the level represented by the fictitious budget line CC'. The movement from Q to R (the decrease in consumption from Ox_2 to Ox_3) indicates the income effect. Since CC' and LM' are parallel, the movement does not involve a change in relative prices. It is once more a real income phenomenon since the reduction in quantity demanded measures the change in purchases attributable exclusively to the decline in real income, the change in relative prices already having been ac-

FIGURE 4.4.5

Substitution and Income Effects for an Inferior Good Not Subject to Giffen's Paradox

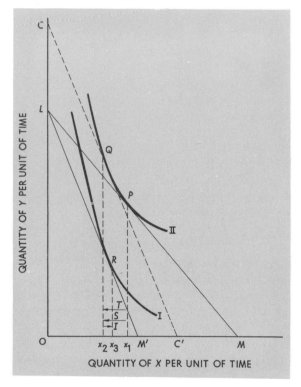

QUANTITY OF X PER UNIT OF TIME

counted for by the substitution effect. Note that X is a normal good: the decrease in real income causes a decrease in consumption.

Figures 4.4.5 and 4.4.6 show the effects of an increase in the price of X under the same assumptions as those of Figure 4.4.4, except that X is an inferior good. In fact, in Figure 4.4.6, X is a Giffen good.

Figure 4.4.5 illustrates the effects of an increase in the price of X, which changes the budget line from LM to LM'. Following the now familiar analysis, the consumer changes from point P to point R; he decreases his consumption of X from Ox_1 to Ox_3 (the total effect). The substitution

FIGURE 4.4.6

Substitution and Income Effects for Giffen's Paradox

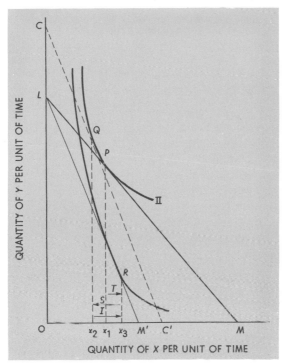

QUANTITY OF X PER UNIT OF TIME

effect, derived by giving the consumer just enough additional money income to compensate him for the decrease in real income occasioned by the price rise, is $P - Q$ (from Ox_1 to Ox_2). The income effect is from Q to R (an *increase* in consumption from Ox_2 to Ox_3). This partial offset to the substitution effect is to be expected since X is an inferior good; a decrease in income causes an increase in the consumption of X.

Exercise: The student should follow the same type of analysis in the case of a price increase for the good subject to Giffen's Paradox, illustrated in Figure 4.4.6.

4.5 CONCLUSION

The basic principles of consumer behavior and of demand have now been developed. The fundamental conclusion of this chapter is that, if consumers behave so as to maximize satisfaction from a limited money income, quantity demanded (with one relatively unimportant exception) will vary inversely with price.

4.6 ANALYTICAL EXERCISE

The tools developed in this chapter can be used to analyze certain theoretical problems not directly related to the demand for a specific commodity. We will analyze two of these problems in this section: (*a*) an individual's willingness to supply labor and (*b*) some possible effects of a minimum guaranteed income.

Figure 4.6.1 contains a portion of an individual's indifference map

FIGURE 4.6.1

Indifference Curve Analysis of Labor Supply

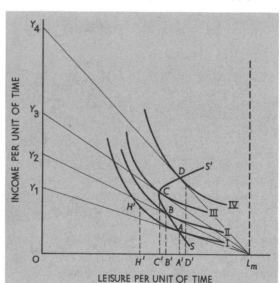

between income and leisure. Utility is regarded as a function of income and leisure. Note from the shape of the indifference curves that we have assumed both income and leisure are considered desirable by the individual; that is, he does not become satiated with leisure within the relevant range.

Before considering the problem of how the consumer maximizes utility, a word of explanation about the unit of measurement for leisure and the vertical line at L_m is in order. The unit of measurement along the horizontal axis can be hours per day, days per year, or any other period of time. Obviously if the unit is hours per day, the maximum hours of leisure is 24. If the unit is days of leisure, the maximum is 7 per week or 365 per year. The line L_m indicates the maximum attainable units of leisure per time period. If the individual chooses OH' units of leisure per period, he also chooses $H'L_m$ for work; or if he chooses OL_m of leisure, he does not work at all. The unit of measurement chosen for the horizontal axis clearly specifies the unit for the vertical. For example, when leisure is designated as hours per day, the vertical axis must measure income per day. Each indifference curve specifies the various combinations of income and leisure that yield the same level of satisfaction. For example, the consumer considers OH' leisure (and hence $H'L_m$ work) and income $H'H$ equivalent to OA' leisure (and hence $A'L_m$ work) and income $A'A$ since both points lie on the same indifference curve. The slopes of the curves indicate the rates at which an individual is willing to trade leisure for income. We assume for analytical convenience that both income and leisure are continuously divisible.

The budget lines are determined by the payment per unit of time. If the unit is hours per day, the budget line is determined by the individual's hourly wage rate; if days per year, by the earnings per day. Consider budget line Y_1L_m. If the individual works the entire time period (say 24 hours per day) and consequently takes no leisure, he could make OY_1 per time period. Assuming he specializes in leisure and does not work, he earns zero income. The slope of the budget line is the relevant wage rate or payment per unit of time. The "cost" of a unit of leisure is the sacrificed earnings for that period of time.[3] Y_2L_m, Y_3L_m, and Y_4L_m are the relevant budget lines for higher wage rates, OY_2/OL_m, OY_3/OL_m, and OY_4/OL_m respectively.

With a given wage rate, the highest attainable level of utility is the point where the relevant budget line is tangent to the indifference curve. An individual with the wage rate indicated by Y_1L_m achieves his highest attainable level of utility at point A. He chooses OA' leisure, $A'L_m$ work, and receives an income of $A'A$. Points B, C, and D indicate the equilibria leisure, work, and income for the other three budget lines, and SS' connects these and all intermediate equilibria. Thus SS' indicates the amount of time the individual is willing to work (or the amount of labor he is willing to supply) at each of a series of wages.

Note that at relatively low wage rates, the individual is willing to work more, or to consume less leisure, as the wage rate increases. Since an increase in potential earnings causes leisure to *cost* more (in lost earnings), he chooses less leisure and more work. After point C, however, further increases in the wage rate induce him to take more leisure and work less.

Thus far in our analysis we have considered only the effect of market-

---

[3] For simplicity we assume a constant wage rate regardless of the amount of time worked. Certainly "overtime" work might be at overtime pay or a second job could be taken at a lower wage than the primary job. We also assume that the individual is free to choose the amount of time he works; sometimes this may not be the case.

determined variables (wage rates) upon the individual's choice between leisure and work. Let us now examine the effect of a nonmarket force upon an individual's willingness to supply labor.

Despite the seriousness of the problem, many discussions of guaranteed minimum income ignore the problem of work incentives. In its most familiar form a guaranteed minimum income would allow people to work, but those who are unable to earn the minimum income would receive the difference between what they earn and the designated minimum from the state. It has been asserted that a person who could not make the minimum income would not work, but that anyone who could

FIGURE 4.6.2

Indifference Curve Analysis of a Minimum Guaranteed Income

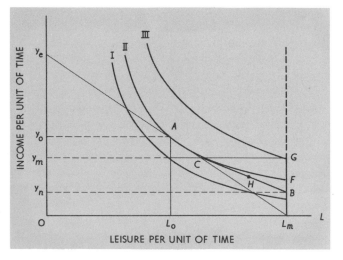

make more would choose to work. We can analyze the theoretical aspects of the problem rather simply.[4]

Consider an individual with an indifference map for leisure and earnings depicted by curves I, II, and III and earning possibilities shown by budget line $Y_e L_m$ in Figure 4.6.2. Following the type of analysis previously developed, we can see that he chooses income OY_0, leisure OL_0, and work time L_0L_m per period of time. Now suppose the government declares that income OY_m per period is a "necessary" income. No one should receive less. The state will make up any difference between what one earns and Y_m assuming, of course, that one earns less than Y_m. Since

[4] The analysis is based upon an article by C. T. Brehm and T. R. Saving, "The Demand for General Assistance Payments," *American Economic Review*, December, 1964, pp. 1002–18.

the individual under consideration is earning more than Y_m, the question is whether the minimum will affect him or not.

Note the way that the guaranteed minimum changes the budget line. The budget line from C to Y_e remains the same; but since the individual can have at least Y_m no matter how much he works and no matter what his wage rate, the income possibility line changes at point C. The new budget line becomes Y_eCGL_m. The individual can now attain the highest possible level of utility on indifference curve III by choosing OL_m leisure and no work. Since III is clearly higher than II, the utility maximizing individual will move from A to G even though he could earn more than the guaranteed minimum.

Under the circumstances, three factors could change and cause the person to choose to work some portion of the time. First, the minimum income could be decreased to some level below the intersection of indifference curve II with the perpendicular at L_m. Then the person would choose point A on II. Second, the wage or potential earnings rate could increase enough to induce him to work. A sufficient increase would raise the budget line at least enough for it to become tangent to indifference curve III. Third, the individual might not consider relief payments as desirable as equal payments for work.

Suppose then that the person attaches some stigma to receiving income from the state. Since he receives less satisfaction from a dollar given him by the state than from an "earned" dollar, he tends to discount state payments by some fraction between zero and one. Say $1 of relief payments is equivalent to $0.50 received for work. The closer to one the discount factor, the less stigma attached. In Figure 4.6.2 let k be the discount factor. Since we assume that the person does not value relief income more than an earned income, $0 < k < 1$. An income of Y_m received from the state would be valued by the individual as equivalent to kY_m "earned" income. Starting from L_m the individual views his income as his earned income plus some fraction k times the difference between the guaranteed minimum and the income he receives from working. His new "budget" line is the broken line L_mBCY_e, i.e., he views his income as Earned Income $+ k(Y_m -$ Earned Income$)$.

Given the value of his discount factor k (or we might call it his degree of "puritan ethic"), the individual chooses point A on indifference curve II, the highest indifference level attainable by budget line L_mBCY_e. If his discount factor k were not as large as that in Figure 4.6.2 and kY_m were raised to (say) the level F, the person would choose OL_m leisure and no work in order to reach the highest utility level. With a still different k the highest attainable level could be reached at a point of tangency on segment BC, say at H. The consumer would work some, earn less than OY_m and receive the difference from the state.

The decision concerning whether or not to receive income from the state, therefore, theoretically depends upon three factors: (1) the individual's possibility of earning income; (2) the amount at which the state sets the minimum; and (3) the discount factor applied to relief payments.

QUESTIONS AND PROBLEMS

1. Using an indifference map, construct a consumer's demand curve for a good.
2. Using an indifference map construct an Engel curve for a normal good. According to the shape of the curve you have constructed, what else can you say about the good?
3. Isolate the substitution, income, and total effect of a price increase for an inferior, non-Giffen good.
4. Using the tools developed in the Analytical Exercise comment upon the following statement: An increase in the income tax causes laborers to work more in order to maintain their income level.

chapter 5

Theory of Production

5.1 INTRODUCTION

Demand is only half of the theory of price; supply is the other half. In order to understand supply one must have a thorough understanding of the theory of production. In fact, the theories of cost, distribution, and resource allocation, as well as the theory of supply, are in large part based upon production theory.

Production in a general sense refers to the creation of any *good* or *service* that people will buy. However the concept of production is much clearer when we speak only of goods, since it is simpler to specify the precise inputs and to indentify the quantity and quality of outputs. Therefore, although this discussion is restricted to the production of goods, one should be aware that problems of resource allocation in service trades and government are equally serious even though they are not as fully covered in this text. The principles of production studied here are as applicable to the output of services as to the output of goods, though the application may be more difficult in the former case.

5.2 PRODUCTION FUNCTIONS

Production processes typically require a wide variety of inputs. They are not as simple as "labor", "capital", and "materials"; many qualitatively different types of each are normally used to produce an output. With a given state of technology, the quantity of output depends upon the quantities of the various inputs used. This relation is more formally described by a *production function* associating physical output with physical rates of input.

Definition: A production function is a schedule (or table, or mathematical equation) showing the maximum amount of output that can be produced from any specified set of inputs, given the existing technology or "state of the art." In short, the production function is a catalog of output possibilities.

5.2.a—Fixed and Variable Inputs, the Short and Long Runs

In analyzing the process of physical production it is convenient to introduce an analytical fiction: classification of inputs as fixed and variable. Accordingly, a *fixed input* is defined as one whose quantity cannot readily be changed when market conditions indicate that an immediate change in output is desirable. To be sure, no input is ever *absolutely* fixed, no matter how short the period of time under consideration. But frequently, for the sake of analytical simplicity, we hold some inputs fixed, reasoning perhaps that while these inputs are in fact variable, the cost of immediate variation is so great as to take them out of the range of relevance for the particular decision at hand. Buildings, major pieces of machinery, and managerial personnel are examples of inputs that cannot be rapidly augmented or diminished. A *variable input*, on the other hand, is one whose quantity may be changed almost instantaneously in response to desired changes in output. Many types of labor services and the inputs of raw and processed materials fall in this category.

Corresponding to the fiction of fixed and variable inputs, economists introduce another fiction, the short and long runs. The *short run* refers to that period of time in which the input of one or more productive agents is fixed. Therefore, changes in output must be accomplished exclusively by changes in the usage of variable inputs. Thus if a producer wishes to expand output in the short run, he must usually do so by using more hours of labor service with the existing plant and equipment. Similarly, if he wishes to reduce output in the short run, he may discharge certain types of workers; but he cannot immediately "discharge" a building or a diesel locomotive, even though its usage may fall to zero.

In the long run, however, even this is possible, for the *long run* is defined as that period of time (or planning horizon) in which all inputs are variable. The long run, in other words, refers to that time in the future when output changes can be accomplished in the manner most advantageous to the businessman. For example, in the short run a producer may be able to expand output only by operating his existing plant for more hours per day. This, of course, entails paying overtime rates to workers. In the long run, it may be more economical for him to install additional productive facilities and return to the normal workday.

5.2.b—Fixed or Variable Proportions

Our attention here is restricted mainly to production under conditions of *variable proportions. The ratio of input quantities* may vary; the businessman, therefore, must determine not only the level of output he wishes to produce but also the optimal proportion in which to combine inputs (in the long run).

There are two different ways of stating the principle of variable proportions. First, variable proportions production implies that output can be changed in the short run by changing the amount of variable inputs used in cooperation with the fixed inputs. Naturally, as the amount of one input is changed, the others remaining constant, the *ratios* change. Second, when production is subject to variable proportions, the *same* output can be produced by various combinations of inputs—that is, by different input ratios. This may apply only to the long run, but it is relevant to the short run when there is more than one variable input.

Most economists regard production under conditions of variable proportions as typical of both the short and long run. There is certainly no doubt that proportions are variable in the long run. When making an investment decision a businessman may choose among a wide variety of different production processes. As polar opposites, an automobile can be almost handmade or it can be made by assembly line techniques. In the short run, however, there may be some cases in which output is subject to fixed proportions.

Fixed-proportions production means that there is one, and only one, ratio of inputs that can be used to produce a good. If output is expanded or contracted, all inputs must be expanded or contracted so as to maintain the fixed input ratio. At first glance this might seem the usual condition: one man and one shovel produce a ditch, two parts hydrogen and one part oxygen produce water. Adding a second shovel or a second part of oxygen will not augment the rate of production.

But in actuality examples of fixed-proportions production are hard to come by. Even the production of most chemical compounds is subject to variable proportions. It is true, for example, that hydrogen and nitrogen must be used in the fixed ratio 3:1 to produce ammonia gas. But if three volumes of hydrogen and one volume of nitrogen are mixed in a glass tube and heated to 400° C., only minute traces of ammonia will be found (and that only after heating for a very long time). However, if finely divided iron is introduced into the tube under the same conditions, almost the entire amount of hydrogen and nitrogen are converted to ammonia gas within minutes. That is to say, the *yield* of ammonia for any given amount of hydrogen and nitrogen depends upon the amount of the catalyst (finely divided iron) used. Proportions are indeed variable from the standpoint of the catalyst not only in this instance but in the production of almost every chemical compound.

The hydrogen-nitrogen-ammonia illustration serves as a convenient introduction to a general view of production processes. One might say that, in the short run, there are three classes of productive inputs. First, there are certain fixed inputs whose quantity cannot be varied. Second, there are variable inputs whose usage may be readily changed. Finally, there are "ingredient" inputs whose quantities may be readily changed but must bear fixed proportions to one another and to output.

It is not difficult to find examples of ingredient inputs. Each brand of cigarettes contains its own special blend of tobaccos. That is, various tobaccos are blended in fixed proportions. And a fixed amount of tobacco blend must be used in each cigarette produced. But the production of cigarettes requires more than the fixed-proportion ingredient inputs. Certain capital equipment—rolling machines, packaging machines, and the like—must be used and human labor services are necessary. In the short run, the building and capital equipment are fixed inputs and most labor services are variable.

In the discussion of production the fixed and variable inputs are stressed. Ingredient inputs are necessary; and they must be used in fixed or relatively fixed proportions or else the quality or character of the product will change. The businessman has little or no choice in this regard. Hence our attention is directed to those aspects of production over which a businessman can exert control.

5.3 PRODUCTION WITH ONE VARIABLE INPUT

To clarify analysis we first introduce some simplifying assumptions whose purpose is to cut through the complexities of dealing with hundreds of different inputs. Thus our attention is focused upon the essential principles of production. More specifically, we assume that there is only one variable input, usually called "labor," although any other input could just as well be used. This variable input can be combined in different proportions with fixed inputs to produce various quantities of output. Note that these assumptions also imply the tacit assumption that inputs may be combined in *various* proportions to produce the commodity in question.

5.3.a—Total Output or Product

The short-run production function in Figure 5.3.1 shows the maximum output per unit of time obtainable from different amounts of the variable input (labor), given a specified amount of the fixed inputs and the required amounts of the ingredient inputs. For example Ox_0 is the *maximum* amount of output obtainable when OL_0 workers are combined with the fixed and ingredient inputs. Likewise OL_1 workers can produce a maximum of Ox_1, and so forth. Certainly, the specified number of inputs could produce less than the amount indicated by the total product curve, but not more than that amount.

This total product curve illustrates some assumptions frequently made

FIGURE 5.3.1

Total Product Curve

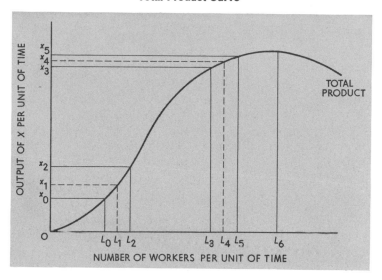

NUMBER OF WORKERS PER UNIT OF TIME

about production with only one variable input. First, maximum output increases with increases in the variable input up to a point, in this case OL_6 workers. After that so many workers are combined with the fixed inputs that output diminishes when additional workers are employed. Second, production at first increases at an increasing rate, then increases at a decreasing rate until the maximum is reached. Increasing the number of workers from OL_0 to OL_1 increases output by x_0x_1. Increasing the number of workers from OL_1 to OL_2 ($L_0L_1 = L_1L_2$) increases output by x_1x_2, which is greater than x_0x_1. At a greater level of output, an increase of L_3L_4 workers increases output by x_3x_4, while an increase of L_4L_5 ($= L_3L_4$) increases production by x_4x_5, which is obviously less than x_3x_4. The reasons for this type of curvature lie in the principle of diminishing marginal returns, discussed in subsection 5.3.c. Note that we have assumed throughout this section that both output and the variable input are continuously divisible. This assumption sacrifices little realism yet adds a great deal of analytical convenience.

5.3.b—Average and Marginal Products

The average product of an input is total product divided by the amount of the input used to produce this output. Thus average product is the output-input ratio for each level of output and the corresponding volume of input.

FIGURE 5.3.2

Derivation of Average Product from Total Product

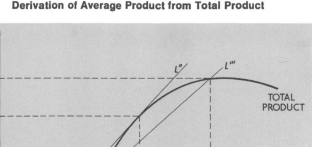

Consider the "typical" total product curve in Figure 5.3.2. Given the specified amounts of fixed factors, OL_0 workers can produce a maximum product of Ox_0. The average product of OL_0 workers is therefore Ox_0/OL_0, the slope of the ray from the origin OL'. In like manner, the average product of any number of workers can be determined by the slope of a ray from the origin to the relevant point on the total product curve; the steeper the slope, the larger the average product. It is easy to see that the slopes of rays from the origin to the total product curve in Figure 5.3.2 increase with additional labor until OL'' becomes tangent at OL_1 workers and Ox_1 output then decrease thereafter (say, to OL''' at OL_2 workers). Hence typical average product curves first increase and then decrease thereafter. This is illustrated by the AP curve in Figure 5.3.4.

The marginal product of an input is the addition to total product attributable to the addition of one unit of the variable input to the production process, the fixed inputs remaining constant. If the total product of 10 workers is 500 units and the total product of 11 workers is 520, fixed factors remaining constant, the marginal product of 11 workers is 20 units.[1] As with average product, we can derive a marginal product

---

[1] Technically speaking marginal product refers only to comparisons of the results of simultaneous experiments and not to the successive addition of units of the variable input in one experiment. Note that we do not speak of the marginal product of the 11th worker but of 11 workers.

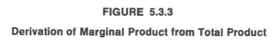

FIGURE 5.3.3

Derivation of Marginal Product from Total Product

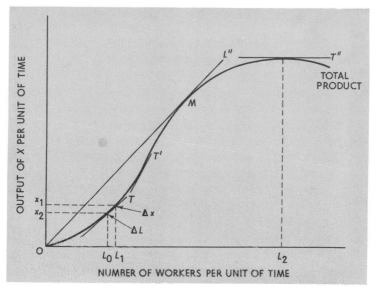

curve from a total product curve. In Figure 5.3.3 OL_0 workers can produce Ox_0 units of output and OL_1 can produce Ox_1. L_0L_1 additional workers increase total product by x_0x_1. Marginal product is therefore x_0x_1/L_0L_1 or $\Delta x/\Delta L$, where the symbol Δ denotes "the change in." Let L_1 become very close to L_0; hence x_1 is very close to x_0; $\Delta x/\Delta L$ approaches the tangent T to the total product curve. Therefore, at any point on the total product curve, marginal product, which is the rate of change of total product, can be *estimated* by the slope of the tangent at that point.

On inspection we see that marginal product first increases; note that T' is steeper than T. It then decreases, OL'' at point M being less steep than T'. Marginal product becomes zero when OL_2 workers are employed (the slope of T''' is zero) and then becomes negative. At point M the slope of the tangent OL'' is also the slope of the ray from the origin to that point. As noted above, average product attains a maximum when a ray from the origin is tangent to the total product curve. Therefore, marginal product equals average product at the latter's maximum point.

An example will elucidate the last point. Consider a student who has taken three tests in a course; his grades are 92, 88, and 96. His *average* grade at this point is accordingly 92. Now suppose he makes less than 92 on his fourth test. His average grade must fall even though his total number of points increases. On the other hand, if he makes more than

92, his average grade rises; and obviously, if he makes exactly 92, his average grade remains unchanged.

In order to improve his average, the *marginal* (or last) test grade must exceed the previous average. If it is less, his average grade must fall. The same reasoning applies to production. If three workers, in co-operation with a fixed amount of other factors, can produce 276 units of output, the average product per worker is 92 units. If hiring an additional worker adds more than 92 units to output (i.e., the marginal product of four workers exceeds 92), average product rises; if hiring an additional

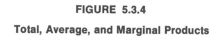

FIGURE 5.3.4

Total, Average, and Marginal Products

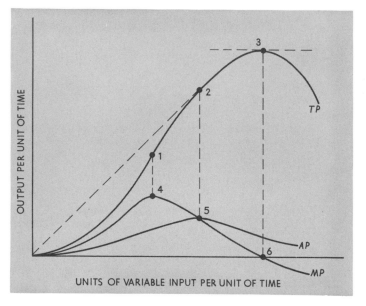

worker adds less than 92 units to output, average product must fall. Thus so long as marginal product exceeds average product, the latter must rise; when marginal product is less than average product, the latter must fall. Thus average product must attain its maximum when it is equal to marginal product.

Figure 5.3.4 illustrates these relations. In this graph one can see not only the relation between marginal and average products but also the relation of these two curves to total product.

Consider first the total product curve. For very small amounts of the variable input, total product rises gradually. But even at a low level of input it begins to rise quite rapidly, reaching its maximum slope (or rate of increase) at point one. Since the slope of the total product curve equals marginal product, the maximum slope (point one) must correspond to the maximum point on the marginal product curve (point four).

After attaining its maximum slope at point one, the total product curve continues to rise. But output increases at a decreasing rate, so the slope is less steep. Moving outward along the curve from point one, the point is soon reached at which a ray from the origin is just tangent to the curve (point two). Since tangency of the ray to the curve defines the condition for maximum average product, point two lies directly above point five.

As the quantity of variable input is expanded from its value at point two, total product continues to increase. But its rate of increase is progressively slower until point three is finally reached. At this position total product is at a maximum; thereafter it declines until it (conceivably) reaches zero again. Over a tiny range around point three, additional input does not change total output. The slope of the total product curve is zero; thus marginal product must also be zero. This is shown by the fact that points three and six occur at precisely the same input value. And since total product declines beyond point three, marginal product becomes negative.

Most of the important relations have so far been discussed with reference to the total product curve. To emphasize certain relations, however, consider the marginal and average product curves. Marginal product at first increases, reaches a maximum at point four (the point of diminishing marginal physical returns) and declines thereafter. It eventually becomes negative beyond point six, where total product attains its maximum.

Average product also rises at first until it reaches its maximum at point five, where marginal and average products are equal. It subsequently declines, conceivably becoming zero when total product itself becomes zero. Finally, one may observe that marginal product exceeds average product when the latter is increasing and is less than average product when the latter is decreasing.

5.3.c—Law of Diminishing Marginal Physical Returns

The slope of the marginal product curve in Figure 5.3.4 illustrates an important principle, the law of diminishing marginal physical returns. As the number of units of the variable input increases, other inputs held constant, after a point the marginal product of the variable input declines. When the amount of the variable input is small relative to the fixed inputs (the fixed inputs are plentiful relative to the variable input), more intensive utilization of fixed inputs by variable inputs may increase the marginal output of the variable input. Nonetheless a point is quickly reached beyond which an increase in the use of the variable input yields progressively less additional returns. Each additional unit has, on average, fewer units of the fixed inputs with which to work.

Principle (the law of diminishing marginal physical returns):   As the amount of a variable input is increased, the amount of other (fixed) inputs held constant, a point is reached beyond which marginal product declines.

This is a simple statement concerning physical relations that have been observed in the real economic world. While it is not susceptible of mathematical proof or refutation, it is of some worth to note that a contrary observation has never been recorded. Psychologists have even found that the law holds true for consecutive study time.[2]

5.3.d—Three Stages of Production

Economists use the relations among total, average, and marginal products to define three stages of production, illustrated in Figure 5.3.5. Stage I covers that range of variable input usage over which average product increases. In other words, stage I corresponds to increasing *average returns* to the variable inputs. The fixed input is present in uneconomically large proportion relative to the variable input. As we will show in the chapter dealing with wage theory, a rational producer would never operate in this range of production: such a small amount of output could be produced by using fewer units of some of the fixed inputs (i.e., by allowing some of the fixed input to remain idle, even though payment must be made for all units).

Production would also never occur in stage III, as is more or less obvious from the graph. Stage III is defined as the range of negative marginal product or declining total product. Additional units of variable input during this stage of production actually cause a decrease in total output. Even if units of the variable input were free, a rational producer would not employ them beyond the point of zero marginal product because their use entails a reduction in total output; additional units of the fixed input must be used if output is to be expanded.

In stage III the variable input is combined with the fixed input in uneconomically large proportions. In terms of agriculture, land is cultivated too intensively. Indeed, the point of zero marginal product of the variable input is called the *intensive margin*. Similarly, in suggestive terminology, at the point of maximum average product the cultivation of land is extensive; and the point of maximum average product is called the *extensive margin*.

---

[2] Do not make the common mistake, however, of saying that you stopped studying because diminishing returns set in. The term "diminishing returns" is frequently heard in noneconomic usage and is almost as frequently misused. Diminishing returns may set in with the first unit of study time, but you may continue studying. You cease studying when the marginal utility of the (expected) increase in grade (or of the pleasure of studying) from an additional unit of study time is less than the expected marginal utility of using that time for something else.

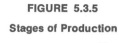

FIGURE 5.3.5

Stages of Production

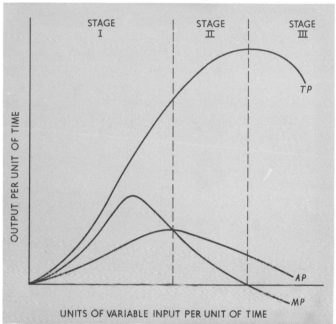

We have now eliminated stages I and III. Production must occur in stage II—between the extensive and intensive margins, or over the range of variable input usage from maximum average product to zero marginal product. If output must be produced in quantities not covered by production in stage II, there must be some change in the quantity of fixed input. If a smaller output is desired, the units of fixed input must be reduced; if a larger output is required, it can be achieved only by augmenting fixed input.

5.4 PRODUCTION WITH TWO VARIABLE INPUTS

In our discussion of the fundamental physical relations of production, we have thus far assumed that there is only one variable input. The analysis is continued here for a more general case. Graphically production is studied under the assumption that there are two variable inputs. One may regard these inputs either as cooperating with one or more fixed inputs or as the only two inputs. The latter situation, of course, is relevant only for the long run. In either case, however, the results of the two-input model are easily extended to cover multiple inputs.

5.4.a—Product Curves for Different Amounts of Fixed Input

When analyzing production with two variable factors, we cannot simply use two sets of average and marginal product curves, such as those discussed in Section 5.3. When the amount of the *now* variable, but *formerly* fixed, factor changes the total, marginal, and average product curves of the variable factor shift. Generally, the greater the amount of fixed input available the greater also are the total, average, and marginal

FIGURE 5.4.1

Total, Average, and Marginal Products for Two Different Amounts of the Fixed Factor

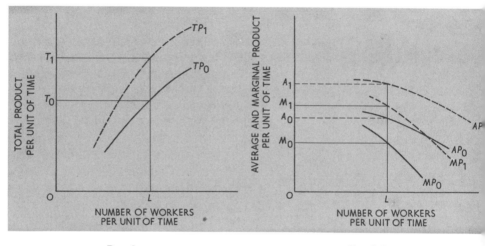

Panel *a*

Total Product

Panel *b*

Average and Marginal Products

products of a given amount of the variable input. Increasing the fixed input increases the amount of this input per unit of variable input. This normally results in an increase in the marginal, and hence in the average and total, product of the variable input.[3]

This proposition is illustrated in Figure 5.4.1. TP_0 in panel *a* and AP_0 and MP_0 in panel *b* are the total, average, and marginal product curves of labor for a fixed amount of another factor, say capital. If the amount of capital increases, the three curves increase to (say) TP_1, AP_1, and MP_1. This means that for each amount of labor over the relevant range total, average, and marginal products are greater. For example, for OL units

---

[3] The results of this subsection hold only for the range of production in stage II. Since this is where production takes place, it is of course the stage of greatest interest.

of labor, an increase in capital increases total product from OT_0 to OT_1, average product from OA_0 to OA_1, and marginal product from OM_0 to OM_1.

If both labor and capital are variable, each factor has an infinite set of product curves, one for every amount of the other factor. Therefore another tool of analysis is necessary when there is more than one variable factor. This tool is the *production isoquant*.

5.4.b—Production Isoquants

An isoquant in production theory is analogous to an indifference curve in consumer theory.

Definition: An isoquant is a curve showing all possible combinations of inputs physically capable of producing a given level of output.

Figure 5.4.2 illustrates two typical isoquants. Isoquant I is the locus of combinations of capital and labor yielding 100 units of output. One can produce 100 units of output by using 50 units of capital and 15 of labor, by using 10 units of capital and 75 of labor, or by using any other combination on I. Similarly II shows the different combinations of capital and labor that can produce 200 units of output.

FIGURE 5.4.2

Typical Isoquants

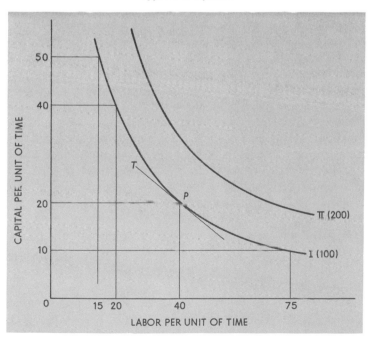

Relations: Any isoquant lying above another represents a larger level of output. Two isoquants never intersect. There are an infinite number of isoquants between I and II in Figure 5.4.2 because there are an infinite number of production levels between 100 and 200 units, provided the product is infinitesimally divisible.

The isoquants in Figure 5.4.2 are concave from above, as are all isoquants over the range in which production takes place. This concavity implies that as capital decreases by equal amounts, proportionately more labor must be added in order to maintain the same output level. Either 50 units of capital and 15 units of labor or 40 units of capital and 20 units of labor can be used to produce 100 units of output (Figure 5.4.2). This means that reducing capital by 10 units requires the addition of only 5 units of labor in order to produce 100 units of output. On the other hand, moving from 20 to 10 units of capital requires changing from 40 to 75 units of labor. The firm now substitutes 35 units of labor for 10 units of capital.

One of the chief features of production under conditions of variable proportions is that different combinations of inputs can be used to produce a given level of output. In other words, one input can be *substituted* for another in such a way as to maintain a constant level of output. Great theoretical and practical importance attaches to the *rate* at which one input must be substituted for another in order to hold output constant.

Analogous to indifference curve theory, the *rate* at which one input can be substituted for another at a given level of output is measured by the slope of a tangent to the isoquant. In Figure 5.4.2 the slope of the tangent T shows the rate at which labor can be substituted for capital in the neighborhood of point P, always maintaining an output of 100 units. For very small movements along an isoquant, the negative of the slope of the tangent is called *the marginal rate of technical substitution,* just as the negative of the slope of a consumer's indifference curve is called the marginal rate of substitution in consumption. There is one slight difference in terminology. In production theory the negative slope of the isoquant is called the marginal rate of technical substitution of K for L, whereas in consumption theory it would be called the marginal rate of substitution of L for K.

For very small movements along an isoquant the marginal rate of technical substitution of capital for labor is the ratio of the marginal product of labor to the marginal product of capital:

$$MRTS_{K \text{ for } L} = -\frac{\Delta K}{\Delta L} \text{ (output constant)} = \frac{MP_L}{MP_K}.$$

The proof is similar to that in Chapter 3 concerning $MRS_{x \text{ for } y} = \frac{MU_x}{MU_y}.$

FIGURE 5.4.3

Interpretation of MRTS

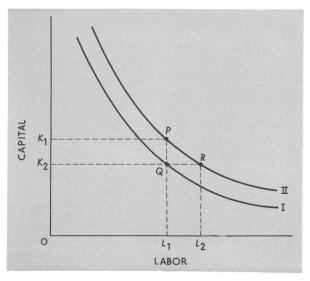

Let the producer originally be at point P, Figure 5.4.3. Next let capital be reduced by a small amount from OK_1 to OK_2, labor held constant at OL_1. The reduction in output is represented by the difference between II and I.

The marginal product of capital for this small reduction in output is the decrease in output divided by the decrease in capital:

$$MP_K = \frac{II - I}{K_1K_2}.$$

Now let the producer return to the II − level of production by holding capital constant at OK_2 and increasing labor from OL_1 to OL_2. The marginal product of labor, by the argument above, is

$$MP_L = \frac{II - I}{L_1L_2}.$$

Taking the ratio of the two marginal products, we obtain

$$\frac{MP_L}{MP_K} = \frac{II - I}{L_1L_2} \div \frac{II - I}{K_1K_2} = \frac{K_1K_2}{L_1L_2}.$$

But by the figure,

$$\frac{K_1K_2}{L_1L_2} = \frac{PQ}{QR} = MRTS_{K \text{ for } L} = \frac{MP_L}{MP_K},$$

which completes the proof.

Relations: The marginal rate of technical substitution measures the reduction in one input per unit increase in the other that is just sufficient to maintain a constant level of output. The marginal rate of technical substitution of input K for input L at a point on an isoquant is equal to the negative of the slope of the isoquant at that point. It is also equal to the ratio of the marginal product of input L to the marginal product of input K.

5.4.c—Diminishing Marginal Rate of Technical Substitution

The marginal rate of technical substitution of capital for labor diminishes as more and more labor is substituted for capital. This proposition sounds plausible; and it is not difficult to explain.

As additional units of labor are added to a fixed amount of capital the marginal product of labor diminishes. Furthermore, as shown in Figure 5.4.1, if the amount of the fixed input is diminished the marginal product of labor diminishes. Thus two forces are working to diminish the marginal product of labor: (a) less of the fixed input causes a downward *shift* of the marginal product of labor curve; (b) more units of the variable input (labor) causes a downward movement *along* the marginal product curve. Thus as labor is substituted for capital the marginal product of labor must decline. For analogous reasons the marginal product of capital increases as less capital and more labor is used. With the quantity of labor fixed, the marginal product of capital rises as fewer units of capital are used. But simultaneously there is an increase in labor input thereby shifting the marginal product of capital curve upward. The same two forces are present in this case: a movement along a marginal product curve and a shift in the location of the curve. In this situation, however, both forces work to increase the marginal product of capital. Thus as labor is substituted for capital, the marginal product of capital increases.

As already defined, the marginal rate of technical substitution is the ratio of the marginal product of labor to the marginal product of capital. As labor is substituted for capital, the marginal product of labor declines and the marginal product of capital increases. Hence the marginal rate of technical substitution of capital for labor declines as labor is substituted for capital so as to maintain a constant level of output. This may be summarized as follows:

Relation: As labor is substituted for capital along an isoquant (so that output is unchanged), the marginal rate of technical substitution declines.

The fact that the marginal rate of technical substitution falls as labor is substituted for capital means that isoquants must be concave from above (that is, in the neighborhood of a point of tangency, the isoquant must lie above the tangent line). This has been mentioned above and is restressed in Figure 5.4.4.

FIGURE 5.4.4

Diminishing Marginal Rate of Technical Substitution

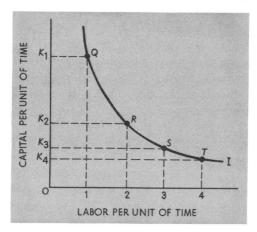

LABOR PER UNIT OF TIME

Q, R, S, and T are four input combinations lying on the isoquant I. Q has the combination OK_1 units of capital and one unit of labor; R has OK_2 units of capital and two units of labor; and so on. For the movement from Q to R, the marginal rate of technical substitution of capital for labor is, by formula,

$$\frac{OK_1 - OK_2}{1 - 2} = OK_1 - OK_2 .$$

Similarly, for the movements from R to S and S to T, the marginal rates of technical substitution are $OK_2 - OK_3$ and $OK_3 - OK_4$ respectively.

Since the marginal rate of technical substitution of capital for labor diminishes as labor is substituted for capital, it is necessary that $OK_1 - OK_2 > OK_2 - OK_3 > OK_3 - OK_4$. Visually, the amount of capital replaced by successive units of labor will decline if, and only if, the isoquant is concave from above. Since the amount *must* decline, the isoquant must be concave from above.

Relation: Isoquants must be concave from above at every point in order to satisfy the principle of diminishing marginal rate of technical substitution.

5.4.d—Economic Region of Production

Many production functions lead to initial isoquant graphs such as shown in Figure 5.4.2. Others, however, generate an isoquant map such as that shown in Figure 5.4.5. It is like the map in Figure 5.4.2 in that the isoquants do not intersect; the higher the isoquant the greater the level of output; and over a range of input values they are negatively sloped. The only difference lies in the fact that the isoquants in Figure 5.4.5 "bend back upon themselves" or have positively sloped segments.

The parallel dashed lines in Figure 5.4.5 indicate the points at which the isoquants bend back upon themselves. The lines OK and OL join these points and form, as we will see, the boundaries of the economic region of production (or the stage II region).

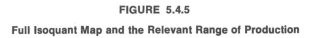

FIGURE 5.4.5

Full Isoquant Map and the Relevant Range of Production

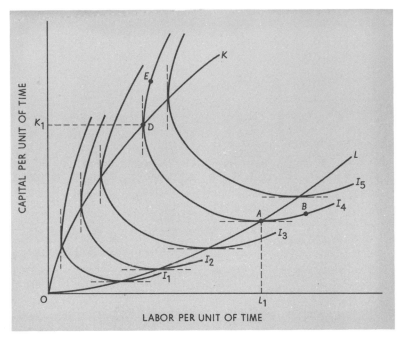

To see why the lines OL and OK form the boundary of production, first consider a movement along I_4 from A to B. An increase in the amount of labor must be accompanied by an *increase* in the amount of capital in order to maintain the same output. On the other hand we could keep the amount of labor constant at OL_1, increase the amount of capital and increase output; i.e., reach a higher isoquant. Therefore, labor must have a negative marginal product along I_4 to the right of A, since additional capital is required to offset the decreased product from additional labor.

Consider now a movement along I_4 from D to E. Increasing the amount of capital requires an offsetting increase in the amount of labor in order to maintain the same level of production. Keeping capital the same at

OK_1 and increasing labor would allow a higher isoquant to be attained and hence a greater output. Therefore, along I_4 above D, capital must have a negative marginal product. By similar argument it is simple to show that along any isoquant in Figure 5.4.5, capital has a negative marginal product above OK and labor has a negative marginal product below OL.

Since an increase in either factor must be accompanied by an off-setting decrease in the other to maintain the same output between OL and OK, both factors must have positive marginal products.[4] Therefore OL is the locus of points for which the marginal product of labor is zero, and OK is the locus of points for which the marginal product of capital is zero. Since no firm would produce where the marginal product of either factor is negative, production occurs within the boundary of OL and OK. These "ridge" lines separate the economic from the uneconomic regions of production. To summarize:

Relations: If the production function is such that intensive and extensive margins for each input exist, the total isoquant map is like the one in Figure 5.4.5. Only those portions of the isoquants lying between the ridge lines (the loci of zero marginal products) are relevant to production. These economic portions of the isoquants are uniquely associated with stage II production.

5.5 OPTIMAL COMBINATION OF RESOURCES

So far the theory of production has been analyzed from the standpoint of an individual entrepreneur. However, nothing has been said about the *optimal* way in which he should combine resources. Any desired level of output can normally be produced by a number of different combinations of inputs. Our task now is to determine the specific combination a producer should select.

5.5.a—Input Prices and Isocosts

Inputs, as well as outputs, bear specific market prices. In determining his *operating* input combination a producer must pay heed to relative input prices if he is to minimize the cost of producing a given output or maximize output for a given level of cost.

Input prices are determined, as are the prices of goods, by supply and demand in the market. For producers who are not monopsonists or oligopsonists (i.e., the sole purchaser or one of a few purchasers of an input), input prices are given by the market and their rates of purchase

---

[4] In more advanced texts it is shown that the intensive margin for one factor is the extensive margin for the other provided the production function is homogeneous of degree one. Thus in the range between OL and OK both factors are in stage II.

do not change them. Let us now concentrate upon a producer who is a perfect competitor in the input market, even though he may be a monopolist or an oligopolist (i.e., a single seller or one of a few sellers) in his output market.

Let us continue to assume that the two inputs are labor and capital, although the analysis applies equally well to any two productive agents. Denote the quantity of capital and labor by K and L, respectively, and their unit prices by r and w. The total cost $\bar{C}$ of using any volume of K and L is $\bar{C} = rK + wL$, the sum of the cost of K units of capital at r per unit and of L units of labor at w per unit.

FIGURE 5.5.1

Isocost Curves for $r =$ \$1,000 and $w =$ \$2,500

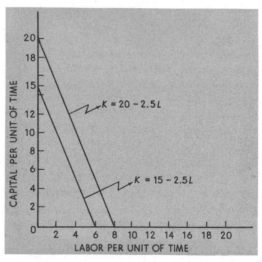

To take a more specific example, suppose capital costs \$1,000 per unit ($r =$ \$1,000) and labor receives a wage of \$2,500 per man-year ($w =$ \$2,500). If a total of \$15,000 is to be spent for inputs, the equation above shows that the following combinations are possible: \$15,000 = \$1,000 $K +$ \$2,500 L, or $K = 15 - 2.5\ L$. Similarly, if \$20,000 is to be spent on inputs, one can purchase the following combinations: $K = 20 - 2.5\ L$. More generally, if the fixed amount $\bar{C}$ is to be spent, the producer can choose among the combinations given by

$$K = \frac{C}{r} - \frac{w}{r} L .$$

This is illustrated in Figure 5.5.1. If \$15,000 is spent for inputs and no labor is purchased, 15 units of capital may be bought. More generally, if

$\overline{C}$ is to be spent and r is the unit cost, $\overline{C}/r$ units of capital may be purchased. This is the vertical axis *intercept* of the line. If one unit of labor is purchased at \$2,500, two and five-tenths units of capital must be sacrificed; if two units of labor are bought, five units of capital must be sacrificed; and so on. Thus as the purchase of labor is increased, the purchase of capital must decrease. For each additional unit of labor, w/r units of capital must be foregone. In Figure 5.5.1, $w/r = 2.5$. Attaching a negative sign, this is the *slope* of the lines.

The solid lines in Figure 5.5.1 are called *isocost curves* because they show the various combinations of inputs that may be purchased for a stipulated amount of expenditure. In summary:

Relation: At fixed input prices r and w for capital and labor, a fixed outlay $\overline{C}$ will purchase any combination of capital and labor given by the following linear equation:

$$K = \frac{\tilde{C}}{r} - \frac{w}{r} L .$$

This is the equation for an isocost curve, whose intercept (C/r) is the amount of capital that may be purchased if no labor is bought and whose slope is the negative of the input-price ratio (w/r).

5.5.b—Production of a Given Output at Minimum Cost

Whatever output an entrepreneur chooses to produce, he wishes to produce it at the least possible cost. To do this he must organize production in the most efficient way.

Suppose at given input prices r and w an entrepreneur wishes to produce the output indicated by isoquant I in Figure 5.5.2. Isocost curves KL, $K'L'$, and $K''L''$ represent the infinite number of isocost curves from which the producer can choose at the given input prices. Obviously he chooses the lowest one that enables him to attain output level I. That is, he produces at the cost represented by isocost curve $K'L'$. Any resource expenditure below that, for example that represented by KL, is not feasible since it is impossible to produce output I with these resource combinations. Any resource combinations above that represented by $K'L'$ are rejected because the entrepreneur wishes to produce the desired output at *least* cost. If he produced at either A or B, at the cost represented by $K''L''$, he can reduce his costs by moving along I to point E. This is the point of optimal resource combination: he uses OK_0 units of capital and OL_0 units of labor.

Equilibrium is reached when the isoquant representing the chosen output is just tangent to an isocost curve. Since tangency means that the two slopes are equal, least cost production requires that the marginal

FIGURE 5.5.2

**Optimal Input Combination to Minimize Cost
Subject to a Given Level of Output**

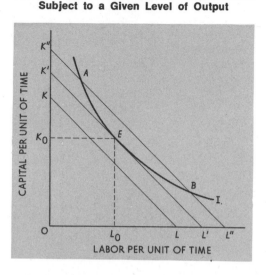

rate of technical substitution of capital for labor be equal to the ratio of the price of labor to the price of capital. The market input-price ratio tells the producer the rate at which he *can substitute* one input for another *in purchasing*. The marginal rate of technical substitution tells him the rate at which he *can substitute in production*. So long as the two are not equal, a producer can achieve a lower cost by moving in the direction of equality.

Principle: To minimize cost subject to a given level of output and given input prices, the producer must purchase inputs in quantities such that the marginal rate of technical substitution of capital for labor is equal to the input-price ratio (the price of labor to the price of capital). Thus

$$MRTS_{K \text{ for } L} = \frac{MP_L}{MP_K} = \frac{w}{r}.$$

The most realistic way of examining the problem is to assume that the entrepreneur chooses a level of output and then chooses the input combination which enables him to produce that output at least cost. As an alternative we could assume that the entrepreneur can spend only a fixed amount on production and wishes to attain the highest level of production consistent with that amount of expenditure. Not too surprisingly, the results turn out the same as before. The entrepreneur produces where the isocost curve representing the amount to be spent on production is tangent to an isoquant. This is the highest isoquant attainable. The marginal rate of technical substitution of capital for labor equals the input-price ratio (the price of labor to the price of capital).

Exercise: Draw some isoquants above and below 1 in Figure 5.5.2. Assume that the producer wishes to obtain the maximum possible output at the cost represented by *K'L'*. Establish that the producer will produce at *E*, using *OL₀* labor and *OK₀* capital.

Principle: In order either to maximize output subject to a given cost or to minimize cost subject to a given output, the entrepreneur must employ inputs in such amounts as to equate the marginal rate of technical substitution and the input-price ratio.

We can now examine how factor proportions change when output changes, the factor-price ratio held constant. In Figure 5.5.3 the curves

FIGURE 5.5.3

Expansion Path

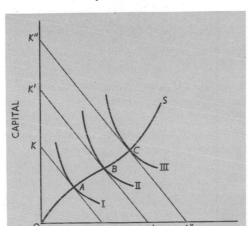

I, II, III are isoquants depicting a representative production function; *KL*, *K'L'*, and *K"L"* represent the least cost of producing the three output levels. Since the factor-price ratio does not change, they are parallel.

To summarize: first, factor prices remain constant. Second, each equilibrium point is defined by equality between the marginal rate of technical substitution and the factor-price ratio. Since the latter remains constant, so does the former. Therefore, *OS* is a locus of points along which the marginal rate of technical substitution is constant. But it is a curve with a special feature. Specifically, it is the locus along which output will expand when factor prices are constant. We may accordingly formulate this result as a

Definition: The expansion path is the curve along which output expands when factor prices remain constant. The expansion path thus shows how factor proportions change when output or expenditure changes, input prices remaining constant throughout. The marginal rate of technical substitution remains constant also since the factor-price ratio is constant.

5.6 CONCLUSION

This chapter contains an explanation of the theory of production and of the optimal combination of inputs when input prices are constant. We turn next to the theory of cost, which relies upon the physical laws of production and upon the prices an entrepreneur must pay for his inputs.

5.7 ANALYTICAL EXERCISE

Problem: Suppose that Transport Service must produce a certain output of cargo and passenger service per year. The Service is confronted with the following combinations of HC100 aircraft and mechanics that can be used to yield this required output over its route pattern.

Combination	Number of Aircraft	Number of Mechanics
No. 1.................60		1000
2.................61		920
3.................62		850
4.................63		800
5.................64		760
6.................65		730
7.................66		710

1. If Transport Service is using 60 aircraft and 1,000 mechanics, how many men can it dismiss and still maintain its output if it acquires an additional HC100?

2. Your answer in (1) is called the _____ _____ of _____ in economic theory.

3. If the additional annual cost resulting from the operation of another HC100 is $250,000, and if mechanics cost Transport Service $6,000 each annually, should the Service acquire a 61-st HC100?

4. Which combination of aircraft and mechanics should Transport Service use to minimize its costs?

5. Suppose the *annual* cost of an HC100 drops to $200,000 and the cost of mechanics rises to $7,000 per year. What combination should now be employed to minimize annual costs?

6. Can the data presented above be used to illustrate the law of variable proportions? Why or why not?

QUESTIONS AND PROBLEMS

1. Below are hypothetical data for a manufacturer, possessing a fixed plant, who produces a commodity that requires only one variable input. Total product is given. Compute and graph the average and marginal product curves. Save your basic calculations because they form the basis for a subsequent problem in Chapter 6.

Units of Variable Input	Total Product	Average Product	Marginal Product
1	100		
2	250		
3	410		
4	560		
5	700		
6	830		
7	945		
8	1,050		
9	1,146		
10	1,234		
11	1,314		
12	1,384		
13	1,444		
14	1,494		
15	1,534		
16	1,564		
17	1,584		
18	1,594		

After completing the table and graph, answer the following questions:

a) When marginal product is increasing, what is happening to average product?

b) Does average product begin to fall as soon as marginal product does? That is, which occurs first, the point of diminishing marginal or average returns?

c) When average product is at its maximum, is marginal product less than, equal to, or greater than average product?

d) Does total product increase at a decreasing rate: (i) when average product is rising? (ii) when marginal product is rising? (iii) when average product begins to fall? (iv) when marginal product passes its maximum value?

e) When average product equals zero, what is total product?

f) (i) If average product is to the left of its maximum, which type of input is present in too large proportion? (ii) Which is in too small proportion? (iii) What are two ways of changing the proportion so as to increase average product? (iv) If either of these were done, what would happen to total product? (v) In view of these facts, is it desirable or undesirable, from a social point of view, for a producer to operate with average product below its maximum (to the left)? With marginal product at its maximum? Why is your answer true in each case?

2. Suppose that a product requires two inputs for its production. Then is it correct to say that if the prices of the inputs are equal, optimal behavior on the part of producers will dictate that these inputs be used in equal amounts?

3. Assume that a curve is drawn showing along the abscissa the amounts of a factor *A* employed in combination with a fixed amount of a group of factors called *B*, and along the ordinate the amount of physical product obtainable from these combinations of factors.

   a) How can you find (geometrically) the amount of *A* for which the average physical product per unit of *A* is a maximum?

   b) How can you find (geometrically) the amount of *A* for which the marginal physical product of *A* is a maximum?

   c) Between the two points defined in questions (*a*) and (*b*), will the marginal physical product of *A* increase or decrease as more of *A* is used?

   d) Between these two points, will the average physical product per unit of *A* increase or decrease as more of *A* is used?

   e) At the point defined in (*a*), will the marginal physical product of *A* be higher or lower than the average physical product per unit of *A*? Give reasons.

   f) At the point defined in (*b*), will the marginal physical product of *A* be higher or lower than the average physical product per unit of *A*? Give reasons.

   g) How can you find (geometrically) the amount of *A* for which the marginal physical product of *A* is zero?

4. An expansion path can be derived under the assumption either that firms attempt to produce each output at minimum cost or that they attempt to gain maximum output at each level of cost. The paths are identical in both cases. Explain.

chapter
6

Theory of Cost

6.1 INTRODUCTION

When people speak of the cost of something they generally mean the price that must be paid for the item in question. To a businessman the cost of producing a good usually means the number of dollars that must be paid for enough raw materials, labor, machinery, and so on to produce the good. In economics, however, cost means somewhat more.

Consider the cost of attending college for one year. As a first approximation one might say that attending college for one year costs the year's tuition, room, board, book purchases, and incidental expenses. Using that approach it would appear that the cost of attending a particular college is essentially the same for any two students. Under certain circumstances that may not be quite correct. Assume that there are two students at the same school paying approximately the same tuition, board, and so forth. One student, however, is an exceptional baseball player who has been offered a major league contract with a large bonus. The *real* cost to him of attending college is not just the sum of his expenses; it is also what he had to give up to attend college. He must *sacrifice* or *give up* the amount he cound have made by playing baseball in order to attend college.

The other student must also sacrifice something in addition to his direct outlays for expenses. Assuming that he is not so athletically inclined, perhaps his best alternative earning possibility might lie in working as a bank teller if he does not attend college. Thus he must sacrifice this amount of potential income. Since bank tellers generally do not receive a large bonus for signing with a bank, the athlete must sacrifice a greater amount; hence the *real* cost of attending college is greater for him than for the nonathlete. The athlete's *best alternative* is greater, so his real total cost is greater.

We use a similar type of analysis when discussing the cost of production. For convenience we speak of two types of cost: (1) the social cost of production, and (2) the private cost of production. Before turning to the mechanics of cost analysis, we must first distinguish between these two costs.

6.1.a—Social Cost of Production

Economists are principally interested in the social cost of production; that is, the cost that society incurs when a resource is used to produce a given commodity. The cost of a productive resource in a particular use (say producing good X) is the amount it could produce in its best alternative (say in producing Y). The foregone Y the resource could have produced had it not been used to produce X is the cost to society. To use a popular wartime example, devoting more resources to the production of guns means using fewer resources to produce butter. The social cost of guns is the amount of butter foregone. The social cost of sending a man to the moon is the goods that society gives up by devoting resources to the trip.

Economists speak of this as the alternative or opportunity cost of production.

Definition: The alternative or opportunity cost of producing one unit of commodity X is the amount of commodity Y that must be sacrificed in order to use resources to produce X rather than Y. This is the social cost of production.

6.1.b—Private Cost of Production

There is a close relation between the opportunity cost of producing commodity X and a calculation the producer of X must make. The use of resources to produce X rather than Y entails a social cost; there is a private cost as well because the entrepreneur must pay a price to get the resources he uses. He must pay a certain amount to the resources in order to bid them away from alternative uses. These payments are *explicit* costs to the firm. He incurs some *implicit costs* also, and a complete analysis of costs must take these implicit costs into consideration.

To aid in analyzing the nature of implicit costs, consider two firms that produce good X and are in every way identical, with one exception. Both use identical amounts of the same resources to produce identical amounts of X. The first entrepreneur rents the building he uses. The second inherited his building and therefore pays no rent. Whose costs are higher? An economist would say both are the same, even though the second entrepreneur makes lower payments to outside factors of production. The reason costs are the same is that using his building to produce X costs the second entrepreneur the amount of income he could have received had he leased it at the prevailing rent. Since these two buildings are the same, presumably the market rental would be the same. In other words, a part of the cost incurred by the second entrepreneur is the payment from himself as entrepreneur to himself as the owner of a resource (the building).

Similarly the implicit cost would also include what he could make in the best alternative use of his time and his capital in another occupation had he not been associated with his firm.

Definition: The implicit costs incurred by an entrepreneur in producing a specific commodity consist of the amounts he could earn in the best alternative use of his time and of any other of his resources currently used to produce the commodity in question.

Implicit costs are thus charges that must be added to explicit costs in order to obtain total private costs.

6.2 PLANNING HORIZON

Let us begin our analysis of costs in the following way. Assume that an individual considers establishing a firm in a particular industry. One of the first things our prospective entrepreneur must decide is the *scale* of operation or the *size* of his firm. To make this decision properly he must know the cost of producing each level of output.

6.2.a—Beginning the Firm

Let us assume for analytical purposes that the individual knows his actions will not affect the price he must pay for the resources he uses. Further, assume that he knows the least cost technology for every level of output. Figure 6.2.1 specifies this *least cost schedule* for various rates of production of good X per period of time. For example, given the existing set of productive techniques and resource prices, the lowest cost of producing Ox_1 units of X is Oc_1. Obviously he could pay more to produce Ox_1 by using a less efficient productive process or by paying some factors of production more than their market prices. He could not, however, produce Ox_1 units at a cost lower than Oc_1.

The total least cost of producing Ox_1 units of output consists of two components, the explicit costs and the implicit costs. The explicit costs are the payments the entrepreneur must make to the factors of production he uses to produce Ox_1. The implicit costs are the market values of the resources he owns and uses in production, including the wages he pays himself. The payments to himself must be included since they cost the entrepreneur what he could receive for the services of these resources had he not chosen to use them himself.

The same type of explanation applicable to Ox_1 units of output and

FIGURE 6.2.1

Long-Run Total Cost Curve

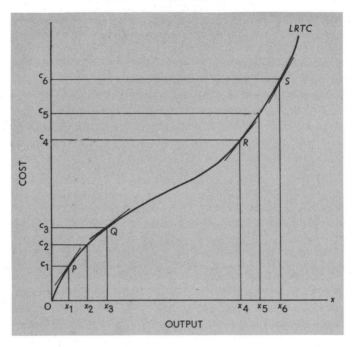

cost Oc_1 applies to every other combination of output and cost specified by the cost curve in Figure 6.2.1.[1] It is important to note that the entrepreneur may use different amounts and combinations of resources. Nothing is fixed to him except the set of technological possibilities, or state of the arts, and the prices at which he can purchase resources. Thus completely different production processes may be used to achieve minimum cost at (say) Ox_1 and Ox_2 units of output. This "planning horizon" in which nothing is fixed to the entrepreneur except factor prices and technology is called the long run, and the associated curve that shows the minimum cost of producing each level of output is called the *Long-Run Total Cost Curve*.

Definition: Long-run total cost is the least cost at which each quantity of output can be produced when no resource is fixed in quantity or rate of usage.

---

[1] Note that since the cost curve begins at the origin and not at some positive amount on the vertical axis, we tacitly assume that the entrepreneur can readily vary the amount of his time and other resources he "invests" in the business. That is to say, the implicit costs are as readily variable as the explicit cost when one is considering the long run, or planning horizon. It is only in the short run, as we shall see below, that implicit costs are fixed.

6.2.b—Shape of Long-Run Total Cost Curves

The slope of the long-run total cost ($LRTC$) curve depends exclusively upon the production function and prevailing factor prices. The curve in Figure 6.2.1 reflects some of the commonly assumed characteristics of long-run total costs.

Two characteristics are apparent on inspection. First, costs and output are *directly related;* that is, the curve has a positive slope. It costs more to produce more, which is just another way of saying that resources are scarce or that one never gets "something for nothing" in the real economic world. The second characteristic is that costs first increase at a decreasing rate and then at an increasing rate. For example, Figure 6.2.1 is constructed so that $x_1x_2 = x_2x_3$, whereas c_1c_2 is clearly greater than c_2c_3. This means that the added total cost is greater when the entrepreneur moves from Ox_1 to Ox_2 than when he increases output from Ox_2 to Ox_3. On the other hand, $x_4x_5 = x_5x_6$ but c_4c_5 is less than c_5c_6; over this range the additional cost incurred by producing more output increases. Alternatively stated, the slope at P (indicated by the tangent at that point) is greater than that at the larger output corresponding to Q. Incremental costs decrease over this range, even though total costs increase. The slope at R is less steep than that at S, indicating that incremental costs increase over this range.

Let us now summarize and, at the same time, relate long-run total cost to factor prices and the production function. Consider Figure 6.2.2, in which we suppose that output is produced by two inputs, K and L. The known and fixed input prices give us the constant input price ratio, represented by the isocost curves l_1I_1', I_3I_3', etc. Next, the known production function gives us the isoquant map, partially represented by x_1, x_3, etc., in Figure 6.2.2.

As is familiar from Chapter 5, when all inputs are readily variable (i.e., the long run), the entrepreneur will choose input combinations that minimize the cost of producing each level of output. This gives us the expansion path $OP'\ Q'\ R'\ S'$. Now let us relate Figures 6.2.1 and 6.2.2. Given the factor-price ratio and the production function, the expansion path shows the combinations of inputs that enable the entrepreneur to produce each level of output at the least possible cost. Given the same production function and factor prices, $LRTC$ also shows the least possible cost of producing each level of output. The points P, Q, R, and S in Figure 6.2.1 correspond exactly to the points P', Q', R', and S', respectively, in Figure 6.2.2. For example, the cost Oc_1 of producing Ox_1 units of output (Figure 6.2.1) is precisely the cost of using QK_1 units of K and OL_1 units of L to produce the x_1 output at the optimal combination represented by P' (Figure 6.2.2).

FIGURE 6.2.2

The Expansion Path and Long-Run Cost

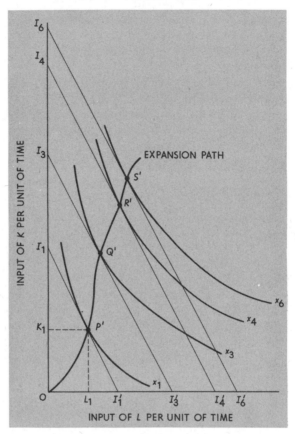

6.2.c—Long-Run Average and Long-Run Marginal Costs

The assumed slopes of the long-run total cost curve specify a particular form for the long-run average cost curve and for the long-run marginal cost curve.

Definition: Average cost is the total cost of producing a particular quantity of output divided by that quantity.

Definition: Long-run marginal cost is the addition to total cost attributable to an additional unit of output when all inputs are optimally adjusted. It is thus the change in total cost as one moves along the expansion path or the long-run total cost curve.

Figure 6.2.3 shows the method of deriving the long-run average cost curve (*LRAC*) from the long-run total cost curve (*LRTC*). Since average

FIGURE 6.2.3

Derivation of Average Total Cost Curve

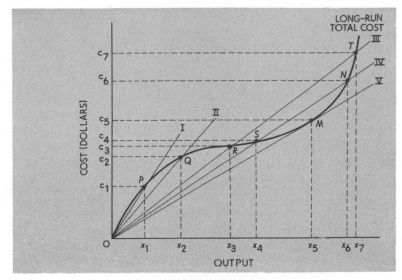

Panel a
Long-Run Total Cost

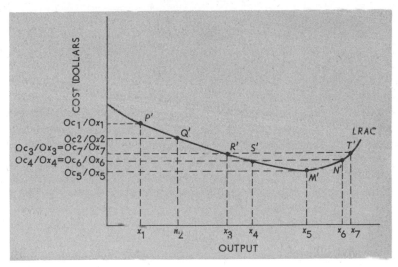

Panel b
Long-Run Average Cost

cost is total cost divided by the corresponding output, the average cost of a particular quantity is given by the slope of a ray from the origin to the relevant point on $LRTC$. For example, at output Ox_1 in panel a average cost is Oc_1/Ox_1, the slope of the ray I from the origin to point P on the curve. The average cost Oc_1/Ox_1 of Ox_1 units of output is plotted as P' in panel b (the scale of the vertical axis of panel b differs from that of panel a). Point Q' in panel b, showing an average cost of Oc_2/Ox_2 at output Ox_2, is derived similarly. Since the slope of ray II is less than the slope of ray I, average cost is less for Ox_2 units than for Ox_1; this can be seen in panel b.

Note that since ray II is steeper than ray III and ray III steeper than ray IV, average cost is greater at output $Ox_2(Oc_2/Ox_2)$ than at Ox_3 and greater at Ox_3 than at Ox_4. In fact it is clear by inspection that the rays become less and less steep until output Ox_5 is reached, where ray V is tangent to the total cost curve at M. Thus $LRAC$ decreases until, at output Ox_5, it reaches its lowest point (M' in panel b). Further increases in output lead to increases in $LRAC$ since the slopes of the rays begin to increase after output Ox_5. For example $LRAC$ is the same at $Ox_6(N')$ as at Ox_4; the same is true for Ox_7 and Ox_3. Thus while $LRTC$ continuously increases, $LRAC$ at first decreases (negative slope), reaches a minimum, then rises (positive slope).

The derivation of marginal cost is illustrated in Figure 6.2.4. Panel a contains the same total cost curve $LRTC$ as that in Figure 6.2.3. As output increases from Ox' to Ox'', one moves from point P to point Q and total cost increases from Oc' to Oc''. Marginal cost, the least possible additional cost of producing one more unit of output, is thus

$$MC = \frac{Oc'' - Oc'}{Ox'' - Ox'} = \frac{QR}{PR}.$$

As P moves along $LRTC$ toward point Q, the distance between P and Q becomes smaller and the slope of the tangent T at point Q becomes a progressively better estimate of QR/PR. For movements in a tiny neighborhood around point Q, the slope of the tangent is marginal cost at output Ox''.

As one moves along $LRTC$ through points such as P and Q the slope of $LRTC$ diminishes until point S is reached at output Ox_m. Therefore the marginal cost curve (LMC) is constructed in panel b so that it decreases (as the *slope* of $LRTC$ decreases) until output Ox_m is attained and increases thereafter (as the *slope* of $LRTC$ increases).

One point should be noted. As indicated in Figure 6.2.3, the ray V gives minimum $LRAC$. But at this point ray V is tangent to $LRTC$, hence the slope of V also gives LMC at point M. Thus $LMC = LRAC$ when $LRAC$ attains its minimum value. Ray V in Figure 6.2.4, panel a, also illustrates this point. Since the slope of $LRTC$ is less than the slope of a

FIGURE 6.2.4

Derivation of Marginal Cost Curve

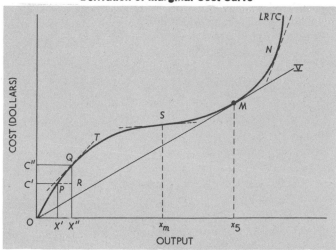

Panel a
Long-Run Total Cost

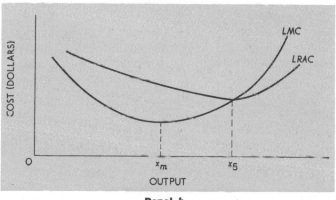

Panel b
Long-Run Marginal Cost

ray from the origin to any point on the curve to the left of M, LMC is less than LRAC from the origin to Ox_5. Since the slope of LRTC is greater than the slope of a ray from the origin to any point on the curve to the right of M, LMC is greater than LRAC at outputs larger than Ox_5.

Exercise: The student should illustrate this point in panel a for points Q and N.

The previously derived LRAC is constructed in Figure 6.2.4 in order to show more clearly the relations between LRAC, LMC, and LRTC.

Relations: (1) *LRTC* rises continuously, first at a decreasing rate then at an increasing rate. (2) *LRAC* first declines, reaches a minimum, then rises. When *LRAC* reaches its minimum, *LMC* equals *LRAC*. (3) *LMC* first declines, reaches a minimum, and then increases. *LMC* lies below *LRAC* over the range in which *LRAC* declines; it lies above *LRAC* when *LRAC* is rising.

6.2.d—Economies of Scale

We have thus far concentrated exclusively upon describing the typical shapes of the long-run cost curves and have not analyzed the economic forces behind them. These forces are called economies and diseconomies of scale.

Economies of scale cause long-run average cost to decline. As the size of plant and the scale of operation are larger, certain economies of scale are usually realized. That is, after adjusting *all* inputs optimally the unit cost of production is reduced as the size of output is increased.

Adam Smith gave one of the chief reasons for this: specialization and division of labor. When the number of workers is expanded, fixed inputs remaining fixed, the opportunities for specialization and division of labor are rapidly exhausted. The marginal product curve rises, to be sure; but not for long. It very quickly reaches its maximum and declines. When workers and equipment are expanded together, however, very substantial gains may be reaped by division of jobs and the specialization of workers in one job or another.

Proficiency is gained by concentration of effort. If a plant is very small and employs only a small number of workers, each worker will usually have to perform several different jobs in the production process. In doing so he is likely to have to move about the plant, change tools, and so on. Not only are workers not highly specialized but a part of their worktime is consumed in moving about and changing tools. Thus important savings may be realized by expanding the scale of operation. A larger plant with a larger work force may permit each worker to specialize in one job, gaining proficiency and obviating time-consuming interchanges of location and equipment. There naturally will be corresponding reductions in the unit cost of production.

Technological factors constitute a second force contributing to economies of scale. If several different machines, each with a different rate of output, are required in a production process, the operation may have to be quite sizable to permit proper "meshing" of equipment. Suppose only two types of machines are required, one which produces and one which packages the product. If the first machine can produce 30,000 units per day and the second can package 45,000, output will have to be 90,000 per day in order to utilize fully the capacity of each type of machine.

Another technological element is the fact that the cost of purchasing and installing larger machines is usually proportionately less than the cost of smaller machines. For example, a printing press that can run 200,000 papers per day does not cost 10 times as much as one that can run 20,000 per day—nor does it require 10 times as much building space, 10 times as many men to work it, and so forth. Again, expanding size tends to reduce the unit cost of production.

A final technological element is perhaps the most important of all: as the scale of operation expands there is usually a qualitative, as well as a quantitative, change in equipment. Consider ditchdigging. The smallest scale of operation is one man and one shovel. But as the scale expands beyond a certain point one does not simply continue to add men and shovels. Shovels and most workers are replaced by a modern ditchdigging machine. In like manner, expansion of scale normally permits the introduction of various types of automation devices, all of which tend to reduce the unit cost of production.

Thus two broad forces—specialization and division of labor and technological factors—enable producers to reduce unit cost by expanding the scale of operation.[2] These forces give rise to the negatively sloped portion of the long-run average cost curve.

But why should it ever rise? After all possible economies of scale have been realized, why doesn't the curve become horizontal?

6.2.e—Diseconomies of Scale

The rising portion of *LRAC* is usually attributed to diseconomies of scale, which means limitations to efficient management. Managing any business entails controlling and coordinating a wide variety of activities—production, transportation, finance, sales, and so on. To perform these managerial functions efficiently the manager must have accurate information; otherwise the essential decision making is done in ignorance.

As the scale of plant expands beyond a certain point, top management necessarily has to delegate responsibility and authority to lower echelon employees. Contact with the daily routine of operation tends to be lost

---

[2] This discussion of economies of scale has concentrated upon physical and technological forces. There are financial reasons for economies of scale as well. Large-scale purchasing of raw and processed materials may enable the buyer to obtain more favorable prices (quantity discounts). The same is frequently true of advertising. As another example, financing of large-scale business is normally easier and less expensive; a nationally known business has access to organized security markets, so it may place its bonds and stocks on a more favorable basis. Bank loans also usually come easier and at lower interest rates to large, well-known corporations. These are but examples of many potential economies of scale attributable to financial considerations. For a more detailed discussion, see William G. Husband and James C. Dockeray, *Modern Corporation Finance* (6th ed.; Homewood, Ill.: R. D. Irwin, Inc., 1966).

and efficiency of operation to decline. Red tape and paper work expand; management is generally not as efficient. This increases the cost of the managerial function and, of course, the unit cost of production.

It is very difficult to determine just when diseconomies of scale set in and when they become strong enough to outweigh the economies of scale. In businesses where economies of scale are negligible, diseconomies may soon become of paramount importance, causing *LRAC* to turn up at a relatively small volume of output. Panel *a*, Figure 6.2.5, shows a long-run average cost curve for a firm of this type. In other cases, economies of scale are extremely important. Even after the efficiency of management begins to decline technological economies of scale may offset the diseconomies over a wide range of output. Thus the *LRAC* curve may not turn upward until a very large volume of output is attained. This case,

FIGURE 6.2.5

Various Shapes of *LRAC*

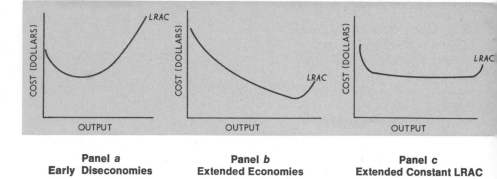

Panel *a*	Panel *b*	Panel *c*
Early Diseconomies	**Extended Economies**	**Extended Constant LRAC**

typified by the so-called natural monopolies, is illustrated in panel *b*, Figure 6.2.5.

In many actual situations, however, neither of these extremes describes the behavior of *LRAC*. A very modest scale of operation may enable a firm to capture all of the economies of scale; however, diseconomies may not be incurred until the volume of output is very great. In this case, *LRAC* would have a long horizontal section as shown in panel *c*. Many economists and businessmen feel that this type of *LRAC* curve describes most production processes in the American economy. For analytical purposes, however, we will assume a "representative" *LRAC*, such as that illustrated in Figure 6.2.4.

6.2.f—Summary

The conventional definition of the long run is "a period of time (not calendar time) of such length that all inputs are variable." Another aspect of the long run has also been stressed, an aspect that is, perhaps, the most important of all. The long run is a *planning horizon*. All production, indeed all economic activity, takes place in the short run. The long run refers to the fact that economic agents, consumers and entrepreneurs, can plan ahead and choose many aspects of the short run in which they will operate in the future. Thus in a sense the long run consists of all possible short-run situations among which an economic agent may choose.

6.3 THEORY OF COST IN THE SHORT RUN

Now that our entrepreneur has investigated all possibilities open to him, he can decide upon a specific scale of output and hence build a plant of such size as to produce this output at the least possible cost. For economic theory, this may be regarded as either *money* cost or *resource* cost because, in the last analysis, they are the same (except in one situation, which is discussed in the last chapter of the book).

6.3.a—Short-Run Total Cost

Prior to investing money resources in buildings, machinery, and so on, the amounts of all resources are variable. That is, the usage of each type of resource can be determined so as to obtain the most efficient (i.e., least cost) combination of inputs. But once money resources have been congealed into buildings, machinery, and other *fixed* assets, their amounts cannot be readily changed, although their rates of utilization can be decreased by allowing fixed assets to lie idle (note, however, that idle assets cost as much, perhaps more, than utilized assets). To summarize, in the *short run* there are certain resources whose amounts cannot be changed when the desired rate of output changes, while there are other resources (called variable inputs) whose usage can be changed almost instantaneously.[3]

Suppose an entrepreneur, whose *LRTC* or planning horizon is that indicated in Figure 6.3.1, builds a plant to produce Ox_0 units of output at total cost Oc_0. Since the inputs of certain resources are fixed, the cost to the firm of these resources is fixed also. We can now examine the effect of varying output when the usage of certain resources cannot be changed.

---

[3] It is not quite precise to say that the inputs of some resources cannot be changed. Certainly the firm could scrap a very expensive piece of capital equipment, buy another one twice as large, and have it installed before lunch, *if it is willing to pay the price*. In fact the firm can probably change any input rather rapidly given, once more, its willingness to pay. The short run is thus a convenient but important analytical device. It is frequently helpful in analyzing problems to suppose some inputs are fixed for a period of time. Moreover, it does not deviate too much from reality to make this assumption since entrepreneurs often consider certain resources as fixed over a period of time. The student should not be overly concerned about the time factor in the short and long run. The fixity of resources is the important element.

FIGURE 6.3.1

Short- and Long-Run Total Cost

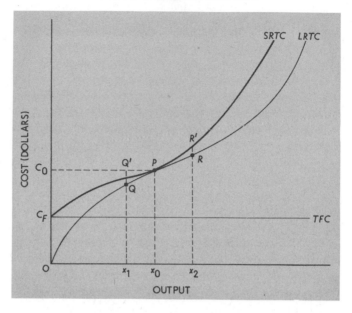

The firm operates in the short run—that period of time in which the input of one or more factors of production is fixed, hence the cost of these factors to the firm is fixed also. Since output can be changed in the short run only by changing variable inputs, the cost of these inputs is a variable cost. The sum of the variable and the fixed costs at any level of output is the *total cost* of producing that output.

Definition: Total fixed cost is the sum of the short-run explicit fixed costs and the implicit cost incurred by an entrepreneur.

Definition: Total variable cost is the sum of the amounts spent for each of the variable inputs used.

Definition: Total cost in the short run is the sum of total variable and total fixed cost.

Consider the short-run total cost curve ($SRTC$) in Figure 6.3.1. This is the curve indicating the firm's total cost of production for each level of output when the input of certain resources is fixed. One characteristic of this curve is that $SRTC$ (Oc_0) equals $LRTC$ at output level Ox_0. This equality is apparent when we remember that the plant was built (and the input of all resources chosen) so as to produce Ox_0 at the least possible cost. Short-run cost at Ox_0 is therefore also the lowest attainable cost for this output.

A second characteristic is that for any output other than Ox_0, $SRTC$

must be greater than $LRTC$. At output Ox_1 or Ox_2, for example, $SRTC$ could not, by definition, be lower than $LRTC$ because $LRTC$ is defined as the *least cost* for *every* level of output. We should therefore expect that $SRTC$ exceeds $LRTC$ at all rates of output except Ox_0. This point is clearly illustrated in Figure 6.3.2. Again we assume that there are two inputs, K and L. Isoquants x_0, x_1, and x_2 indicate the rates of output corresponding to Ox_0, Ox_1, and Ox_2 in Figure 6.3.1. Given constant input prices, the associated isocost curves are I_0I_0', I_1I_1', and I_2I_2'.

If the entrepreneur believes that x_0 will be the most profitable rate of

FIGURE 6.3.2

Input Combinations and Short-Run Cost

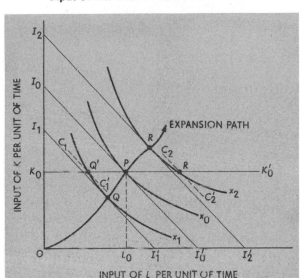

output, he will hire OL_0 units of labor and invest OK_0 in *fixed* assets. Once his money resources are congealed in the fixed assets OK_0, he operates in the short run. But so long as he produces Ox_0 units of output, he operates at the least possible unit cost; $LRTC$ and $SRTC$ are the same, as indicated by the point of tangency P in Figure 6.3.1.

Now suppose it becomes desirable to change output from x_0 to x_2. In the short run, the entrepreneur cannot move along his expansion path; or to put it differently, with the fixed plant OK_0, K_0K_0' is his *short-run* expansion path. The entrepreneur expands output by expanding labor input operating the same quantity of fixed assets (for example, he expands output by operating overtime in his fixed plant, with the higher overtime pay to his labor force). That is, in the short run he must move to R' instead of R. Cost is higher, as indicated by the dashed line c_2c_2', which lies above I_2I_2'. Further, the *reason* for a higher cost in the short run is apparent: at R' the marginal rate of technical substitution is not equal to the input price ratio. The marginal product of a dollar's worth of K exceeds the marginal product of a dollar's worth of L. But in the short run, with K fixed, the entrepreneur can do no better. In the long run, he can; he will expand plant size and reduce labor usage, moving to point R on his expansion path.

Exercise: Using Figures 6.3.1 and 6.3.2, carry out the same argument for a reduction of output to x_1.

A third characteristic of $SRTC$ is the positive cost, OC_F, at zero output. Since we have fixed the input of some resources, the firm must pay these resources the same amount at all outputs. Figure 6.3.1, therefore, shows both components of short-run total costs: (1) total fixed costs (TFC) OC_F, which must be paid regardless of output and (2) total variable costs (TVC), the difference between $SRTC$ and OC_F. TVC changes as output changes since variable costs are the payments to the resources that the firm can vary with output.

6.3.b—Average and Marginal Costs

The short-run total cost of production, including implicit cost, is very important to an entrepreneur. However, one may obtain a deeper understanding of total cost by analyzing the behavior of short-run average cost and marginal cost. The method used in deriving these curves is similar to that used to derive long-run average and marginal costs.

We assume a specific short-run situation such as that developed in subsection 6.3.a. First consider average fixed costs (AFC).

Definition: Average fixed cost is total fixed cost divided by output.

The derivation of AFC, illustrated in Figure 6.3.3, is quite simple. Total fixed cost, OC_F, is shown by the horizontal line TFC in panel a; outputs Ox_1, Ox_2, and Ox_3 are such that $Ox_1 = x_1x_2 = x_2x_3$. Since AFC at a particular output equals TFC divided by that output, average fixed cost is given by the slope of a ray to the relevant point on the TFC curve. For output Ox_1, AFC is the slope of the ray OP, OC_F/Ox_1. Similarly, for output Ox_2, AFC is OC_F/Ox_2, and so on. These values are plotted and connected in panel b. TFC equals AFC times quantity at any point on the curve. Since TFC is a constant (OC_F), $x_1P' \times Ox_1 = x_2Q' \times Ox_2 = x_3R' \times Ox_3$, and so on. A curve such as this is called a rectangular hyperbola. It is negatively sloped and approaches, but never reaches, the horizontal axis as output increases. The AFC curve derived from panel a is plotted in panel b.

FIGURE 6.3.3

Derivation of the Average Fixed Cost Curve

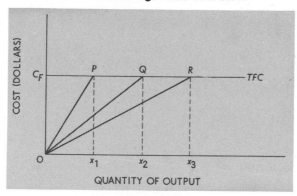

Panel a
Total Fixed Cost

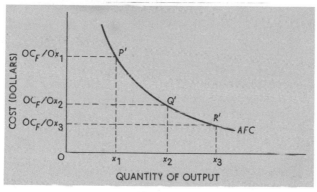

Panel b
Average Fixed Cost

Now we examine average variable cost (AVC), a concept completely analogous to long-run average costs, since all costs are variable in the long run.

Definition: Average variable cost is total variable cost divided by output.

Having spent considerable time developing the concept of long-run average cost, we need not spend much time deriving the average variable cost curve, since the two techniques are similar.

Figure 6.3.4 shows how AVC is derived from TVC. As is true of all "average" curves, the average variable cost associated with any level of output is given by the slope of a ray from the origin to the corresponding point on the TVC curve. As may easily be seen from panel a, the slope of a ray from the origin to the curve steadily diminishes as one passes through points such as P; and it diminishes until the ray is just tangent to the TVC curve at point Q, associated with output Ox_2. Thereafter the slope increases as one moves from Q toward points such as R. This is reflected in panel b by constructing AVC with a negative slope until output Ox_2 is attained. After that point, the slope becomes positive and remains positive.

Note the difference in the slopes of AVC and AFC: the latter has a negative slope throughout, while AVC first declines, reaches a minimum, then rises. Although the U-shapes of AVC and long-run average cost are similar, the reasons for their decline and rise are different. The explanation for the curvature of AVC lies in the short-run theory of production.

FIGURE 6.3.4

Derivation of the Average Variable Cost Curve

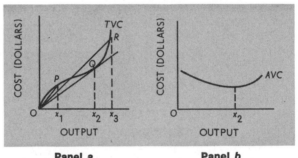

Panel a	Panel b
Total Variable Cost	**Average Variable Cost**

Total variable cost at any output consists of the payments to the variable factors of production used to produce that output. TVC, therefore, equals the sum of the number of units of each variable input (V) multiplied by unit price (P) of that input. For example, at output Q produced by n variable inputs, $TVC = P_1V_1 + P_2V_2 + P_3V_3 + \ldots + P_nV_n$. For the one-variable case, $TVC = PV$. Average variable cost is TVC divided by output (Q), or

$$AVC = \frac{TVC}{Q} = \frac{PV}{Q} = P\left(\frac{V}{Q}\right).$$

The term (V/Q) is the number of units of input divided by the number of units of output. In Chapter 5, we defined the average product (AP) of an input as total output (Q) divided by the number of units of input (V). Thus

$$\frac{V}{Q} = \frac{1}{(Q/V)} = \frac{1}{AP},$$

and

$$AVC = P\frac{V}{Q} = P\frac{1}{(Q/V)} = P\left(\frac{1}{AP}\right).$$

Thus average variable cost is the price of the input multiplied by the reciprocal of average product. Since by the law of variable proportions average product normally rises, reaches a maximum, then declines, average variable cost normally falls, reaches a minimum, then rises.

FIGURE 6.3.5

Derivation of the Average Total Cost or Unit Cost Curve

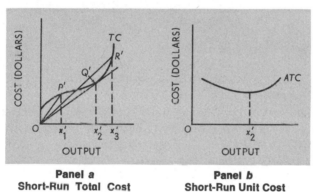

Panel *a*
Short-Run Total Cost

Panel *b*
Short-Run Unit Cost

Figure 6.3.5 shows the derivation of short-run average total cost, which may be called average cost or unit cost.

Definition: Average total cost is total cost divided by output.

Exactly the same analysis used for AVC holds for panels a and b, which show the derivation of ATC from TC. The slope of the ray diminishes as one moves along TC until point Q' is reached. At Q' the slope of the ray is least, so minimum ATC is attained at output level Ox_2'. Thereafter the slope of the ray increases continuously, and the ATC curve has a positive slope. (Note: the output level Ox_2' *does not* represent the same quantity as Ox_2 in Figure 6.3.4. As we shall see, AVC reaches its minimum at a lower output than that at which ATC reaches its minimum.)

ATC may also be computed by an alternative method. Since $TC = TFC + TVC$,

$$ATC = \frac{TC}{Q} = \frac{TFC + TVC}{Q} = \frac{TFC}{Q} + \frac{TVC}{Q} = AFC + AVC.$$

Thus one may calculate average cost as the sum of average fixed and average variable cost.

This method of calculation helps to explain the shape of the average total cost curve. Over the range of values for which AFC and AVC both decline, ATC, the sum of AFC and AVC, must obviously decline as well. But even after AVC turns up, the decline in AFC causes ATC to continue to decline. Finally, however, the increase in AVC more than offsets the decline in AFC; ATC therefore reaches its minimum and increases thereafter.

Finally let us examine marginal cost in the short run.

Definition: Marginal cost is the change in total cost attributable to a one-unit change in output.

The definitions of long- and short-run marginal cost that we have given are virtually identical. The concepts are not quite the same, however. Long-run marginal cost refers to the change in cost resulting from a change in output when *all inputs are optimally adjusted*. Short-run marginal cost, on the other hand, refers to the change in cost resulting from a change in output when *only the variable inputs change*. Since the fixed inputs cannot be changed in the short run, input combinations are not optimally adjusted. Thus the short-run marginal cost curve reflects suboptimal adjustment of inputs.

Although the concept of marginal cost differs slightly between the long run and the short run, the process of deriving marginal cost is similar. The marginal cost of, say, the second unit produced is the increase in the total cost caused by changing production from one unit to two units; or, $MC_2 = TC_2 - TC_1$. Since only variable cost changes in the short run, however, the marginal cost of producing an additional unit is the increase in variable cost. Thus the marginal cost of the second unit is also $MC_2 = TVC_2 - TVC_1$.

The derivation of marginal cost is illustrated in Figure 6.3.6. Panel a shows the short-run total cost curve TC. As output increases from Ox_1 to Ox_2, one moves from point P to point Q, and total cost increases from Oc_1 to Oc_2. Marginal cost is thus QR/PR. As before, the slope of the tangent T at point Q becomes a progressively better estimate of MC (QR/PR) as the distance between P and Q becomes smaller and smaller. Thus for small changes, the slope of the total cost curve is marginal cost.

As TC increases the slope decreases (MC decreases) until point S is reached at output Ox_3. Thereafter, the slope increases (MC increases). The MC curve is constructed in panel b so that it decreases until output Ox_3 is attained and increases thereafter.

FIGURE 6.3.6

Derivation of the Marginal Cost Curve

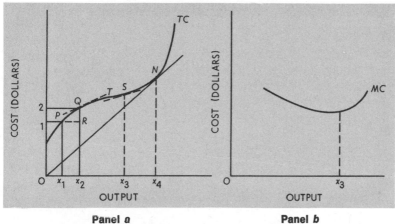

Panel *a*	Panel *b*
Short-Run Total Cost	**Short-Run Marginal Cost**

One final point concerning the relation of short-run marginal and average cost curves should be noted. As already implied and as Figure 6.3.7 reillustrates, TC and TVC have the same slope at each output level. TC is simply TVC displaced upward by the constant amount TFC (see Figure 6.3.7).

FIGURE 6.3.7

Relation of *MC* to Variable and Total Costs

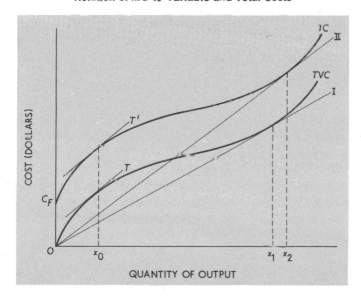

At output Ox_0 the tangent (T) to TVC has the same slope as the tangent (T') to TC. Since the slopes of the two tangents at output Ox_0 are equal, MC at Ox_0 is given by the slope of either curve. The same holds true for any other output level. The slope of ray I from the origin gives minimum AVC. But at this point (output Ox_1) ray I is just tangent to TVC; hence it also gives MC at output Ox_1. Thus $MC = AVC$ when the latter attains its minimum value. Similarly the slope of ray II gives minimum ATC (at output Ox_2). At this point the ray is tangent to TC; thus its slope also gives MC at output Ox_2. Consequently $MC = ATC$ when the latter attains its minimum value. Finally, as is easily seen from Figure 6.3.7, AVC attains its minimum at a lower output than the output at which ATC attains its minimum.

FIGURE 6.3.8

Typical Set of Cost Curves

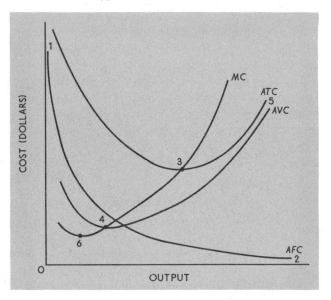

The properties of the average and marginal cost curves, as derived in this section, are illustrated by the "typical" set of short-run cost curves shown in Figure 6.3.8. The curves indicate the following

Relations: (a) AFC declines continuously, approaching both axes asymptotically, as shown by points one and two in the figure. *AFC* is a rectangular hyperbola. (b) AVC first declines, reaches a minimum at point four, and rises thereafter. When *AVC* attains its minimum at point four, *MC* equals *AVC*. As *AFC* approaches asymptotically close to the horizontal axis, *AVC* approaches *ATC* asymptotically, as shown by point five. (c) *ATC* first declines, reaches a minimum at point three, and rises thereafter. When *ATC* attains its minimum at point three, *MC* equals *ATC*. (d) MC first declines, reaches a minimum at point six, and rises thereafter. *MC* equals both *AVC* and *ATC* when these curves attain their minimum values. Furthermore, *MC* lies below both *AVC* and *ATC* over the range in which the curves decline; it lies above them when they are rising.

6.4 RELATIONS BETWEEN SHORT- AND LONG-RUN AVERAGE AND MARGINAL COSTS

Suppose an entrepreneur has the planning horizon labeled *LRTC* in all three panels of Figure 6.4.1. By the process developed in Section 6.2 we may derive his long-run average and marginal cost curves and plot these in Figure 6.4.2, the scale of which differs from that of Figure 6.4.1. These curves are labeled *LRAC* and *LRMC* respectively. Suppose now that the entrepreneur only considers plants of three different sizes: small, medium, and large.

The three short-run total cost curves ($SRTC_1$, $SRTC_2$, $SRTC_3$) for the three different plants are given in Figure 6.4.1. The total cost curve $SRTC_1$ in panel *a* is associated with the "small" plant. The fixed resources are fixed to produce output Ox_s at the least possible total cost Oc_1. $SRTC_2$ in panel *b* is the cost curve for the "medium" plant; the fixed resources are fixed to produce Ox_m at least cost (Oc_2). The cost curve $SRTC_3$ in panel *c* is associated with the "large" plant, built to produce Ox_l at least cost (Oc_3). LRTC is the same in all three panels.

First consider the small plant. Since $SRTC_1$ lies above *LRTC* at every output except Ox_s, short-run average cost exceeds long-run average cost at every output except Ox_s.

Exercise: The student should test this assertion by constructing a few rays from the origin to the two total cost curves at the same output level.

At output Ox_s, short- and long-run average costs are equal since the same ray from the origin (II) strikes both total cost curves at this point. Or $SRAC_1 = LRAC = Oc_1/Ox_s$ at output Ox_s. The minimum point on *LRAC* is attained at an output greater than Ox_s (note ray I from the origin).

Exercise: The student should pivot ray II downward around the origin until II is tangent to *SRTC₁*, in order to ascertain that the output of minimum *SRAC₁* is greater than Ox_s and less than the output at which *LRTC* reaches its minimum.

In Figure 6.4.2 (which, as noted above, differs in scale) the short-run average cost curve associated with the small plant is plotted. Note that all of the relations described are apparent in this figure. $SRAC_1$ is greater than *LRAC* everywhere except at point S' (output Ox_s), at which the two are equal. Both curves attain a minimum at outputs greater than Ox_s, but $SRAC_1$ reaches a minimum at a lower output than does *LRTC*.

It should be obvious that since $SRTC_1$ is tangent to *LRTC* at S (output Ox_s), short-run and long-run marginal costs (given by the slope of the

FIGURE 6.4.1

Long-Run and Short-Run Cost Curves

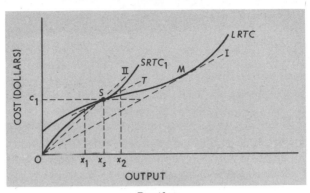

Panel *a*
Small Plant

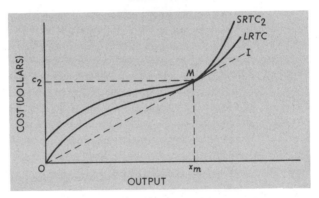

Panel *b*
Medium Plant

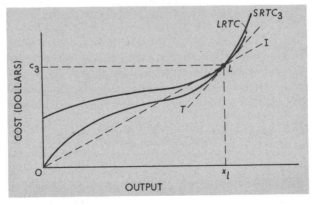

Panel *c*
Large Plant

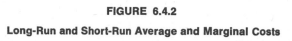

FIGURE 6.4.2

Long-Run and Short-Run Average and Marginal Costs

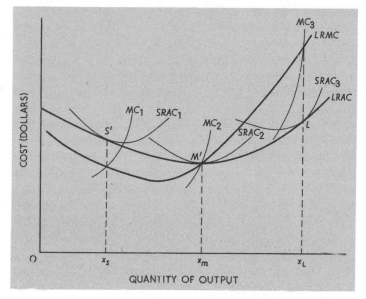

tangent T in Figure 6.4.1, panel a) are equal at output Ox_s. When moving from Ox_s to any greater output (say Ox_2), the *additional* cost of producing the *added* output is greater in the short run than in the long run because the short run is characterized by suboptimal adjustment. $SRTC_1$ lies further above Oc_1 at Ox_2 than does $LRAC$; thus the *increase* in cost associated with the movement from Ox_s to Ox_2 is greater in the short run. Hence at outputs greater than Ox_2, short-run marginal cost exceeds long-run marginal cost.

When moving from Ox_s to a smaller output (say Ox_1), the reduction in cost associated with that movement is greater in the long run than in the short run because a firm can adjust optimally in the long run. At output Ox_1, $SRTC_1$ exceeds $LRTC$; or $SRTC_1$ is closer to Oc_1 than is $LRTC$ at that output. Since the costs are the same (Oc_1) at Ox_s, the reduction in cost of moving from Ox_s to Ox_1 is less in the short run. Thus short-run marginal cost for the small plant is less than long-run marginal cost at outputs less than Ox_s and greater for outputs larger than Ox_s, the output at which both marginal costs are equal. These relations are shown in Figure 6.4.2.

Turning now to the medium plant in panel b, Figure 6.4.1, we see that $SRTC_2$ is tangent to $LRTC$ at output Ox_m with cost Oc_2 (point M). Since the ray from the origin (I) is tangent to both $SRTC_2$ and $LRTC$ at M, $LRAC$, $LRMC$, $SRAC_2$, and $SRMC_2$ are all equal at output Ox_m. Both short- and long-run average costs are at their minima at this point. By the analysis developed for the small plant, we can see that $SRMC_2$ is less (greater) than $LRMC$ at outputs less (greater) than Ox_m. These relations are shown by $SRAC_2$ and MC_2 in Figure 6.4.2. We see therefore that the medium plant is that which achieves the least long-run average cost.

Using the same methods we can see in panel c that for the large plant short-run average cost equals long-run average cost and short-run marginal cost equals long-run marginal cost at output Ox_l (point L).

Exercise: The student should determine for himself from panel *c* that *(a)* $SRMC_s$ and $LRMC$ lie above both average cost curves at output Ox_l; *(b)* the minimum point on $SRAC_s$ is attained at an output less than Ox_l; *(c)* $SRMC_s$ is less (greater) than $LRMC$ at outputs less (greater) than Ox_l; *(d)* $SRAC_l$ is greater than $LRAC$ at every output except Ox_l.

These relations are shown in Figure 6.4.2 as MC_3 and $SRAC_3$.

In the short run the entrepreneur must operate with one of the three sizes, large, medium, or small. But in the long run, he can build the plant whose size leads to least average cost for any given output. Thus he regards his long-run average cost curve as a planning device, because this curve shows the least cost of producing each possible output. An entrepreneur therefore is normally faced with a choice among quite a wide variety of plants. In Figure 6.4.3, six short-run average and marginal cost curves are shown; but this is really far from enough. Many curves could be drawn between each of those shown. These six curves are only representative of the wide variety that could be constructed.

These many curves generate LAC as a planning device. Suppose the

FIGURE 6.4.3

Average and Marginal Cost Curves

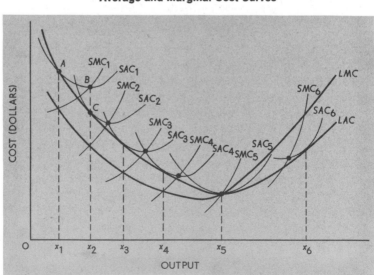

entrepreneur thinks the output associated with point A in Figure 6.4.3 will be most profitable. He will build the plant represented by SAC_1 because it will enable him to produce this output at the least possible cost per unit. With the plant whose short-run average cost is given by SAC_1, unit cost could be reduced by expanding output to the amount associated with point B (Ox_2), the minimum point on SAC_1. If demand conditions were suddenly changed so this larger output were desirable, the entrepreneur could easily expand, and he would add to his profitability by reducing unit cost. Nevertheless, when setting his future plans the entrepreneur would decide to construct the plant represented by SAC_2 because he could reduce unit costs even more. He would operate at point C thereby lowering unit cost from the level at point B on SAC_1.

The long-run planning curve, LAC, is a locus of points representing the least unit cost of producing the corresponding output. The entrepreneur determines the size of plant by reference to this curve. He selects that short-run plant which yields the least unit cost of producing the volume of output he anticipates.

Figure 6.4.3 illustrates the following

Relations: (a) LMC intersects LAC when the latter is at its minimum point. One, and only one, short-run plant has minimum SAC that coincides with minimum LAC (SAC_i). SMC_i equals LMC at this common minimum. *(b)* At each output where a particular SAC is tangent to LAC, the relevant SMC equals LMC. At outputs below (above) the tangency output, the relevant SMC is less (greater) than LMC. *(c)* For all SAC curves the point of tangency with LAC is at an output less (greater) than the output of minimum SAC if the tangency is at an output less (greater) than that associated with minimum LAC.

6.5 CONCLUSION

The physical conditions of production and resource prices jointly establish the cost of production. If the set of technological possibilities changes, the cost curves change. Or if the prices of some factors of production change, the firm's cost curves change. Therefore, it should be emphasized that cost curves are generally drawn under the assumptions of *constant factor prices* and a *constant technology.*

While the cost of production is important to business firms and to the economy as a whole, it is only half the story. Cost gives one aspect of economic activity; to the individual businessman it comprises his obligation to pay out funds; to the society as a whole it represents the resources that must be sacrificed to obtain a given commodity. The other aspect is revenue or demand. To the individual businessman revenue constitutes the flow of funds from which his obligation may be met. To society, demand hopefully represents the social valuation placed on a commodity.

Thus both demand and cost must be taken into consideration. It is to this combination of demand and cost that we turn in Chapter 7.

6.6   ANALYTICAL EXERCISE

Consider an entrepreneur who, for simplicity, we shall assume produces a commodity by means of a fixed asset (capital) and one particular type of labor. At present, he has a fixed plant and he hires the labor he wants at a fixed market wage. The given technology and the given factor prices establish a set of short-run cost curves such, for example, as those shown in Figure 6.3.8.

FIGURE 6.6.1

Some Effects of Featherbedding

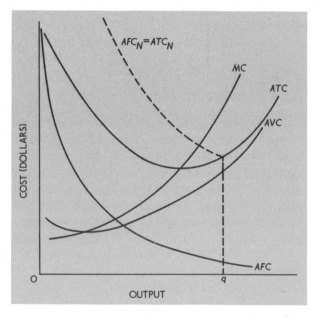

Now suppose the workers organize a labor union. They do not attempt to raise wages, but they are successful in obtaining an effective "featherbedding" contract, i.e., the entrepreneur is required to *hire* at least x workers whether he *uses* them or not. What is the effect of the featherbedding contract on the short-run cost curves of this entrepreneur?

To get an answer, let us first note that to be effective featherbedding, the required x workers must equal or exceed the number of workers the entrepreneur would voluntarily choose to employ. Under these conditions, the entrepreneur has no *variable* cost and hence no *marginal* cost at all (i.e., until more than x workers are employed). The AVC and MC curves are coincident with the horizontal axis until output exceeds the output producible in this plant by x workers.

Yet while variable and marginal cost decline to zero, average cost and average fixed cost must rise. Until $x + 1$ workers are hired, all the entrepreneur's costs are fixed costs. Thus the new AFC and ATC curves are identical over that range of output for which used labor is equal to or less than x workers.

The situation is illustrated schematically by means of Figure 6.6.1. The solid curves represent the short-run cost situation prior to featherbedding, where we assume that Oq units of output are produced by the full utilization of x workers. After featherbedding, MC and AVC simply become the line segment Oq. The new average fixed cost (AFC_N) equals the new average total cost (ATC_N) over the output range from zero to Oq. These new curves are represented by the dashed line, whose upward displacement from both AFC and ATC indicates that total cost has risen even though variable cost has declined.

QUESTIONS AND PROBLEMS

1. Return to Problem 1 at the end of Chapter 5. Total product is given; and you have computed average and marginal product. You are also given the following information:

> Total fixed cost (total price of fixed inputs) is $220 per period.
>
> Units of the variable input cost $100 per unit per period.
>
> Using this information, complete the following table:

Units of Variable Input	Product			Cost			Average Cost			Marginal Cost
	Total	Average	Marginal	Fixed	Variable	Total	Fixed	Variable	Total	
1.........	100									
2.........	250									
3.........	410									
4.........	560									
5.........	700									
6.........	830									
7.........	945									
8.........	1,050									
9.........	1,146									
10........	1,234									
11........	1,314									
12........	1,384									
13........	1,444									
14........	1,494									
15........	1,534									
16........	1,564									
17........	1,584									
18........	1,594									

A. Graph the total cost curves on one sheet and the average and marginal curves on another.

B. By reference to table and graph, answer the following questions.

1) When marginal product is increasing, what is happening to:
   a) Marginal cost?
   b) Average variable cost?

2) When marginal cost first begins to fall, does average variable cost begin to rise?

3) What is the relation between marginal cost and average variable cost when marginal and average product are equal?

4) What is happening to average variable cost while average product is increasing?

5) Where is average variable cost when average product is at its maximum? What happens to average variable cost after this point?

6) What happens to marginal cost after the point where it equals average variable cost?
   a) How does it compare with average variable cost thereafter?
   b) What is happening to marginal product thereafter?
   c) How does marginal product compare with average product thereafter?

7) What happens to total fixed cost as output is increased?

8) What happens to average fixed cost as:
   a) Marginal product increases?
   b) Marginal cost decreases?
   c) Marginal product decreases?
   d) Marginal cost increases?
   e) Average variable cost increases?

9) How long does average fixed cost decrease?

10) What happens to average total cost as:
    a) Marginal product increases?
    b) Marginal cost decreases?
    c) Average product increases?
    d) Average variable cost decreases?

11) Does average cost increase:
    a) As soon as the point of diminishing marginal returns is passed?
    b) As soon as the point of diminishing average returns is passed?

12) When does average cost increase? Answer this in terms of:
    a) The relation of average cost to marginal cost.
    b) The relation between the increase in average variable cost and the decrease in average fixed cost.

2. A student once was asked to show a cost schedule for a firm where "increasing returns" prevail. He gave the following schedule of average total cost:

Output	*ATC*
60 units	$15
70 units	12
80 units	8

What would you say to the student?

3. Explain why $SMC = LMC$ at the output where SAC is tangent to LAC, why $LMC > SMC$ at lower outputs, and why $LMC < SMC$ at greater outputs.

4. Is the recognition by entrepreneurs of implicit costs merely a theoretical abstraction or do real world businessmen actually take these costs into consideration.

chapter
7

Theory of Price in Perfectly Competitive Markets

7.1 INTRODUCTION

In Chapter 2 we emphasized that supply and demand are the basic determinants of the price of goods. Since goods are produced by firms, an understanding of price theory requires an understanding of the firm's behavior. The two broad general topics covered in Chapters 3–6 supply the framework upon which the theory of the firm is based. *Demand* establishes the revenue side of business operation. *Production and cost* establish the supply conditions. Brought together, revenue and cost for the individual business firm and demand and supply for the entire market determine the market price and output of the firm and industry. Furthermore, as we shall see in this and subsequent chapters, these forces also determine the allocation of resources among industries.

Our analysis is based upon two fundamental assumptions:

7.1.a—Free Markets

First, we assume that each market is free and operates freely in the sense that no external control of market forces exists. One form of external control is governmental intervention—for example, farm crop controls, public utility regulations, or presidential threats to steel or aluminum producers. All such controls establish artificial market conditions to which business firms must adjust. Another type of control is collective behavior or collusion of firms in a market. Such behavior limits the free exercise of market forces.

While many markets are not free in the sense used here, a large number are. The object is to analyze the efficiency of resource allocation in free markets. In cases in which the market is not free, one may draw inferences concerning the relative efficiency of free as against controlled markets. Thus the perfectly competitive market serves as a yardstick to measure the performance of other types of market structures.

7.1.b—Profit Maximization

The second fundamental assumption is that entrepreneurs try to maximize profits.[1] This does not mean that businessmen may not be seekers after other goals. Nonetheless, a business cannot remain in business very long unless some profits are earned. It would be a very unusual businessman who treats profits in a cavalier fashion or who, other things remaining the same, prefers less profit to more. Notwithstanding several criticisms of the profit-maximization assumption, this assumption is the only one providing a general theory of firms, markets, and resource allocation that is successful both in explaining and predicting business behavior.

7.2 PERFECT COMPETITION

The theory of the firm set forth in this chapter is based upon the exacting concept of *perfectly competitive markets.* Perfect competition forms the basis of the most important and widely used model of economic behavior. The essence of perfect competition is that neither buyers nor producers recognize any competitiveness among themselves; no *direct* competition among economic agents exists.

The theoretical concept of competition is diametrically opposed to the businessman's concept of competition. For example, a businessman might maintain that the automobile industry or the cigarette industry is quite competitive since each firm in these industries must consider what its rivals will do before it makes a decision about advertising campaigns, design changes, quality improvements, and so forth.

That type of market is far removed from what the economist means when he speaks of perfect competition.[2] Perfect competition permits no personal rivalry (i.e., personal in the sense that the firm considers the reaction of competitive firms in determining its own policy). All relevant economic magnitudes are determined by impersonal market forces.

Four important conditions define perfect competition. Taken together, these conditions guarantee a free, impersonal market in which the forces

---

[1] For the purpose of explaining business behavior it is sufficient to assume that entrepreneurs act *as if* they tried to maximize profit. For the purpose of predicting business behavior the "as if" assumption is the justifiable one.

[2] This does not imply that the model of perfect competition is not relevant in predicting the consequences of a disturbance in an economy containing industries that are comprised of a few interdependent firms (economists call such industries oligopolistic). The competitive model is a useful approach to many problems in which the conditions differ from the assumptions set forth here.

of demand and supply, or of revenue and cost, determine the allocation of resources and the distribution of income.

7.2.a—Small Size, Large Numbers

First, perfect competition requires that every economic agent be so small, relative to the market as a whole, that it cannot exert a perceptible influence on price. From the standpoint of buyers this means that each consumer taken individually must be so unimportant he cannot obtain special considerations from the sellers. Perhaps the most familiar special consideration is the rebate, especially in the area of transportation services. But there can be many others, such as special credit terms to large buyers, or free additional services. None of these can prevail if the market is perfectly competitive.

From the seller's standpoint, perfect competition requires that each producer be so small he cannot affect market price by changes in his output. If all producers act collectively, changes in quantity will definitely affect market price. But if perfect competition prevails, each producer is so small that individual changes will go unnoticed.

7.2.b—Homogeneous Product

A closely related provision is that the product of each seller in a perfectly competitive market must be identical to the product of every other seller. This ensures that buyers are indifferent as to the firm from which they purchase. Product differences, whether real or imaginary, are precluded by the existence of perfect competition.

In this context the word "product" has a much more detailed meaning than it does in ordinary conversation, where one might regard an automobile or a haircut as a product. For us, this is not adequate to describe a product: every changeable feature of the good must be included. When this is done it is possible to determine whether the market is characterized by a homogeneous, or perfectly standardized, commodity. If it is not, the producer who has a slightly differentiated product has a degree of control over the market and, therefore, over the price of his specific variety; he can thus affect market price by changes in his output. This condition is incompatible with perfect competition.

7.2.c—Free Mobility of Resources

A third precondition for perfect competition is that all resources are perfectly mobile—that each resource required can move in and out of the market very readily in response to pecuniary signals.

The condition of perfect mobility is an exacting one. First, it means that labor must be mobile, not only geographically but among jobs. The latter, in turn, implies that the requisite labor skills are few, simple, and easily learned. Next, free mobility means that the ingredient inputs are not monopolized by an owner or producer. Finally, free mobility means that new firms (or new capital) can enter and leave an industry without extraordinary difficulty. If patents or copyrights are required, entry is not free. Similarly, if vast investment outlays are required, entry certainly is not easy. If average cost declines over an appreciable range of output, established producers will have cost advantages that make entry difficult. In short, free mobility of resources requires free and easy entry and exit of firms into and out of an industry—a condition very difficult to realize in practice.

7.2.d—Perfect Knowledge

Consumers, producers, and resource owners must possess perfect knowledge if a market is to be perfectly competitive. If consumers are not fully cognizant of prices, they might buy at higher prices when lower ones are available. Then there will not be a uniform price in the market. Similarly, if laborers are not aware of the wage rates offered, they may not sell their labor services to the highest bidder. Finally, producers must know costs as well as price in order to attain the most profitable rate of output.

But this is only the beginning. In its fullest sense, perfect knowledge requires complete knowledge of the future as well as the present. In the absence of this omniscience, perfect competition cannot prevail.

The discussion to this point can be summarized by the following:

Characteristics: Perfect competition is an economic model of a market possessing the following characteristics: each economic agent is so small relative to the market that it can exert no perceptible influence on price; the product is homogeneous; there is free mobility of all resources, including free and easy entry and exit of business firms into and out of an industry; and all economic agents in the market possess complete and perfect knowledge.

7.2.e—Conclusion

Glancing at the four requirements above should immediately convince one that no market has been or can be perfectly competitive. Even in basic agricultural markets, where the first three requirements are frequently satisfied, the fourth is obviated by vagaries of weather conditions. One might therefore reasonably ask why such a palpably unrealistic model should be considered at all.

The answer can be given in as much or as little detail as desired. For our present purposes, it is brief. First, generality can be achieved only by means of abstraction. Hence no theory can be perfectly descriptive of real world phenomena. Furthermore, the more accurately a theory describes one specific real world case the less accurately it describes all others. In any area of thought a theoretician does not select his assumptions on the basis of their presumed correspondence to reality; the conclusions, not the assumptions, are tested against reality.

This leads to a second point of great, if somewhat pragmatic, importance. The conclusions derived from the model of perfect competition have, by and large, permitted accurate explanation and prediction of real world phenomena. That is, perfect competition frequently works as a theoretical model of economic processes even though it does not accurately describe any specific industry. The most persuasive evidence supporting this assertion is the fact that despite the proliferation of more sophisticated models of economic behavior, economists today probably use the model of perfect competition in their research more than ever before.

7.3 PLANNING THE FIRM

At the beginning of Chapter 6 we assumed that a prospective entrepreneur was considering entry into an industry. We assumed that "Demand conditions are such that he builds his plant to operate at a particular scale of production, and after the plant is built he operates in the short run." Assuming the industry is perfectly competitive, we can now examine the long-run conditions that determine the size plant he should build. We do this first because operating *plans* are based upon the long run, or planning horizon. It is only after these plans have congealed that a short-run situation exists. We therefore postpone analysis of the short run, in which the firm actually operates, until we analyze the long run, in which the entrepreneur chooses the specific short-run situation that is to be applicable.

7.3.a—Demand of a Firm in Perfect Competition

Suppose that panel *a*, Figure 7.3.1 depicts the equilibrium of the market for the perfectly competitive industry our prospective entrepreneur is planning to enter. Equilibrium price is Op_0 and quantity demanded and supplied Ox_0.

Let us say there are 50,000 firms of approximately the same size in the market. The entrepreneur recognizes that if he enters the industry at approximately the same size as existing firms, sales will rise by only $\frac{1}{500}$ of 1 percent. Such a change would be both graphically and *economically* so small as to have an imperceptible influence on price. The entrepreneur may assume with confidence that any variation in his own output and sales will have a negligible effect upon market price. Concerted action by a large number of sellers can influence market price; but one seller acting alone cannot. The individual firm may therefore assume that the demand curve facing *him* is a horizontal line at the level of price established by demand and supply equilibrium in the market.

The demand curve for any firm in this perfectly competitive industry is shown in panel *b*, Figure 7.3.1. Each producer knows that changes in his volume of output will have no perceptible effect upon market price. A change in his rate of sales per period of time will change his revenue, but it will not affect market price.

FIGURE 7.3.1

Derivation of Demand for a Perfectly Competitive Firm

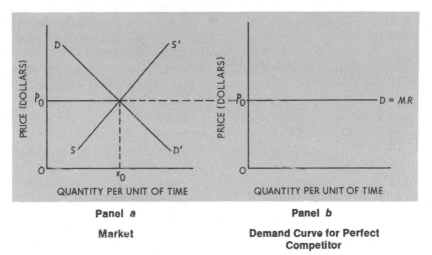

Panel *a*

Market

Panel *b*

Demand Curve for Perfect
Competitor

The producer in a perfectly competitive market, therefore, does not have to reduce his price in order to expand his rate of sales. Any number of units per period of time can be sold at the market equilibrium price. If he were to charge a higher price, he could sell nothing. A lower price would result in a needless loss of revenue. He thus charges the market price for whatever quantity he wishes to produce and sell.

Since price remains constant, each additional unit sold increases total revenue by its (constant) price. In this special case, therefore, price and marginal revenue are equal at every level of sales. Therefore, the demand curve and the marginal revenue curve are identical for a producer in a perfectly competitive market. For this reason, the curve in panel *b* is labeled $D = MR$. When the demand curve is horizontal, demand is said to be perfectly elastic.

The results of this section may be summarized as follows:

Relations: The demand curve (also called the average revenue curve) for a producer in a perfectly competitive market is a horizontal line at the level of the market equilibrium price. The output decisions of the seller do not affect market price. In this case, the demand and marginal revenue curves are identical (i.e., $D = AR = MR$); demand is perfectly elastic and the coefficient of price elasticity approaches infinity.[3]

7.3.b—Total Revenue, Total Cost, and Profit

In deciding the size plant to build, the entrepreneur attempts to achieve maximum profit, which is the difference between his total receipts from selling the product (total revenue) and his total cost of producing it. Figure 7.3.2 shows the long-run total cost curve (or planning curve), the total revenue curve (at the prevailing market price), and the profit at each rate of output. The long-run cost curve is essentially the same as those discussed in Chapter 6. The slope of this curve at any point is marginal cost; the slope of a ray from the origin to the curve is average cost.

Total revenue is the price per unit of output (given supply and demand in the market) times the quantity of output (for example, the sale of 400 units of X at a market price of $3 per unit obviously yields $1,200 total revenue, the sale of 401 units at the same price yields $1,203). The TR line in Figure 7.3.2 indicates total revenue at each level of output. This curve begins at the origin (since at zero units sold, revenue is zero regardless of price), and it is a straight line (since under perfect competition price does not change regardless of the firm's output). The slope of the total revenue curve is, therefore, both price and marginal revenue (in the example above, increasing output from 400 to 401 increases revenues from $1,200 to $1,203 or by $3, which is the price).

Relations: Total revenue is price times quantity sold; $TR = px$. Average revenue is total revenue divided by output; $AR = \dfrac{TR}{x} = \dfrac{px}{x} = p$. Marginal revenue is the additional revenue from selling one more unit, or the slope of the total revenue curve; $MR = p$ since the additional revenue from one more unit is the market price of that unit.

---

[3] A perfectly elastic demand means that the coefficient of price elasticity increases without bound as the percentage change in price becomes smaller and smaller. Let us take a numerical example. Suppose the market equilibrium price is $5 and a particular producer is selling 1,000 units at that price. If he increased his price to $5.01, his sales would fall to zero. Thus

$$\frac{\Delta q}{q} = \frac{-1000}{1000} \text{ and } \frac{\Delta p}{p} = \frac{1}{500}; \text{ so } \eta = 500.$$

If he increased the price to only $5.001, his sales would also fall to zero, and η would be 5,000. Thus one generalizes by saying that for infinitesimally small price changes the coefficient of price elasticity approaches infinity under condition of perfect competition.

In Figure 7.3.2 total profit $(TR - TC)$ is represented by the curve so labeled or by the vertical distance between the cost and revenue curves. Since total cost exceeds total revenue at outputs greater than Ox_1 and less than Ox_0, profit is negative over these ranges. At Ox_0 and Ox_1 total revenue equals total cost, and profit is zero. These are called break-even points; but remember that the entrepreneur's opportunity cost is included in total cost, so at the break-even points he makes the potential income of the next best use of his resources. From Ox_0 to Ox_1 profit is positive since total revenue exceeds total cost. This "pure profit" is in addition to his opportunity cost.

FIGURE 7.3.2

Long-Run Cost, Total Revenue, and Profit

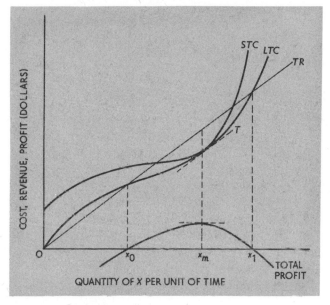

Profit is at a maximum when the total profit curve reaches its peak, when the vertical distance between TR and TC is the greatest (at output Ox_m). The maximum profit output occurs when the slope of a tangent (labeled T) to the total cost curve is equal to the slope of the total revenue curve; the vertical distance between total revenue and total cost is maximized.[4] The slope of total revenue being marginal revenue or price

---

[4] Note that the slope of TC equals the slope of TR also at some output between zero and Ox_0. This output, however, would give a loss or negative profit (actually it would give the *largest* loss of any output less than Ox_0). With the assumption of perfect knowledge and profit maximization, no entrepreneur would choose this loss position when positive profits could be made at any output between Ox_0 and Ox_1.

and the slope of total cost being marginal cost, maximum profit occurs where marginal cost equals marginal revenue (price).

This is a most important proposition for the theory of the firm under perfect competition. Any time an additional unit of output adds more to receipts than to the cost of production, the entrepreneur will increase his profit by producing it. For example, if producing one more unit adds $6 to cost and the firm can sell it for $7, the extra unit adds $1 to profit. It follows that the entrepreneur increases production so long as price exceeds marginal cost. On the other hand, if producing an additional unit adds more to cost than the price at which it can be sold, that unit would decrease profit and thus would not be produced. It follows, therefore, that the entrepreneur will not increase production when marginal cost exceeds price. At the output where marginal cost equals price, profit is a maximum and the entrepreneur has no incentive to change his level of production. The firm is in equilibrium; the entrepreneur would therefore choose to build a plant of such size as to produce Ox_m at minimum cost. This plant is represented by STC in Figure 7.3.2.

7.3.c—Alternative Approach to Long-Run Planning

Let us examine these relations using the long-run average cost, long-run marginal cost, and demand curves. Figure 7.3.3 specifies the same conditions as Figure 7.3.2 by using marginal and average curves rather than total curves. LAC and LMC are the long-run average and marginal cost curves. The vertical axes differ in scale, but the horizontal scales are

FIGURE 7.3.3

Profit Maximization by the Marginal Approach

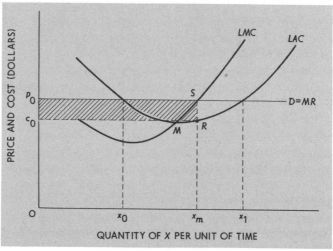

the same. The demand curve indicates the market price (p_0) used in the preceding subsection.

The break-even outputs are Ox_0 and Ox_1. These occur where LAC equals price and are at the same break-even outputs shown in Figure 7.3.2. This is apparent when we note that $LAC = \dfrac{LTC}{x}$ and $p_0 = \dfrac{TR}{x}$, when $TR = LTC$, $LAC = p_0$.

Since the profit maximizing output Ox_m is that at which the slope of the total cost curve (marginal cost) equals the slope of the revenue curve (price), $LMC = p_0$ at Ox_m in Figure 7.3.3. Note that the firm would not attempt to produce at the least unit cost (point M). At M price exceeds LMC; the firm can gain by producing more output. In Figure 7.3.3 total revenue (price times quantity) is given by the area of rectangle $O\ p_0\ S\ x_m$. Total cost (average cost times quantity) is given by the area of $O\ c_0\ R\ x_m$. Thus profit $(TR - TC)$ is given by the area of $c_0\ p_0\ S\ R$.

To summarize, the firm will plan to build its plant of such size that long-run marginal cost equals price. It will be the plant, of course, in which the desired rate of output can be produced for the least unit cost.

7.3.d—Zero and Negative Profit Solutions

Before developing the theory of the firm in the short run (after the entrepreneur builds his plant), let us analyze some alternative situations that may confront an entrepreneur planning to enter the industry. While our prospective entrepreneur was drawing his graphs and deciding upon the scale of operation, suppose other firms, lured by the prospect of profits, entered the industry and increased supply so much that market price fell. We assume for simplicity that all firms face the same cost curves and that the entry of new firms or output changes by old firms do not change costs.[5]

Figure 7.3.4 illustrates the planning situation now facing our prospective entrepreneur at the new price Op_L, all cost conditions remaining the same as before. In panel a the new total revenue curve is TR_L, whose slope reflects the new lower price Op_L. As constructed, it lies below long-run total costs at each nonnegative output. At zero output the two are equal. At each positive output LTC exceeds TR_L and a loss results. The minimum loss *at a positive output* (that is, the least vertical distance between LTC and TR_L) occurs at output Ox_L, where the slope of LTC (MC) equals the slope of TR_L (Op_L). Zero output would lead neither to profit nor to loss; the firm would therefore choose not to enter the industry (that is, to produce zero output).

---

[5] We will drop this assumption later in the chapter when analyzing an industry's supply curve.

FIGURE 7.3.4

Zero and Negative Profit Solutions

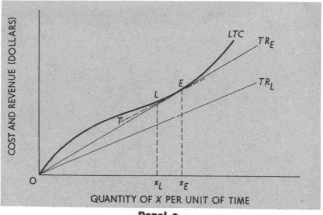

Panel a
Total Curves

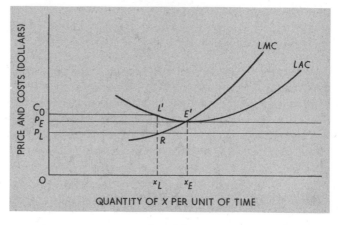

Panel b
Average Curves

Panel b shows the same situation. Op_L lies below LAC at every output; no positive profit can result. The minimum loss at a positive output occurs at Ox_L, where $LMC = Op_L$. This loss is given by the area of the rectangle $p_L c_L L' R$, the difference between LTC and TR_L. It is once more clear that the firm would not be induced to enter the industry. In fact under the assumption that all firms have the same cost curves, some firms already in the industry would be induced to leave the industry.[6]

---

[6] The student might note that we violate our assumption of perfect knowledge by positing that enough firms enter to drive the price down to Op_L. Why would a firm

If an increase in the number of firms increases supply and lowers price, a decrease in the number of firms decreases supply and raises price. Firms are motivated to leave the industry until market price rises sufficiently to eliminate losses. Let us assume that price rises to Op_E, the slope of TR_E in panel a. Since LTC is tangent to TR_E at output Ox_E, total cost equals total revenue, and the firms in the industry make neither profit nor loss at this output. We are assuming, of course, that firms in the industry have sufficient time to make long-run adjustments and attain least cost output. At any other positive output LTC is greater than TR_E and losses would result. Since LTC is tangent to TR_E at Ox_E, $p = MC = $ minimum LAC.

These relations are apparent in panel b. Although no profit results, no firm is induced to leave since each makes its opportunity cost; neither is any other firm induced to enter since it would make only its opportunity cost, which presumably it makes already. Each firm is in a profit-maximizing equilibrium, since $LMC = MR$; of course, the maximum pure profit is zero. The industry is also in equilibrium since $p = LAC$. Since maximum profit is zero pure profit, no firms leave the industry and none is induced to enter.

We will further analyze the long-run equilibrium of the firm and the industry later in this chapter. Before doing so, however, an analysis of the firm in the short run is in order.

7.4 SHORT-RUN EQUILIBRIUM OF A FIRM

Assume that the entrepreneur, rather than waiting for profits to be competed away, built a plant of optimal size when price was Op_0 and when profits were positive. He now operates in the short run, in which the rate of output per period of time can be expanded or diminished only by changing the rate of use of variable inputs. The firm can adjust its rate of output over a wide range subject only to the limitation imposed by its fixed inputs (generally, plant and equipment).

7.4.a—Short-Run Profit Maximization

The analysis of short-run profit maximization is essentially the same as that described for the long run. The firm produces where short-run

---

with perfect knowledge enter knowing full well it would make losses? We could assume that demand suddenly falls and drives price to Op_L. The explanation given, however, is more consistent with the model of long-run industry equilibrium to be analyzed later in this chapter.

The reason we know all firms are making losses is that the firms in the industry are operating in the short run and, except for the one point at which they are equal, short-run average cost is everywhere greater than long-run average cost. Thus if price is less than LAC it is also at least as far below SAC, if not further.

FIGURE 7.4.1

Short-Run Equilibrium

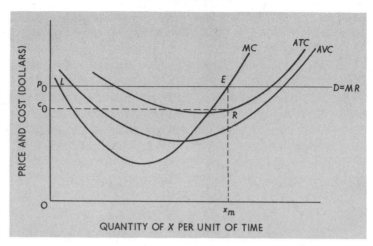

QUANTITY OF X PER UNIT OF TIME

marginal cost equals price, point E at output Ox_m in Figure 7.4.1. Producing another unit would add more to costs than the firm would receive from the sale of that unit; MC exceeds MR. The firm would not stop short of output Ox_m, however, since at lesser outputs producing another unit adds more to revenue than to cost; MR exceeds MC. Total cost is the area $Oc_0 Rx_m$; total revenue is the area $Op_0 Ex_m$; profit is the difference, the area $c_0 p_0 E R$. The firm makes a positive profit.

Note that at point L in Figure 7.4.1 marginal cost also equals price. That is not, however, a point of equilibrium since the firm would not choose to produce this output under the circumstances depicted. In the first place, average cost exceeds price at this output so losses would occur, whereas at other outputs profits could be realized. Second, the firm could clearly gain by producing an additional unit. Price is greater than marginal cost; thus the firm would be motivated to increase output.[7]

7.4.b—Profit, Loss, and the Firm's Short-Run Supply Curve

The equality of price and short-run marginal cost guarantees either that profit is a maximum or that loss is a minimum. Whether a profit is made or a loss incurred can be determined only by comparing price and average total cost at the equilibrium rate of output. If price exceeds unit cost, the entrepreneur enjoys a short-run profit; on the other hand, if unit cost exceeds price, a loss is suffered.

---

[7] Economists say that $MC = P$ is the *necessary* condition for profit maximization and that the second order or *sufficient* condition is that where $MC = P$, MC must be positively sloped.

FIGURE 7.4.2

Profit, Loss, or Ceasing Production in the Short Run

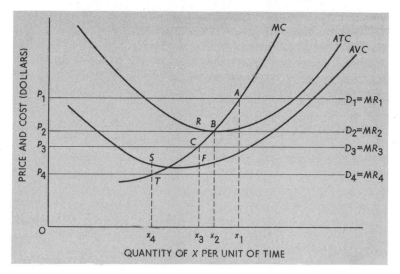

Figure 7.4.2 illustrates four possible short-run situations for the firm. First the market established price may be Op_1; the firm settles at point A where $MC = Op_1$, produces Ox_1 units, and since ATC is less than price, receives a profit. Second, market price may be Op_2. Now MC equals price at point B; the firm produces Ox_2. Since B is the lowest point on ATC, the firm makes neither profit nor loss. Third, if price is Op_3, the firm produces Ox_3; price equals MC at C. Because average cost is greater than price at the optimal output, total cost is greater than total revenue, and the firm suffers a loss. That loss is CR times Ox_3.

When demand is $D_3 = MR_3$, there is simply no way the firm can earn a profit. At every output level average total cost exceeds price. If output were either smaller or greater than Ox_2 units per period of time, the loss would simply be greater. One might, therefore, ask why the firm does not go out of business since a loss is incurred at any rate of output.

The basic answer to this question is that an entrepreneur incurring a loss in the short run will continue to produce if, and only if, he loses less by producing than by closing the plant entirely. Remember there are two types of costs in the short run: fixed costs and variable costs. The fixed costs cannot be changed and are incurred whether the plant is operated or not. Fixed costs are unavoidable in the short run and are the same at zero output as at any other.

Therefore, at zero output total revenue would be zero also and total cost would be the total fixed cost. The loss would thus be the amount of total fixed costs. If the firm can produce where $MC = MR$, and if at this output total revenue is greater than total variable cost, a smaller loss is suffered when production takes place. The firm covers all of its variable cost and some revenue is left over to cover a part of fixed cost. The loss is that part of fixed cost not covered and is clearly less than the entire fixed cost.

Returning to Figure 7.4.2 one can see more easily why the firm in the short run would produce at C and not shut down. The firm loses CR dollars per unit produced. However, variable cost is not only covered but there is an excess of CF dollars per unit sold. The excess of price over average variable cost, CF, can be applied to fixed costs. Thus not all of the fixed costs are lost, as would be the case if production were discontinued. Although a loss is sustained, it is smaller than the loss associated with zero output.

This is not always the case, however. Suppose market price is Op_4, so demand is given by $D_4 = MR_4$. If the firm produced, its equilibrium would be at T where $MC = Op_4$. Output would be Ox_4 units per period of time. Here, however, the average variable cost of production exceeds price. Not only would the firm lose all of its fixed costs, it would also lose ST dollars per unit on its variable costs as well. The firm could improve its earnings situation by producing nothing and losing only fixed cost. Thus when price is below average variable cost, the short-run equilibrium output is zero.

As shown in Chapter 6, average variable cost reaches its minimum at the point where marginal cost and average variable cost intersect. If price is less than the minimum average variable cost, the loss-minimizing output is zero. For price equal to or greater than minimum average variable cost, equilibrium output is determined by the intersection of marginal cost and the price line.

Principles: (1) Marginal cost tells *how much* to produce, given the choice of a positive output; the firm produces the output for which $MC = P$. (2) Average variable cost tells *whether* to produce; the firm ceases to produce if price falls below minimum *AVC*. (3) Average total cost tells how much profit or loss is made if the firm decides to produce; profit equals the difference between P and ATC multiplied by the quantity produced and sold.

Using the principles just discussed it is possible to derive the short-run supply curve of an individual firm in a perfectly competitive market. The process is illustrated in Figure 7.4.3. Panel a shows the marginal cost curve of a firm for rates of output greater than that associated with minimum average variable cost. Suppose market price is Op_1. The corresponding equilibrium rate of output is Ox_1. Now on panel b, find the

FIGURE 7.4.3

Derivation of the Short-Run Supply Curve of an Individual Producer in Perfect Competition

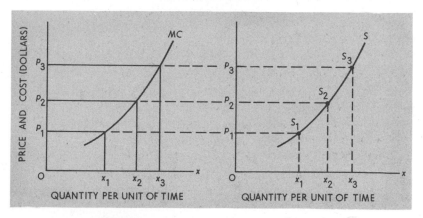

Panel a
Positions of Short-Run Equilibria for the Firm

Panel b
Equilibrium Quantities Supplied by the Firm

point associated with the coordinates Op_1, Ox_1. Label this point S_1; it represents the quantity supplied at price Op_1.

Next, suppose price were Op_2. In this case, equilibrium output would be Ox_2. Plot the point associated with the coordinates Op_2, Ox_2 on panel b—it is labeled S_2. Similarly, other equilibrium quantities supplied can be determined by postulating other market prices (for example, price Op_3 leads to output Ox_3 and point S_3 on panel b). Connecting all the S-points so generated one obtains the short-run supply curve of the firm, the curve labeled S in panel b. But by construction, the S-curve is precisely the same as the MC curve. The following is thus established:

Proposition: The short-run supply curve of a firm in perfect competition is precisely its marginal cost curve for all rates of output equal to or greater than the rate of output associated with minimum average variable cost. For market prices lower than minimum average variable cost, equilibrium quantity supplied is zero.

7.4.d—Short-Run Industry Supply Curve

In earlier chapters it was shown that market demand is simply the horizontal sum of the demand curves of all buyers in the market. Deriving the short-run industry supply curve may not be such an easy matter.

As you will recall from Chapter 6, the short-run marginal cost curve of a firm is derived under the assumption that the unit prices of the variable inputs are fixed; no change by the individual firm acting alone can change a factor's unit cost to the firm. This seems a reasonable assumption under perfect competition because one firm is usually so small, relative to all users of the resource, that variations in its rate of purchase will not affect the market price of the resource. In other words, many resource markets are more or less perfectly competitive, at least on the buying side. Thus production, and therefore resource use, can frequently be expanded in one firm without affecting the market price of the resource.

But when *all* producers in an industry *simultaneously* expand output there may be a marked effect upon the resource market. For example, one small cotton textile manufacturer could probably expand his production by 10 percent or even 100 percent without affecting the world price of raw cotton. The few additional bales he might purchase would not have a significant effect on the total demand for raw cotton. If all cotton textile manufacturers in the United States simultaneously attempt to expand output by 10 percent, however, the demand for cotton would probably increase substantially and the resulting increase in the price of cotton would be significant. When all manufacturers attempt to increase output, raw cotton prices are bid up; and the increase in the price of a variable factor of production (raw cotton) causes an increase in all firms' cost curves, including marginal cost.

As a consequence, the industry supply curve usually cannot be obtained by summing horizontally the marginal cost curves of each producer. As industry output expands, input prices normally increase, thereby shifting each marginal cost curve to the left. A great deal of information would be required to obtain the exact supply curve. However, one may generally presume that the industry supply curve is somewhat more steeply sloped and somewhat less elastic when input prices increase in response to an increase in output. In this case, the concept of a competitive industry supply curve is less precise. Nonetheless, doubt is not cast upon the basic fact that in the short run, quantity supplied varies directly with price. The latter is all one needs to draw a positively sloped market supply curve.

7.4.e—Summary of the Short Run

Given the market demand and supply curves, a short-run market price-quantity equilibrium is attained at the price that equates quantity demanded and quantity supplied. The market equilibrium price establishes the horizontal demand or marginal revenue curve for firms in the industry. If the firm produces at all, it attains its profit-maximizing (or loss-minimizing) output where price equals marginal cost. When, at this output, average total cost is greater (less) than price, the firm makes a loss (profit). When average total cost equals price neither profit nor loss is made. However, when price is below the minimum average variable cost, the firm ceases production in the short run and loses only its fixed costs.

Note: We have now established the process for deriving industry demand and supply curves. The student should return to Chapter 2 to recall how these curves are used in the economic analysis of industry equilibrium and the analysis of comparative static changes.

7.5 LONG-RUN EQUILIBRIUM IN A PERFECTLY COMPETITIVE MARKET

Since all inputs are variable in the long run, an entrepreneur has the option of adjusting his plant size, as well as his output, in order to achieve maximum profit. In the limit, he can liquidate his business entirely and transfer his resources and his command over resources into a more profitable investment alternative. But just as established firms may leave the industry, new firms may enter the industry if profit prospects are brighter than elsewhere. Indeed, adjustment of the number of firms in the industry in response to profit motivation is the key element in establishing long-run equilibrium.

7.5.a—Long-Run Adjustment of an Established Firm

We have already discussed the firm that is contemplating entry into an industry and is deciding what scale plant to build. We have seen that he will build so as to produce at least unit cost the output at which long-run marginal cost equals price. In the long run, an established firm can adjust plant size, and therefore rate of output, in order to attain maximum profit.

Consider a firm in a short-run situation in which it incurs a loss. In looking to the long run, or the planning horizon, the entrepreneur has two options: he can go out of business or he can construct a plant of more suitable size. By the now familiar argument maximum profit is obtained by producing the rate of output in the plant of such size that long-run marginal cost equals price. You will recall that long-run marginal cost shows the addition to total cost attributable to the addition of one unit of output, after plant size has been adjusted so as to produce that rate of output at minimum achievable unit cost.

7.5.b—Long-Run Adjustment of the Industry

The process of attaining long-run equilibrium in a perfectly competitive industry is illustrated in Figure 7.5.1. Suppose each firm in the industry is identical. Its size is represented by SAC_1 and SMC_1 in panel b.

FIGURE 7.5.1

Long-Run Equilibrium Adjustment in a Perfectly Competitive Industry

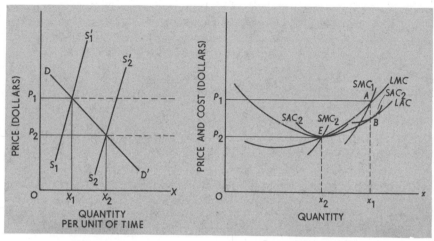

Panel *a*
Long-Run Market Equilibrium

Panel *b*
**Long-Run Equilibrium Adjustment
of a Firm**

The market demand curve is given by DD' in panel *a*, and the market supply is S_1S_1'. Market equilibrium establishes the price of Op_1 per unit and total output and sales of OX_1 units per period of time. At price Op_1 each plant is built to produce Ox_1 units (the output at which $Op_1 = LMC$) at least possible cost $(x_1 B)$. Each firm receives a profit of AB per unit of output. The number of firms multiplied by Ox_1 (each firm's output) equals OX_1 (total output). Although each firm is in equilibrium, the industry itself is not. As we saw earlier in this chapter the appearance of *pure economic profit*, a return in excess of that obtainable elsewhere, attracts new firms into the industry, expanding industry supply (say) to $S_2 S_2'$ and reducing market price. The process of new entry might be very slow, or it might be very fast. It depends primarily upon the liquid assets in other industries. In any event, as time elapses new firms will enter the industry, thereby shifting the supply curve to the right.

When each firm adjusts optimally to the new market price, the output of each will be smaller. The larger number of firms accounts for the increase in output from OX_1 to OX_2 in panel *a*. Now all firms produce the output at which Op_2 equals LMC at output Ox_2. The number of old firms plus the number of new entrants times Ox_2 equals OX_2. Since the new price equals LMC and SMC_2 at E, the minimum LAC and the minimum SAC_2, neither profit nor loss is present for any firm. Both the industry and its firms are in long-run equilibrium.

7.5.c—Long-Run Equilibrium in a Perfectly Competitive Firm

This position of long-run equilibrium is inevitable from and is embodied in the assumption of profit maximization and free entry. Each firm strives to achieve the maximum possible profit. In the short run a firm in perfect competition can do nothing more than adjust its output so that marginal cost equals price. In the long run it can adjust the size of its plant and it can select the industry in which it operates, both with an eye to profit.

The long-run equilibrium position of a firm in a perfectly competitive industry is explained by Figure 7.5.2. As we have seen, if price is above

FIGURE 7.5.2

Long-Run Equilibrium of a Firm in a Perfectly Competitive Industry

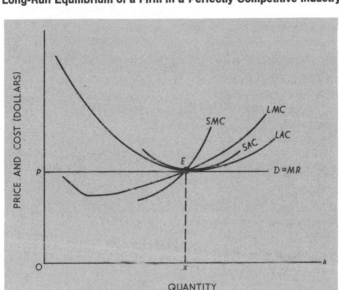

Op, each established firm can adjust plant size and earn a pure profit. New firms are attracted into the industry, shifting the supply curve to the right. Price falls, and hence the horizontal demand curve facing each firm, old and new, falls also. All firms readjust. If "too many" firms enter, market price and each firm's horizontal demand curve may fall below Op. Each firm incurs a loss. As their plants and equipment depreciate, some firms will leave the industry, thereby causing the market supply curve to shift to the left. Market price and, accordingly, the horizontal individual demand curves rise.

So long as the cost curves do not change, the only conceivable point of long-run equilibrium occurs at point E in Figure 7.5.2. Each firm in the industry receives neither profit nor loss. There is no incentive for further entrance because the rate of return in this industry is the same as in the best alternative. But for the same reason there is no incentive for a firm to leave the industry. The number of firms stablilizes, each firm with a short-run plant represented by *SAC* and *SMC*.

Firms will enter or leave the industry if there is either pure profit or pure loss. Therefore, since the position of long-run equilibrium must be consistent with *zero* profit (and zero loss), it is necessary that price equal average cost. For a firm to attain its individual equilibrium, price must be equal to marginal cost. Therefore, price must equal both marginal and average total cost. This can occur only at the point where average and marginal cost are equal, or at the point of minimum average total cost.[8]

The statement, so far, could conceivably apply to any *SAC* and *SMC*. However, unless it applies only to the short-run plant that coincides with minimum long-run average cost, a change in plant size would lead to the appearance of pure profit, and the wheels of adjustment would be set in motion again. These arguments establish the following:

Proposition: Long-run equilibrium for a firm in perfect competition occurs at the point where price equals minimum long-run average cost. At this point minimum short-run average cost equals minimum long-run average cost, and the short- and long-run marginal costs are equal. The position of long-run equilibrium is characterized by a "no profit" situation —the firms have neither a pure profit nor a pure loss, only an accounting

---

[8] Some students may object to the model of long-run equilibrium at the minimum point of each firm's long-run average cost curve on the grounds that the model is based upon the assumption that each firm is exactly like every other firm; that is, each firm's cost curve is the same as that of every other firm. We have made that assumption for simplicity; theory does not require it. To see why the assumption is not necessary, one must understand that any differences in cost are due to differences in the productivity of one or more resources. Assume that all firms except one are alike; that firm, because of (say) a more favorable location, has a lower cost curve. The owner of that location (he might be the owner of the firm) could raise the rent to the firm (if the owner, his opportunity cost would rise) up to the point at which the firm's pure profit disappears. The firm would be motivated to pay the rent since the owner of the firm would still make the equivalent of his best alternative. If he did not pay that rent, some other firm would.

Thus the cost curve of the previously lower cost firm would tend to rise because of increased rent. It would not, of course, rise above those of other firms because any higher rent would occasion looses; hence no firm would pay it. The same type of argument applies to the superiority of other specialized resources, including the superiority of management. If a superior manager, even a manger-owner, could lower his firm's costs, he could presumably lower the costs of other firms as well. His hiring price would be bid up, or if he is the owner, his opportunity cost would rise. At equilibrium all firms' long-run average cost curves would, therefore, reach their low points at the same cost (albeit not necessarily at the same output), and no firm would make pure profit or loss (although some might have differing factor payments or rents).

profit equal to the rate of return obtainable in other perfectly competitive industries.

7.6   CONSTANT AND INCREASING COST INDUSTRIES

The analysis of Section 7.5 was based upon the tacit assumption of "constant cost," in the sense that expanded resource usage does not entail an increase in resource prices. To carry the analysis further, and to make it more explicit, both constant and increasing cost industries are examined in this subsection. The phenomenon of decreasing cost is not examined inasmuch as it is not consistent with all the requirements of perfect competition.

7.6.a—Constant Cost Industries

Long-run equilibrium and long-run supply price under conditions of constant cost are explained by Figure 7.6.1 Panel *a* shows the long- and

FIGURE 7.6.1

Long-Run Equilibrium and Supply Price in a Perfectly Competitive Industry Subject to Constant Cost

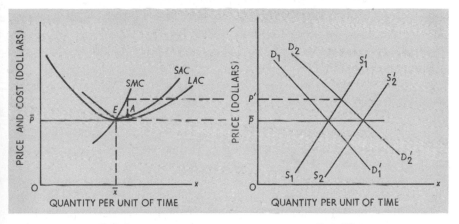

Panel *a*	Panel *b*
Long-Run Equilibrium of the Firm	Long-Run Market Equilibrium

short-run conditions of each firm in the industry, while panel *b* depicts the market as a whole. D_1D_1' and SS_1' are the original market demand and supply curves, establishing a market equilibrium price of $O\bar{p}$ dollars per unit. We assume that the industry has attained a position of long-run equilibrium, so the position of each firm in the industry is depicted by panel *a*—the price line is tangent to the long- and short-run average cost curves at their minimum points.

Now suppose demand increases to D_2D_2'. Instantaneously, with the number of firms fixed, the price will rise to Op' and each firm will move to equilibrium at point A. However, at point A each firm earns a pure economic profit inasmuch as price exceeds average cost. New entrants are thereby attracted into the industry; the industry supply curve shifts to the right. In this case we assume that all resources used are so general that increased usage in this industry does not affect the market price of resources. As a consequence, the entrance of new firms does not increase the costs of existing firms; the LAC curve of established firms does not shift and new firms can operate with an identical LAC curve. Long-run equilibrium adjustment to the shift in demand is accomplished when the number of firms expands to the point at which S_2S_2' is the industry supply curve.

In other words, since output can be expanded by expanding the number of firms producing $O\bar{x}$ units per period of time at average cost $O\bar{p}$, the industry has a constant long-run supply price equal to $O\bar{p}$ dollars per unit. If price were above this level, firms of size represented by SAC would continue to enter the industry in order to reap the pure profit obtainable. If price were less than $O\bar{p}$, some firms would ultimately leave the industry to avoid the pure economic loss. Hence in the special case in which an expansion of resource usage does not lead to an increase in resource price, the long-run industry supply price is constant. This is precisely the meaning of a constant-cost industry.

Exercise: The student should carry out the same type of analysis for a decrease in demand.

7.6.b—Increasing Cost Industries

An increasing cost industry is depicted in Figure 7.6.2. The original situation is the same as in Figure 7.6.1. The industry is in a position of long-run equilibrium. D_1D_1' and S_1S_1' are the market demand and supply curves respectively. Equilibrium price is Op_1. Each firm operates at point E_1, where price equals minimum average cost, both long- and short-run cost. Thus each firm is also in a position of long-run equilibrium.

Let demand shift to D_2D_2' so that price instantaneously rises to a much higher level. The higher price is accompanied by pure economic profit; new firms are consequently attracted into the industry. The usage of resources expands and now, we assume, resource price expands with resource usage. The cost of inputs therefore increases for the established firms as well as for the new entrants. As a result the entire set of cost curves shifts upward, say to a position represented by LAC_2 in panel a.[9]

---

[9] As Figure 7.6.2 is constructed, the minimum point on LAC shifts to the left as LAC shifts upward. In fact, minimum LAC can correspond to either a smaller or a

FIGURE 7.6.2

Long-Run Equilibrium and Supply Price in a Perfectly Competitive Industry Subject to Increasing Cost

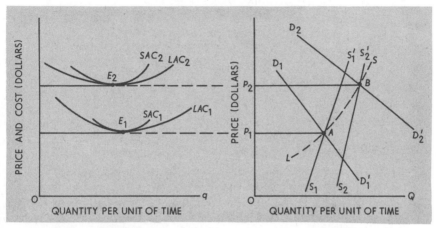

Panel a	Panel b
Long-Run Equilibrium of the Firm	**Long-Run Market Equilibrium**

Naturally, the process of equilibrium adjustment is not instantaneous. The *LAC* curve gradually shifts upward as new entrants gradually join the industry. As shown in Figure 7.6.2, the marginal cost curves of all firms shift to the left as new firms enter and bid up factor prices. Thus two forces tend to work in opposite directions upon the industry's supply curve. Shifting marginal cost to the left tends to shift the industry's supply curve to the left. However, new firms enter the industry, and this tends to shift industry supply to the right. The forces causing a shift to the right (entry) must dominate those causing a shift to the left (rise in marginal costs); otherwise total output could not expand as dictated by the increase in market price.

To see why supply must shift to the right after an increase in demand, let us assume that the opposite happens. In Figure 7.6.2 demand, as before, shifts to D_2D_2'. In the short run price and quantity increase along with profits. The profits attract new firms who, upon entering, bid up resource prices. All cost curves rise as indicated in panel *a*. Suppose, however, that the leftward shift in all marginal cost curves dominates the tendency for an increase in supply caused by entry. Therefore, the new supply curve would lie somewhere to the left of S_1S_1'. If demand remains

---

larger output. The analysis underlying the exact nature of the shift involves an advanced concept not treated in this text. For a detailed treatment, see C. E. Ferguson and Thomas R. Saving, "Long-Run Scale Adjustments of a Perfectly Competitive Firm and Industry," *American Economic Review*, December, 1969.

D_2D_2', price must be greater than Op_2; firms must be making pure profits; entry must continue. If the same process reoccurs, price will rise further, costs will rise, profits will continue, and entry will be further encouraged. Thus a leftward shift in supply is not consistent with equilibrium. At some point the entry of new firms must dominate the increase in costs, and supply must shift to the right, though not by as much as it would in a constant cost industry, since under constant costs no shift in marginal costs occurs.

The process of adjustment must continue until a position of full long-run equilibrium is attained. In Figure 7.6.2, this is depicted by the intersection of D_2D_2' and S_2S_2', establishing an equilibrium price of Op_2 dollars per unit. Each firm produces at point E_2, where price equals minimum average cost. The important point to emphasize is that in constant cost industries new firms enter until price returns to the unchanged level of minimum, long-run average cost. For industries subject to increasing cost, new firms enter until minimum long-run average cost shifts upward to equal the new price.

In the transition from one long-run equilibrium to the other, the long-run supply price increases from Op_1 to Op_2. This is precisely what is meant by an increasing cost industry. In keeping with this, the long-run industry supply curve is given by a line joining such points as A and B in panel b, LS. Thus an increasing cost industry is one with a positively sloped long-run supply curve. Alternatively stated, after all long-run equilibrium adjustments are made, an increasing cost industry is one in which an increase in output requires an increase in long-run supply price.

The result of this section can be summarized as follows:

Relations: Constant or increasing cost in an industry depend entirely upon the way in which resource prices respond to expanded resource usage. If resource prices remain constant, the industry is subject to constant cost; if resource prices increase, the industry is one of increasing cost. The long-run supply curve for a constant cost industry is a horizontal line at the level of the constant long-run supply price. The long-run industry supply curve under conditions of increasing cost is positively sloped, and the long-run supply price increases as long-run equilibrium quantity supplied expands.

7.7   CONCLUSION

Up to this point the salient feature of perfect competition is that, in long-run market equilibrium, market price equals minimum average cost. This means that each unit of output is produced at the lowest possible cost, either from the standpoint of money cost or of resource usage. The product sells for its average (long-run) cost of production; each firm accordingly earns the going rate of return in competitive industries, nothing more or less.

It should be emphasized that firms do not choose to produce the quantity with the lowest possible long-run average cost simply because they believe this level of production is optimal for society and they wish to benefit society. The firms are merely trying to maximize their profits. Given that motivation, the market *forces* firms to produce at that point. If society benefits, it is not through any benevolence of firms but through the functioning of the market. Another point that warrants reemphasis is that the theory of perfect competition is not designed to describe specific real world firms. It is a theoretical model that is frequently useful in explaining real world behavior and in predicting the economic consequences of changes in the different variables contained in the model. The conclusions of the theory, not the assumptions, are the crucial points when analyzing economic problems.

7.8 ANALYTICAL EXERCISE

Suppose demand for coal at the retail level is elastic over the relevant price range. Further, suppose the government feels that the price of coal is too high. It therefore places a price ceiling or maximum on coal at the mine. What will happen to the price of coal at the retail level? Will total receipts of retailers increase or decrease?

As a first step let us consider what happens at the mine (or mining area). Assume for analytical purposes that coal mining is a perfectly

FIGURE 7.8.1

Supply and Demand at the Mine

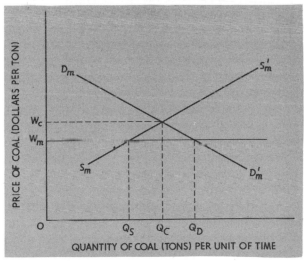

QUANTITY OF COAL (TONS) PER UNIT OF TIME

competitive, increasing cost industry. Assume also that before the imposition of the ceiling price, the industry was in long-run equilibrium;
each firm produced the quantity at which $P = LAC$ and therefore enjoyed
no pure profit. Figure 7.8.1 shows the market demand and supply for
coal at the mine. Demand (D_mD_m') is the demand curve of retailers for
coal at the mine. It is derived holding the demand for coal from retailers
and other factors constant (we assume that individual consumers cannot
purchase coal directly from the mine).

The long-run industry supply curve, S_mS_m', is the type of supply curve
developed in Section 7.6, Figure 7.6.2. It is the locus of long-run equili-

FIGURE 7.8.2

Demand and Supply at Retail

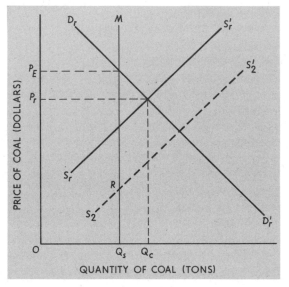

bria for the mining industry. Since we assume an increasing cost industry,
S_mS_m' is upward sloping. The equilibrium price at the mine is OW_c and
equilibrium quantity is OQ_c.

Figure 7.8.2 shows demand and supply conditions at retail. D_rD_r' is
the consumers' demand for coal. S_rS_r', based upon a given cost of coal at
the mines to retailers (OW_c), is the retailers' supply curve. Since coal is
an input for the retailers, the supply curve for coal at retail should shift
when the price of coal at the mines changes, just as a change in the price
of any factor of production changes the supply of the product produced.
Specifically, when the price at the mine falls, other things remaining the
same, the retail supply curve should shift to the right. That is, if retailers
can buy coal cheaper, they would be willing and able to supply more re-

tail coal at every retail price. Equilibrium in the retail market occurs at a price of OP_r (given a price at the mine of OW_c) and a quantity sold of OQ_c, obviously the same as OQ_c in Figure 7.8.1 because the retailers sell all that they buy.

Returning to Figure 7.8.1, assume that the government sets the ceiling price OW_m. Quantity demanded by retailers at the new price is OQ_D. The new price is below OW_c (the price at which neither profit nor loss occurs); thus firms begin to make losses and some leave the industry. Since we assume that mining is an increasing cost industry, the exit of firms and the decrease in quantity produced lowers factor prices and

FIGURE 7.8.3

Cost Curves of an Individual Firm

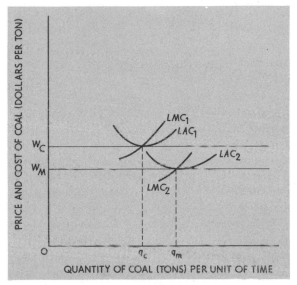

hence lowers the long-run average and marginal cost curves of the remaining firms in the industry. Figure 7.8.3 shows the process. Long-run average and marginal costs fall from LAC_1 and LMC_1 to LAC_2 and LMC_2. The minimum point on LAC_2 equals the ceiling price OW_m. Each remaining firm now produces Oq_m (the new equilibrium output) rather than Oq_c, but there are fewer firms, none of which makes pure profit. The new quantity supplied by the industry, indicated in Figure 7.8.1, is OQ_S.[10] Thus a shortage (excess demand) of Q_SQ_D occurs at the

---

[10] Figure 7.8.3 is drawn under the assumption that the fall in resource prices caused by the exit of firms from the industry shifts the minimum point on LAC to the right. It could just as easily have shifted it to the left (see footnote 9 above). The equilibrium output of each surviving firm is greater, but the output of the industry as a whole is less (see Section 7.6.b above).

mines since retailers now wish to purchase OQ_D but the mines are only willing to sell OQ_S. The mining industry must find some method of allocation (rationing, first come first served, favoritism, and so on) in order to determine which retailers get the available supply. In any case only OQ_S is available to the retailers.

Now according to our analysis the lower price of coal at the mine should cause supply at retail to shift to S_2S_2' (Figure 7.8.2). Retail price should fall and the quantity of coal sold should increase as determined by the intersection of D_rD_r' and S_2S_2'. But remember that only OQ_S is produced, so only OQ_S can be sold. The curve S_2S_2' specifies the quantities that retailers are *willing* to sell at the mine price of OW_m; the vertical line MQ_S indicates the maximum amount retailers are *able* to sell at that price. Therefore, the curve S_2RM shows the quantities that retailers are *willing and able* to sell at each retail price when the mine price is fixed at OW_m.

The intersection of supply and demand now occurs at the price OP_E, clearly higher than the old price. The quantity sold is OQ_S. After the ceiling price at the mine is imposed, consumers pay a higher price for less coal. Since demand was assumed to be elastic, retailers receive less total revenue.

Exercise: Analyze the problem under the assumption that mining is a constant cost industry.

QUESTIONS AND PROBLEMS

1. Use the output-cost data computed from the problem in Chapter 6.
   a) Suppose the price of the commodity is $1.75 per unit.
      i) What would net profit be at each of the following outputs?
         1,314
         1,384
         1,444
         1,494
         1,534
      ii) What is the greatest profit output?
      iii) Is there any output that will yield a greater profit at any price?
      iv) How much more revenue is obtained by selling this number of units than by selling one fewer? What is the relation between marginal revenue and selling price?
      v) If you are given selling price, how can you determine the optimum output by reference to marginal cost?
   b) Suppose price is $0.70.
      i) What would net profit be at each of the following outputs:
         410
         560

700
830
945
1,234
1,444

ii) Is there any output that will earn a net profit at this price?

iii) When price is $0.70, what is the crucial relation between price and average variable cost?

iv) Consider any price for which the corresponding marginal cost is equal to or less than $0.70. At such a price, what is the relation between marginal cost and average variable cost?

v) When the relation in (iv) exists, what is the relation between average and marginal product?

vi) What will the producer do if faced with a permanent price of $0.70?

vii) Why is it not socially desirable to have a producer operating when price is $0.70?

c) Suppose price is $0.80.

i) What will the optimum output be?

ii) Can a profit be made at this price?

iii) Will the producer operate at all at this price?

iv) For how long?

d) Determine the supply schedule of this individual producer.

Price	Quantity Supplied
$0.60	
0.70	
0.80	
0.90	
1.00	
1.10	
1.20	
1.30	
1.40	
1.50	
1.60	
1.70	
1.80	
1.90	
2.00	

2. How can we have a constant cost industry when every firm in the industry operates under conditions of increasing cost?

3. Under what circumstances is the horizontal sum of all firms' marginal cost curves above minimum average variable cost an industry's supply curve? Under what circumstances is it not?

chapter
8

Theory of Price
under Pure Monopoly

8.1 INTRODUCTION

"Perfect competition" provides the economist with a very useful analytical model, even though the exacting conditions of the model never obtain in the real world. The same statement almost applies to the model of pure monopoly, to which we now turn. The conditions of the model are exacting; and it is difficult, if not impossible, to pinpoint a pure monopolist in real world markets. On the other hand, many markets closely approximate monopoly organization, and monopoly analysis often explains observed business behavior quite well.

A pure monopoly exists if there is only *one firm* that produces and sells a particular commodity or service. Since the monopolist is the only seller in the market, he has neither rivals nor direct competitors. Furthermore, no other sellers can enter the market or else a monopoly would not exist. Yet, as we shall see, monopoly does not necessarily guarantee success; it only guarantees that the monopolist can make the best of whatever demand and cost conditions exist without fear of new firms entering the market and competing away his profits.[1]

While the pure monopolist has no *direct competitors* who sell the

---

[1] More advanced economic models sometimes consider the effects of potential competition in the monopolist's market. In these cases the entrepreneur can sometimes maintain his position only if he does not exploit it fully (we shall see below what "exploiting it fully" means). Potential competitors will be induced to enter if profit prospects are particularly bright, or when the monopolist's policy is such that they think they can capture a substantial portion of the market. Whenever entry is possible, the position of an existing monopoly is perilous. While this situation is applicable in many markets, we shall, for simplicity of analysis, assume that entry is blocked. Remember, however, that in many cases the monopolist must consider the effects his actions may have upon potential competitors.

same product, he does have *indirect competition*. In the first place, all commodities compete for a place in the consumer's budget. Thus, to a certain extent, the monopolist's product competes with all other goods and services in the general struggle for the consumer's dollar. Some goods, however, are closer substitutes for the monopolist's product than others. While there are no perfect or nearly perfect substitutes for a monopoly product (otherwise a monopoly would not exist), a second source of indirect competition lies in the existence of imperfect substitutes.

For example, American Telephone and Telegraph almost has a monopoly in providing long-distance telephone service in the United States. However, there are various substitutes that can be used: mail, railway express, messengers, personal visits, smoke signals. When the Aluminum Company of America (Alcoa) was the only manufacturer of aluminum (prior to World War II) it had no direct competitors, but it did have competition from producers of other metals that were imperfect substitutes. More recently, International Nickel has been in a similar situation. Gas is a fairly good substitute for electricity (usually a regional monopoly) in many cases. Any real world monopolist, therefore, has competition to a greater or lesser degree, which in some measure tends to weaken the monopolist's position. There are, however, no other producers of the monopolist's specific product in the market.

To summarize:

Definition: A pure monopoly exists when there is only one producer in a market. There are no direct competitors or rivals in either the popular or technical sense. However, the policies of a monopolist may be constrained by the indirect competition of all commodities for the consumer's dollar and by reasonably adequate substitute goods.

8.2 DEMAND AND MARGINAL REVENUE UNDER MONOPOLY

The most important object of Chapters 3 and 4 was to show that market demand curves are negatively sloped (except for the truly insignificant case of Giffen's Paradox). Since a monopoly is the only firm selling in the market, the market demand *is* the monopolist's demand curve. As you will recall the market demand curve shows, for each specific price, the quantity of the commodity that buyers will take. Of perhaps equal importance for our analysis of monopoly is the market *marginal revenue,* the variation in total revenue resulting from an additional unit of sales.

8.2.a—Calculation of Marginal Revenue

Let us consider first why marginal revenue for a monopolist differs from marginal revenue for a perfect competitor. As previously emphasized, a change in the quantity sold by a competitive firm has no notice-able effect upon market price; therefore, marginal revenue to this firm is the market price. On the other hand, a change in the quantity a monop-olist sells does affect market price. More specifically, since the monopolist *must lower price* if he wishes to increase his rate of sales, his marginal revenue is not the market price. For example, suppose a monopolist can sell 10 units per period of time at $4 each; in order to sell 11 units per period he must lower price to $3.75. At a price of $4 his total revenue is $40. At a price of $3.75 each his total revenue is $41.25. The additional revenue resulting from the increase of one unit is consequently $1.25. Now consider another case: A monopolist can sell 50 units per period of time at $5 each and 51 units per period at $4.50. The additional unit of sales causes total revenue to decline from $250 to $229.50; the marginal revenue is −$20.50. Marginal revenue can be positive, negative, or zero.

The only time a monopolist's marginal revenue equals market price is for the first unit sold. That is, at zero sales total revenue is zero; for the first unit sold total revenue is the demand price for one unit. The change in total revenue is thus the same as price. Since the monopolist must reduce price to sell additional units per period of time, at every other level of output marginal revenue is less than price. As you remember from Chapter 6, when average cost decreases, marginal cost is less than average cost. Similarly, since average revenue (price) decreases over the entire range of outputs, marginal revenue is less than average revenue (price) over this range.

Relations: Marginal revenue is the addition to total revenue attributable to the addition of one unit of output to sales per period of time. After the first unit sold, marginal revenue is less than price.

Figure 8.2.1 illustrates the relations between demand, marginal reve-nue, and total revenue for a monopolist with a linear demand curve. In panels *a* and *b*, the scales of the vertical axes differ but the horizontal axes have the same scale. Note the difference between the total revenue curves of a monopolist and a perfect competitor (you will remember the latter is a monotonically increasing straight line, whose constant slope is the market price). Total revenue (panel *a*) first increases when price is reduced and sales expand; it reaches a maximum at Ox_0 and declines thereafter.

Panel *b* indicates the relations between marginal revenue (MR) and demand. As mentioned above MR is below price at every output level except the first (since we have assumed continuous data, the two are equal infinitesimally close to the vertical axis). Also, since demand is negatively sloped, MR is as well. Finally, when TR reaches its maximum (at output Ox_0), MR is zero (at output Ox_0, price Op_0). At greater rates of output MR is negative. These relations are clearly indicated when we

FIGURE 8.2.1

Total Revenue, Marginal Revenue, Demand

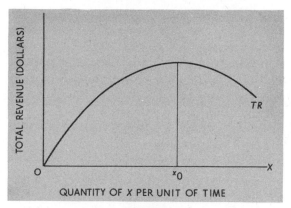

Panel a
Total Revenue

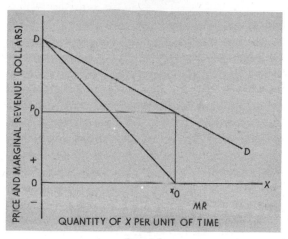

Panel b
Demand and Marginal Revenue

consider the characteristics of marginal revenue: if TR increases, an additional unit of sales per period adds a positive amount to revenue; hence MR is positive. The opposite holds for a decrease in TR.

8.2.b—Graphical Derivation of Marginal Revenue from Linear Demand

We can now be more specific and give a graphical derivation of the marginal revenue curve. Consider Figure 8.2.2, in which we have a *linear*

FIGURE 8.2.2

Derivation of Marginal Revenue When Demand Is Linear

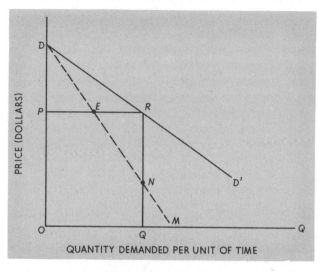

QUANTITY DEMANDED PER UNIT OF TIME

Demand, Total Revenue, and Marginal Revenue

Price	Quantity	Total Revenue	Marginal Revenue	Sum of MR Entries
11	0	0	—	—
10	1	10	10	10
9	2	18	8	18
8	3	24	6	24
7	4	28	4	28
6	5	30	2	30
5	6	30	0	30
4	7	28	−2	28
3	8	24	−4	24
2	9	18	−6	18
1	10	10	−8	10

demand curve DD'. Our task is to determine the marginal revenue associated with any (and hence every) point on DD'.

Suppose price is OP; thus quantity demanded is OQ and total revenue is equal to the area of the rectangle $OPRQ$. Further, it follows from the definition of MR that TR corresponding to any quantity is the sum of all MR figures up to and including MR for the quantity under consideration.[2] Graphically, this means that total revenue for each rate of output is equal to the area under the marginal revenue curve.

---

[2] A numerical example may elucidate this point. A comparison of columns 3 and 5 confirms that the sum of the MR figures exactly equals TR.

If we already knew the marginal revenue curve *DM*, total revenue would also equal the area *ODNQ*. At the moment this curve is not known; indeed, our problem is to determine the marginal revenue (*QN*) associated with quantity *OQ* and price *OP* = *QR*. The only thing we know right now is that there must be an area *ODNQ* which is equal to total revenue, or the area *OPRQ*. Our problem is to locate the point *N*. When the proper *N* is found, we know that area *ODNQ* will equal area *OPRQ*.

These two geometrical shapes have a substantial area in common, namely *OPENQ*. The triangle *ERN* is unique to *OPRQ* and the triangle *EPD* is unique to *ODNQ*. Since *OPENQ* is common, the area of *ODNQ* will equal the area *OPRQ* if the area of *EDP* equals the area of *ERN*.

At this point, we have three pieces of information. First, since the opposite angles formed by two intersecting straight lines are equal, angle *DEP* equals angle *REN*. Second, both figures are right triangles (that is, angles *DPE* and *ERN* are right angles). Since two angles are equal, the third must be as well. The two triangles are, accordingly, similar triangles. Finally, we know that if properly constructed the two triangles have equal area. But similar triangles of equal area are congruent, so the corresponding sides must be equal. Hence *PE* = *ER* and *DP* = *RN*.

We have thus obtained a method for finding marginal revenue corresponding to any point on a linear demand curve. Suppose the point in question is *R*. From *R*, drop a perpendicular *RQ* to the quantity axis and a perpendicular *RP* to the price axis. On the perpendicular *RQ* mark off a distance *RN* that is equal to *DP*. When this is done, the distance *NQ* is the marginal revenue associated with the output *OQ* units. By repeating this process for other points on *DD'*, the *MR* curve is determined.

Another method is equally valid but does not directly follow the logic of locating the point *N*. From the point *R*, drop perpendiculars *RP* and *RQ* to both axes. Find the midpoint *E* of the line *RP*. Draw a straight line from *D* to *E* and extend this line until it intersects *RQ*. The point of intersection is *N*, the point in question.

Relation: When demand is linear, *MR* is a negatively sloped straight line that lies exactly halfway between the vertical axis and the demand curve.

8.2.c—Graphical Derivation of MR when Demand Is Nonlinear

The derivation of *MR* when demand is nonlinear differs but slightly. The mechanics are explained by means of Figure 8.2.3. *DD'* is the demand curve. The problem is to find marginal revenue corresponding to such points as R_1, R_2, and R_3 on *DD'*. From point R_1, first drop perpendiculars

(R_1P_1 and R_1Q_1) to both axes. Next, construct the tangent to DD' at R_1 and extend the tangent so that it cuts the vertical axis at point S_1. Since the slope of the curve and of its tangent are the same at the point of tangency, the marginal quantities are also the same. Thus to find marginal revenue at point R_1, mark off a distance $R_1N_1 = S_1P_1$. Then N_1Q_1 is marginal revenue and N_1 is a point on the marginal revenue curve.

Proceeding in the same fashion, select another point R_2 on DD' and drop perpendiculars (R_2P_2 and R_2Q_2) to the axes. Next, construct the

FIGURE 8.2.3

Derivation of Marginal Revenue from Nonlinear Demand Curve

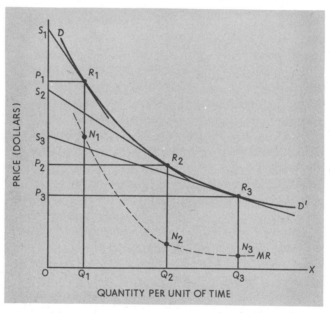

tangent to DD' at R_2 and extend the tangent line to cut the vertical axis at S_2. Finally, mark off the distance $R_2N_2 = S_2P_2$. Marginal revenue is N_2Q_2 and N_2 is another point on the marginal revenue curve. (*Exercise:* carry out the same argument for the point R_3.) Connecting all points so generated—and for accuracy, there must be many of them—establishes the marginal revenue curve corresponding to the given nonlinear demand curve.

Note that when demand is nonlinear, marginal revenue does not lie half the distance from the vertical axis to the demand curve. For demand curves that are concave from above, marginal revenue is less than half the distance from the vertical axis to demand (note where MR crosses P_2R_2 and P_3R_3). For demands concave from below, marginal revenue cuts the perpendicular from the vertical axis to demand to the right of its midpoint.

8.2.d—Marginal Revenue, Demand, and Elasticity

As you will recall from Chapter 2 changes in total expenditure are related to demand elasticity. When demand is elastic, an increase in quantity (decrease in price) causes an increase in total expenditure. Over an inelastic segment of demand, an increase in quantity occasions a decrease in total expenditure, while in the unitary portion, total expenditure remains unchanged. Since total consumer expenditure on a commodity is the same as the monopolist's total revenue, the relation of elasticity to marginal revenue follows directly from the above relations. If marginal revenue is positive (negative), a unit increase in sales leads to an increase (decrease) in total revenue. If marginal revenue is zero, a unit change in sales does not change total revenue. Therefore, a positive (negative) marginal revenue indicates that demand is elastic (inelastic) at that

TABLE 8.2.1
Relations among Marginal Revenue, Elasticity,
and Changes in Total Revenue

	1	*2*	*3*
Marginal revenue	Positive	Negative	Zero
Demand elasticity	Elastic	Inelastic	Unitary
Change in total revenue for an increase in quantity	Increase	Decrease	No change

FIGURE 8.2.4

Relations among Marginal Revenue, Elasticity, and Demand

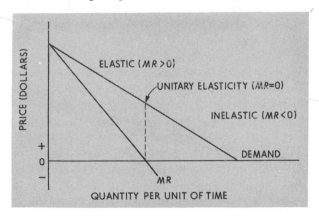

quantity. Zero marginal revenue means unitary elasticity. These relations are summarized in Table 8.2.1. They can be seen also in Figure 8.2.4, which shows a straight line demand curve.

An even more precise relation among price, marginal revenue, and the coefficient of elasticity is given by the equation[3]

$$MR = p\left(1 - \frac{1}{\eta}\right),$$

_____

[3] A formal proof of this relation is relegated to a footnote. Consider the accompanying graph.

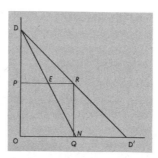

Let DD' be a linear demand curve. This is used merely for convenience because the formula to be developed holds for nonlinear demand curves as well. Consider the point R on DD', corresponding to a price of $OP = QR$ and quantity demanded of $OQ = PR$. NQ is the marginal revenue associated with point R because, by construction, $RN = DP$. Furthermore, at point R the coefficient of price elasticity (η) is RD'/DR.

First note that

$$NQ = RQ - RN.\tag{1}$$

Now since $\dfrac{DP}{PR} = \dfrac{RQ}{QD'}$ and $RN = DP$, it follows that

$$RN = PR\left[\frac{RQ}{QD'}\right] = RQ\left[\frac{PR}{QD'}\right]\tag{2}$$

Substituting equation (2) in equation (1),

$$NQ = RQ - RN$$

$$= RQ - RQ\left[\frac{PR}{QD'}\right]\tag{3}$$

$$= RQ\left[1 - \frac{PR}{QD'}\right].$$

Next, observe that

$$\frac{PR}{QD'} = \frac{OQ}{QD'} = \frac{DR}{RD'} = \frac{1}{\eta}.\tag{4}$$

Finally, substituting equation (4) in equation (3), one obtains where η is the price elasticity of demand. Note that when $\eta > 1$ (demand is elastic), $\dfrac{1}{\eta} < 1$; hence, $(1 - \dfrac{1}{\eta}) > 0$. Since $p > 0$, $p(1 - \dfrac{1}{\eta}) > 0$. Therefore, $MR > 0$.

Exercise: The student should carry out the same type of analysis for $\eta = 1$ and $\eta < 1$.

Relations: When demand is negatively sloped, marginal revenue is negatively sloped and is less than price at all relevant quantities. The difference between marginal revenue and price depends upon the price elasticity of demand as shown by the formula $MR = p(1 - 1/\eta)$. Total revenue increases at first, reaches a maximum, and declines thereafter. The maximum point on the total revenue curve is attained at precisely that rate of output and sales for which marginal revenue is zero and elasticity is unitary.

8.3 SHORT-RUN EQUILIBRIUM UNDER MONOPOLY

The analysis of perfect competition is based upon two important assumptions: (1) each entrepreneur attempts to maximize profit and (2) the firm operates in an environment free from outside control. Monopoly analysis rests upon the same two assumptions.

8.3.a—Cost under Monopoly

The short-run cost conditions confronting a monopolist are essentially similar to those faced by a perfectly competitive firm. The chief difference lies in the potential impact of output changes on factor prices. In the theory of perfect competition we assume that each producer is very small relative to the total factor market. He can thereby change *his* rate of output without affecting factor prices (just as a consumer can change his rate of purchases without affecting commodity price).

The assumption just discussed cannot be imposed on the markets for all factors a monopolist hires. To be sure, a monopolist will purchase some unspecialized inputs, such as unskilled labor, whose prices are not affected by his actions. But he will hire certain specialized inputs as well; and

$$NQ = RQ \left[1 - \frac{1}{\eta} \right] \tag{5}$$

Since NQ is marginal revenue (MR) and RQ is price p, equation (5) can be written to express the relation among marginal revenue, price, and the coefficient of price elasticity as stated in the text:

$$MR = p\left(1 - \frac{1}{\eta}\right).$$

since the monopolist *is* the industry, his rates of purchase will have a definite impact upon the prices of these factors. Generally, factor prices will vary directly with the monopolist's use of them.

Notwithstanding the monopolist's possible effect upon factor prices, his cost curves have the same general shape as those described in Chapter 6. The primary implication of rising supply prices of variable inputs is that the average and marginal cost curves rise more rapidly than if the input supply prices were constant. Thus, for example, marginal cost rises not only because of diminishing marginal productivity but also because input prices rise with increased use.

8.3.b—Short-Run Equilibrium

A monopolist, just as a perfect competitor, attains maximum profit (or minimum loss) by producing and selling at that rate of output for which the positive (negative) difference between total revenue and total cost is greatest (least). This condition occurs when the slope of the total revenue curve equals the slope of the total cost curve; in other words, when marginal revenue equals marginal cost (even though for the monopolist MR does not equal price).

Figure 8.3.1 depicts the marginal cost and marginal revenue curves of a monopolist. Maximum profit or minimum loss occurs at output Ox_0, where MC equals MR. At any lower output, for example Ox_1, the monopolist can gain additional profit or can reduce his loss by producing and selling an additional unit per period of time. Since MR exceeds MC

FIGURE 8.3.1

$MC = MR$ for Profit Maximization

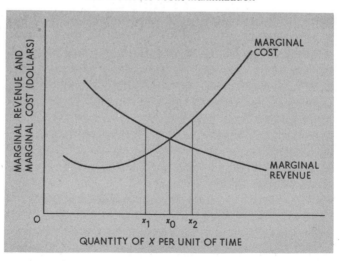

at Ox_1, the added revenue from the sale of another unit per period is greater than the additional cost of producing it. He therefore produces additional units until MR equals MC. Likewise, he would not produce more than Ox_0, for example Ox_2, since at larger outputs the marginal cost of producing another unit per period is greater than the marginal revenue gained from selling it. Thus producing more or less than Ox_0 causes profit (loss) to diminish (increase).

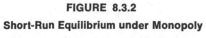

FIGURE 8.3.2

Short-Run Equilibrium under Monopoly

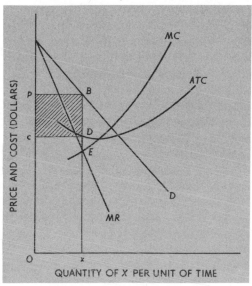

Using the proposition just established, the position of short-run equilibrium is easily described. Figure 8.3.2 shows the relevant cost and revenue curves for a monopolist. Since AVC and AFC are not necessary for exposition, they are omitted. The profit maximizer produces at E where $MC = MR$. Output is Ox, and from the demand curve we see that price must be Op per unit in order to ration the Ox units among those who wish to buy the commodity. Total revenue is $Op \times Ox$, or the area of the rectangle $OpBx$. The unit cost of producing this amount is Oc. Total cost is $Oc \times Ox$, or the area $OcDx$. Profit is $TR - TC$, or the shaded area $cpBD$.

In the example of Figure 8.3.2, the monopolist earns a pure profit in the short run. This need not be the case, however; a monopolistic position does not assure profit. If demand is sufficiently low a monopolist may incur

FIGURE 8.3.3

Short-Run Losses under Monopoly

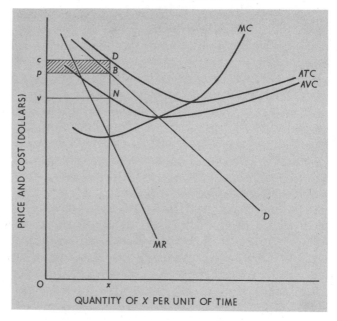

a loss in the short run, just as a pure competitor may. For example, Figure 8.3.3 shows a loss situation. Marginal cost equals marginal revenue at output Ox, which can be sold at price Op. Average cost is Oc. Total cost, $OcDx$ exceeds total revenue $OpBx$; hence the firm makes a loss of $pcDB$.

Note that the monopolist would produce rather than shut down in the short run, since he covers all of his variable cost ($OvNx$) and still has some revenue ($OpBN$) left to apply to fixed cost. If demand decreases so that the monopolist cannot cover all of his variable cost at any price, he would shut down and lose only fixed cost. This situation is analogous to that of the perfect competitor, except that we cannot derive a monopoly short-run supply curve.

In the short run the primary difference between monopoly and perfect competition lies in the slope of the demand curve. Either may earn a pure economic profit; either may incur a loss. Of course, another important difference is that the monopolist who earns pure profit need not worry about new firms entering the industry and competing his profits away.

Principles: If a monopolist produces a positive output, he maximizes profit or minimizes losses by producing the quantity for which *MC = MR*. Since the monopolist's demand is above *MR* at every positive output, equilibrium price exceeds *MC*.

8.4 LONG-RUN EQUILIBRIUM UNDER MONOPOLY

A monopoly exists if there is only one firm in the market. Among other things this statement implies that "entrance" into the market is closed. Thus whether or not a monopolist earns a pure profit in the short run, no other producer can enter the market in the hopes of sharing whatever pure profit potential exists. Therefore, pure economic profit is not eliminated in the long run, as in the case of perfect competition. The monopolist will, however, make adjustments in plant size as demand conditions warrant them, even though entry is prohibited.

8.4.a—Adjustments in Plant Size

A monopolist faced with the cost and revenue conditions depicted in Figure 8.4.1 would build his plant to produce the quantity at which long-run marginal cost equals marginal revenue. He produces Ox units per period at a cost of Oc per unit and sells at a price of Op. Long-run profit is $cpBE$. By the now familiar argument, this is the maximum profit possible under the given revenue and cost conditions. He operates in the short run with plant size indicated by SAC_1 and SMC_1. New entrants cannot come into the industry and compete away his profits.

But demand or cost conditions can change for reasons other than the entry of new firms; and such changes cause the monopolist to make adjustments. Assume that demand and marginal revenue change. At first the firm will adjust without changing plant size. It will produce the quantity at which the new MR equals SMC_1, or it will close down in the

FIGURE 8.4.1

Long-Run Equilibrium under Monopoly

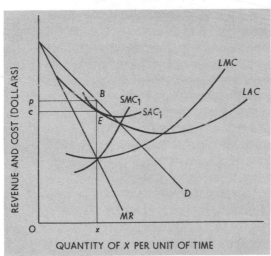

short run if it cannot cover variable costs. In the long run the monopolist can change plant size.

Long-run equilibrium adjustment under monopoly must take one of two possible courses. First, if the monopolist incurs a short-run loss, and if there is no plant size that will result in pure profit (or at least, no loss), the monopolist goes out of business. Second, if he suffers a short-run loss or earns a short-run profit with his original plant, he must determine

FIGURE 8.4.2

Long-Run Equilibrium for a Monopolist

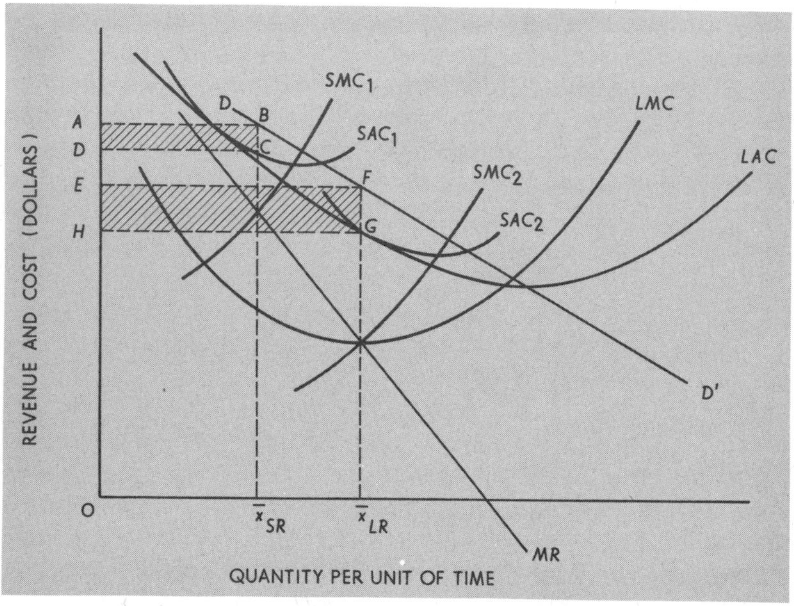

whether a plant of different size (and thus a different price and output) will enable him to earn a larger profit.

The first situation requires no comment. The second is illustrated by Figure 8.4.2. DD' and MR show the market demand and marginal revenue confronting a monopolist. LAC is his long-run average cost curve, and LMC is the associated long-run marginal cost curve. Suppose in the initial period the monopolist builds the plant exemplified by SAC_1 and SMC_1. Equality of short-run marginal cost and marginal revenue leads to the sale of $O\bar{x}_{SR}$ units per period at the price OA. At this rate of output unit cost is OD; short-run monopoly profit is represented by the area of the shaded rectangle $ABCD$.

Since a pure economic profit can be reaped, the monopolist would not consider discontinuing production. To this end, long-run marginal cost becomes the relevant consideration. The profit-maximum maximorum is attained when long-run marginal cost equals marginal revenue. The associated rate of output is $O\bar{x}_{LR}$, and price is OE.

By reference to LAC, the plant capable of producing $O\bar{x}_{LR}$ units per period at the least unit cost is the one represented by SAC_2 and SMC_2. Unit cost is accordingly OH, and long-run maximum monopoly profit is given by the area of the shaded rectangle $EFGH$. This profit is obviously (visually) greater than the profit obtainable from the original plant.

Generalizing, we have the following:

Proposition: A monopolist maximizes profit in the long run by producing and marketing that rate of output for which long-run marginal cost equals marginal revenue. The optimal plant is the one whose short-run average cost curve is tangent to the long-run average cost curve at the point corresponding to long-run equilibrium output. At this point short-run marginal cost equals marginal revenue.

The organization described by the proposition above is the best the monopolist can attain; and he *can* attain it because in the long run his plant size is variable and the market is effectively closed to entry.

8.4.b—Comparison with Perfect Competition

Most comparisons between the equilibria of monopoly and perfect competition are tenuous. For example, one sometimes hears that price is lower and output greater under perfect competition than under monopoly.

FIGURE 8.4.3

Price and Output Comparisons

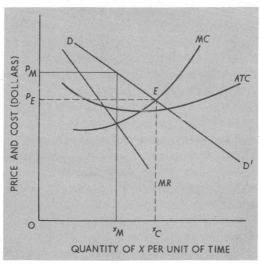

This statement is based upon the following analysis. The monopolist depicted in Figure 8.4.3 produces Ox_M per period of time and sells at a price of Op_M. If we can also assume that MC represents competitive supply, supply equals demand at E. The perfectly competitive industry would sell Ox_C (greater than Ox_M) at a price of Op_C (less than Op_M). There is reason to doubt, however, that MC can represent the supply curve of a perfectly competitive industry. As we have seen, competitive supply is not always the sum of the marginal cost curves. Even if this were so, the sum of n firms' marginal cost curves would not necessarily be the marginal cost curve of a single much larger firm. One can only say that a monopolist is more likely to earn a pure profit because he can effectively exercise some market control.

We can also say that in long-run industry equilibrium under perfect competition production occurs at the point of minimum long- and short-run average cost. The monopolist utilizes the plant capable of producing his long-run equilibrium output at the least unit cost. Only under the extremely rare circumstance in which marginal revenue intersects marginal cost at minimum long-run average cost would this plant be the one associated with the absolute minimum unit cost. In any case the slightest change in demand would upset this equilibrium.

We should also note that while the perfect competitor produces at the point where marginal cost and price are equal, the monopolist's price *exceeds* marginal cost. Under certain conditions, demand represents the social valuation of the commodity. Similarly, long-run marginal cost, with some exceptions, represents the marginal social cost of production. Under monopoly the marginal value of a commodity to a society exceeds the marginal social cost of its production. Society as a whole would, therefore, benefit by having more of its resources used in producing the commodity in question. The profit-maximizing monopolist will not do this, however, for producing at the point where price equals marginal cost would decrease his profit. Alternatively, the perfect competitor in long-run equilibrium produces the quantity at which the marginal social cost of production equals the marginal social valuation; he does so, however, not because of any innate social consciousness but because the market forces him to do so.

8.5 PRICE DISCRIMINATION UNDER MONOPOLY

Earlier in this chapter we stated that a pure monopoly exists if a commodity has only one seller in a well-defined market. Price discrimination can exist under monopoly if the monopolist is the only seller of a commodity in two or more well-defined, separable markets. Price discrimination means that a monopolist charges different prices for the same commodity in different markets. Price discrimination can occur when a

monopolist charges different prices domestically and abroad or perhaps
when a doctor charges one fee for an operation to low-income patients
and another fee for the same operation to high-income patients.

Certain conditions are necessary for the monopolist to be able to dis-
criminate. First, the markets must be *separable*. If purchasers in the lower
price market are able themselves to sell the commodity to buyers in the
higher price market, discrimination will not exist for long. For example,
a lower price patient cannot resell his operation to a higher price patient,
but a lower price buyer of some raw material could perhaps resell it to
someone in the higher price market. Discrimination would not be prac-
ticed in the latter case. Second, as we shall soon see, demand elasticities
must be different in the different markets.

TABLE 8.5.1
Allocation of Sales between
Two Markets

Quantity	Marginal Revenue Market I		Marginal Revenue Market II	
1...............	$45	(1)	$34	(3)
2...............	36	(2)	28	(5)
3...............	30	(4)	22	(7)
4...............	22	(6)	13	(10)
5...............	17	(8)	[10]	(12)
6...............	15	(9)	8	
7...............	[10]	(11)	7	
8...............	7		4	
9...............	4		2	
10.............	0		1	

The analysis of discriminatory pricing is a straightforward application
of the $MC = MR$ rule. As a first step in that analysis, let us assume that a
monopolist has two separate markets for his product. Demand conditions
in each market are such that the marginal revenues from selling specified
quantities are as given in Table 8.5.1. Assume also that for some reason
the monopolist decides to produce 12 units. How should he allocate sales
between the two markets?

Consider the first unit; he can gain $45 by selling it in the first market
or $34 by selling in the second market. Obviously, if he sells only one
unit per period, he will sell it in market I. The second unit per period is
also sold in the first market since its sale there increases revenue by $36,
whereas it would only bring $34 in market II. Since $34 can be gained
in II but only $30 in I, unit three per period is sold in market II. Similar
analysis shows that the fourth unit goes to I and the fifth to II. Since unit
six adds $22 to revenue in either market, it makes no difference where it

is sold; six and seven go to each market. Eight and 9 are sold in I because they yield higher marginal revenue there; 10 goes to II for the same reason. Unit 11 can go to either market, since the additional revenues are the same, and unit 12 goes to the other. Thus we see that the 12 units should be divided so that the marginal revenues are the same for the last unit sold in each market; the monopolist sells 7 units in market I and 5 in market II.

Exercise: The student should establish that any further reallocation of the 12 units diminishes total revenue. He should also establish that 17 units should be divided 8 in II and 9 in I.

Principle: The discriminating monopolist allocates a given output such that the marginal revenues in each market are equal. He sells any additional unit in the market with the higher marginal revenue.

This argument establishes the basis for allocating a given output between two markets. It also permits an easy explanation of the condition that different demand elasticities in the two markets are necessary for price discrimination to exist. Recall that marginal revenue may be expressed in the following way:

$$MR = p\left(1 - \frac{1}{\eta}\right),$$

where p is price and η is the elasticity of demand. As just shown, MR must be the same in each market. Therefore, if $MR_I = MR_{II}$, it is necessary that

$$p_I\left(1 - \frac{1}{\eta_I}\right) = p_{II}\left(1 - \frac{1}{\eta_{II}}\right).$$

Thus

$$\frac{p_I}{p_{II}} = \frac{\left(1 - \frac{1}{\eta_{II}}\right)}{\left(1 - \frac{1}{\eta_I}\right)}.$$

Consequently, if the elasticities are equal $(\eta_I = \eta_{II})$, $\left(1 - \frac{1}{\eta_I}\right) = \left(1 - \frac{1}{\eta_{II}}\right)$. Therefore, p_I must equal p_{II}, and price discrimination does not exist. For $p_I \neq p_{II}$, $\eta_I \neq \eta_{II}$.

As we have seen, the first problem confronting a price discriminating monopolist is to allocate a given level of sales between his markets. The second problem is to determine the optimal level of sales and, therefore, the level of price in each of the submarkets. For this calculation both revenue and cost data are required.

Assume that a monopolist can separate his market into two markets.

FIGURE 8.5.1

Submarket and Total Market Demands and Marginal Revenues

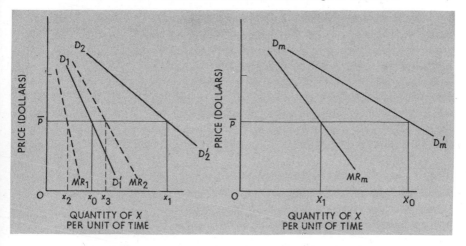

Panel a	Panel b
Demand and Marginal Revenue in Submarkets	**Monopoly Demand and Marginal Revenue**

The demands and marginal revenues of each are shown in panel a, Figure 8.5.1. D_1D_1' and MR_1 are demand and marginal revenue in the first market; D_2D_2' and MR_2 are demand and marginal revenue in the second. Panel b shows the horizontal summation of the two demand and marginal revenue curves. For example, at a price of $O\bar{p}$ consumers in market I would take Ox_0 and consumers in market II would take Ox_1. The total quantity demanded at $O\bar{p}$ is accordingly $Ox_1 + Ox_2 = OX_0$, shown in panel b. All other points on D_mD_m' are derived similarly. $MR_1 = O\bar{p}$ at output Ox_2; $MR_2 = O\bar{p}$ at Ox_3. Therefore, in panel b, $MR_m = O\bar{p}$ at a quantity of $Ox_2 + Ox_3 = OX_1$. Other points on MR_m, the total market MR curve, are derived similarly.

The demand and marginal revenue conditions depicted in panel a, Figure 8.5.1, are reproduced in Figure 8.5.2, along with average and marginal costs of production. The profit maximizing output is $O\overline{X}$, the quantity at which the total market marginal revenue equals marginal cost. The marginal revenue (equals marginal cost) associated with this output is Om.

The market allocation rule, previously determined, requires that marginal revenue be the same in each submarket. Since the total market marginal revenue is the added revenue from selling the last unit in either submarket, $MR_1 = MR_2 = Om$. At a marginal revenue of Om, the quantity sold in submarket one is $O\bar{x}_1$; in submarket two, $O\bar{x}_2$. Since MR_m is

FIGURE 8.5.2

Profit Maximization under Price Discrimination

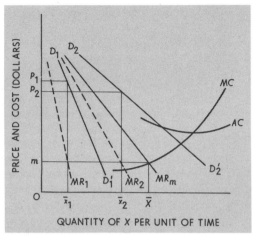

QUANTITY OF X PER UNIT OF TIME

the horizontal summation of MR_1 and MR_2, $O\bar{x}_1 + O\bar{x}_2 = OX$, the total output. Furthermore, from the relevant demand curves the price associated with output $O\bar{x}_1$ in market one is Op_1; the price associated with $O\bar{x}_2$ in market two is Op_2. Because these clearly differ, discrimination can exist.

Summarizing these results:

Proposition: If the aggregate market for a monopolist's product can be divided into submarkets with different price elasticities, the monopolist can profitably practice price discrimination. Total output is determined by equating marginal cost with aggregate monopoly marginal revenue. The output is allocated among the submarkets so as to equate marginal revenue in each submarket with aggregate marginal revenue at the $MC = MR$ point. Finally, price in each submarket is determined directly from the submarket demand curve, given the submarket allocation of sales.

A final relation is worth noting. Since marginal revenue must be the same in each submarket, our MR—p—η formula reduces to

$$p_I \left(1 - \frac{1}{\eta_I} \right) = p_{II} \left(1 - \frac{1}{\eta_{II}} \right).$$

Thus if $\eta_I < \eta_{II}$, p_I must necessarily be greater than p_{II} to preserve the equality. That is, the discriminatory price is greater in the market with the less elastic demand. This helps to explain why students pay more for books and less for airline tickets than professors do. But it explains much more than this. Whenever groups with different demand elasticities exist and there cannot be arbitrage between groups, those who are least willing to substitute other commodities (i.e., those with the least elastic demand) will always pay the highest price.

8.6 CONCLUSION

The pure monopolist chooses the output at which $MC = MR$. In contrast to perfect competition, the market does not force the monopolist in the long run to produce the quantity at which long-run ATC is at its minimum and to charge a price equal to minimum long-run ATC and MC. This does not necessarily indicate that price must be higher and quantity lower under monopoly than under perfect competition. Cost conditions may differ between the two forms of organization. We can only say that price under monopoly will not, in the absence of regulation, equal marginal cost and that the entry of competitors will not reduce pure profit to zero. Demand conditions certainly can change so as to eliminate profit, however, since a monopoly position does not guarantee pure profit.

8.7 ANALYTICAL EXERCISES: MONOPOLY REGULATION

Since some of the social effects of monopoly behavior are thought to be "undesirable," governments from time to time attempt to regulate their behavior by imposing price ceilings and by enacting certain forms of taxation. Without considering social desirability, we can analyze some effects of such regulation upon the price-output behavior of monopolists.

8.7.a—Price Regulation

If a government believes a monopolist is making "too much" profit, is charging "too high" a price, or is "restricting" output,[4] it can set a price ceiling on the commodity. As you will recall from Chapter 2, a ceiling price under perfect competition causes a shortage, and some form of nonprice allocation of the good must develop. This may or may not be the case under monopoly.

Consider first the situation in Figure 8.6.1. Under the cost and revenue conditions depicted, the nonregulated monopolist sells Ox_e at a price of Op_e; he obviously makes a substantial pure profit. Now let us assume that the government imposes a price ceiling (i.e., a price less than Op_e). Suppose Op_c is the maximum price allowed. The segment p_cC becomes the new demand and marginal revenue up to the output Ox_c. The monopolist

---

[4] "Too much" and "too high" are perhaps undefinable except in the sense that they mean more than or higher than someone wishes them to be. The monopolist "restricts" output only in the sense that $P > MC$.

FIGURE 8.6.1

Effects of Price Ceilings under Monopoly

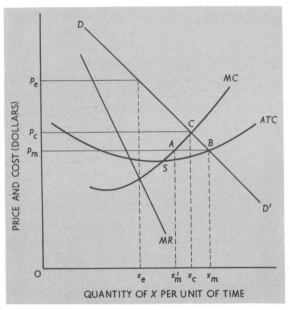

can sell any quantity up to Ox_c at a price of Op_c because over this range actual demand lies above p_cC; he would certainly charge no lower price. Thus over the segment p_cC, the monopolist's effective demand is a horizontal line and $P = MR$. After Ox_c the old demand and marginal revenue curves become effective. The entire new demand is, therefore, the line p_cCD'. With the new demand curve, marginal revenue now equals marginal cost at C; the monopolist sells Ox_c units per period at a price of Op_c. Since C lies on DD', quantity supplied equals quantity demanded and the market is cleared. Price falls, quantity increases, and marginal cost now equals price. Further, profit clearly diminishes. Since Ox_e and Op_e gave *maximum* profit, any other combination, including Op_c and Ox_c, must give less than maximum profit.

At any ceiling price set between Op_e and Op_c, price would equal MC at an output greater than the quantity the market would demand at that price. Therefore the monopolist sells the quantity given by his demand curve (DD') at the ceiling price. Again price falls from Op_e and quantity increases from Ox_e, but in contrast to Op_c, price exceeds the marginal cost of the last unit sold.

You may think, "If Op_c causes price to fall, quantity to rise, and profit to diminish, why not lower price even farther, possibly to Op_m?" True enough, at Op_m the monopolist could sell Ox_m and still cover costs since

$ATC = OP_m$ at Ox_m. Note, however, that the new demand and marginal revenue curve is $p_m BD'$. Therefore $MR = MC$ at A; and the firm would produce Ox_m', which is *less* than Ox_m. Since quantity demanded at Op_m is Ox_m, a shortage of $x_m'\, x_m$ results. In this case the monopolist must allocate by means other than price, the government must ration, and a black market will result. In fact, any price below Op_c causes a decrease in quantity from Ox_c and hence a shortage inasmuch as quantity demanded exceeds quantity supplied. The monopolist will produce along his MC curve over the portion SC; but the market demands a greater quantity at each of these prices. If price is set below minimum ATC (point S), the monopolist will go out of business.

Under the conditions assumed in Figure 8.6.1, the greatest quantity is attained by setting the ceiling price so that the monopolist produces where MC intersects actual demand. This result, however, may not always be obtainable by a ceiling price. Figure 8.6.2 depicts such a case. The non-regulated profit-maximizing monopolist in Figure 8.6.2 sells Ox_1 units per period at price Op_1. If the government sets a ceiling price of Op_3, the price at which MC crosses demand, the monopolist in the long run would go out of business; at this price he could not cover total costs. In fact, the ceiling could be no lower than Op_2 without forcing the firm to cease production. At Op_2 the firm would sell Ox_2 units per period and make no pure profit. The monopolist would like to produce and sell the quantity at which Op_2 equals MC (point A), but demand conditions would not allow him to sell this quantity. A surplus would occur. There-

FIGURE 8.6.2

Effects of Price Ceilings under Monopoly

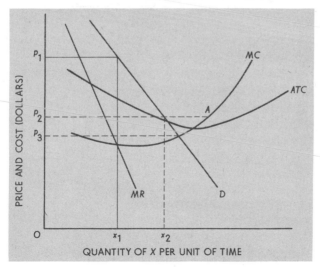

fore, at any ceiling between Op_1 and Op_2, the firm sells the quantity given by the actual demand curve at that price; at any ceiling below Op_2 the firm eventually shuts down.

8.7.b—Taxation

An alternative method of monopoly regulation is some type of special taxation. We examine here the effects of three common types: the excise or per unit tax, the lump-sum tax, and the percentage of profits tax.

FIGURE 8.6.3

Effects of an Excise Tax under Monopoly

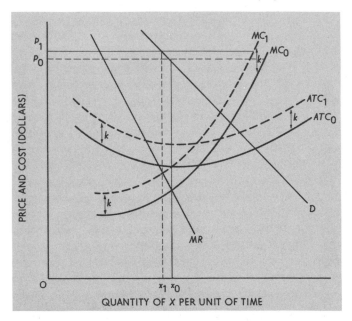

An excise or per unit tax means that for every unit sold, regardless of price, the monopolist must pay a specified amount of money to the government. Assume that the monopolist, whose cost curves ATC_0 and MC_0 are shown in Figure 8.6.3, is charged a tax of k dollars for every unit sold. Total cost after the tax is the total cost of *production* (presumably the same as before) plus k times output; thus average or unit cost must rise by exactly the amount of the tax, k dollars. The after-tax ATC in Figure 8.6.3 rises from ATC_0 to ATC_1, or by the vertical distance k. MC also rises by k dollars. If it costs MC_0 to produce and sell an additional unit of output before the tax, after the tax it costs $MC_0 + k = MC_1$ to produce and sell that unit. This also is shown in Figure 8.6.3.

Before the tax is imposed the monopolist produces Ox_0 and charges a price of Op_0. After the imposition of the tax, the cost curves shift vertically by the amount k to ATC_1 and MC_1. MC_1 now equals MR at the output Ox_1, so price rises to Op_1. This effect, of course, differs completely from the effect of the ceiling price that causes price to fall and quantity to rise.

Note that the firm absorbs some of the tax and shifts some to the consumers in the form of higher prices. The proportion shifted depends upon the slope of marginal cost and the slope of demand. We can extend the horizontal lines from p_1 and p_0 to the MC curves to see the proportion of k that is shifted. This shows the difference between p_0 and p_1, the amount of the tax shifted, as a fraction of the tax k.

A lump-sum tax has a somewhat different effect upon price and quantity. Assume that instead of imposing an excise tax on the monopolist, the government charges (say) a license fee that remains the same regardless of quantity sold. The license fee is, therefore, a fixed cost to the monopolist. ATC rises after the fee is imposed; at very small outputs ATC rises more than at larger outputs because the larger the output the more units the fee is "spread over." Once the fee is paid, however, no additional tax is charged for an additional unit of production per period. MC, therefore, remains unchanged. Since MC and MR do not change after the lump-sum tax, their point of intersection does not change, and thus price and quantity remain the same after the tax is imposed. The lump-sum tax, which does reduce profits, must not, of course, be so large as to cause a loss and drive the monopolist out of business.

A percentage of profit tax, just as the lump-sum tax, does not affect quantity or price. Assume that a monopolist must pay π percent of his profit (regardless of the profit) as a tax. Since π is presumably between 0 and 100, the monopolist retains $(100 - \pi)$ percent of his profits after paying the tax. Revenue and cost curves remain the same. Before the tax is imposed the monopolist chooses price and quantity so as to maximize profit. After the tax he still chooses the same price and quantity so as to maximize his before tax profit, since he obviously prefers $(100 - \pi)$ percent of the maximum profit to $(100 - \pi)$ percent of some smaller amount.

Tax regulation, therefore, differs from price regulation in several ways even though profits are reduced in all cases. In particular, taxation, in contrast to some price ceilings, cannot force the monopolist to set price equal to marginal cost.

QUESTIONS AND PROBLEMS

1. We have stated in this chapter that the monopolist does not have a supply curve. Explain! (Hint: What is the definition of supply? Under some circumstances could one price be the minimum necessary to induce him to supply a specific quantity, while under other conditions, not involving cost changes, a lower price would induce him to supply that amount?)

2. Some time ago, most of the major airlines issued student travel cards at a nominal price. These cards permit college students to fly "space available" (i.e., no reservations allowed) at substantial discounts. All but one of these lines are now wondering whether this strategy has really paid off; older nonstudents have been found using the cards, and some students have been insuring themselves available space by reserving seats for fictitious passengers who then do not show up for the flight.

   a) Do the discounts represent price discrimination?

   b) Do the conditions necessary for successful discrimination exist?

3. From 1923 to 1946, Du Pont was virtually the sole American producer of "moistureproof Cellophane," a product for which it held the key patents. In an opinion which exonerated Du Pont of possessing any economically meaningful monopoly, the Supreme Court held "an appraisal of the 'cross-elasticity' of demand in the trade" to be of considerable importance to the decision. Why?

4. Derive the marginal revenue curve for a demand curve concave from above.

9

Theories of Price
under Imperfect Competition

9.1 INTRODUCTION

Between the extremes of perfect competition and monopoly come a large number of theoretical market structures, none of which lends itself to the rigorous analysis of Chapters 7 and 8. For convenience, we classify all these "intermediate" market structures into two categories: monopolistic competition and oligopoly. Many of the theories of markets in these classifications were developed during the late 1920's and early 1930's because of the reaction to the theories of perfect competition and monopoly. Many economists, after pointing out that the two "extremes" are not accurate pictures of the real world, turned their attention to the middle ground between monopoly and perfect competition.

We first present the theory of monopolistic competition; second, discuss some oligopoly models; third, indicate reasons why some industries are not competitive; and fourth, analyze some effects of attempting to get more "realism" into the theory of the firm. Although we do not dwell upon the matter, it should become obvious that most real world problems can be analyzed within the context of the competition or monopoly model.

9.2 FUNDAMENTALS OF MONOPOLISTIC COMPETITION

One of the most notable achievements of economists who examined the middle ground between competition and monopoly was that of an American economist, Edward Chamberlin. Our attention is directed first to his theory of monopolistic competition.[1]

---

[1] E. H. Chamberlin, *The Theory of Monopolistic Competition* (Cambridge, Mass.: Harvard University Press, 1933).

Chamberlin based his theory of monopolistic competition on a solid empirical fact: there are very few monopolies because there are very few commodities for which close substitutes do not exist; similarly there are very few commodities that are entirely homogeneous. Instead, there is a wide range of commodities, some of which have relatively few good substitutes and some of which have many good, but not perfect, substitutes.

For example, one often speaks of an "automobile industry," knowing full well that automobiles are not a homogeneous product. A Ford is a substitute, albeit not a perfect substitute, for a Cadillac. Fords are perhaps better substitutes for Chevrolets; but, in fact, even a Ford Falcon is not a perfect substitute for a "deluxe" Ford, and the latter is not a perfect substitute for a Thunderbird. Each automobile firm has an absolute monopoly over its own brands of cars; but the various brands are, in greater or lesser degree, substitutes. There is intense *personal* competition or rivalry among the firms. Now consider a case at the other extreme. Haircuts from Sam's Barber Shop are closely related to haircuts from Joe's Barber Shop across the street. They are not the same product, however; one shop has a monopoly on "haircuts from Sam's," the other a monopoly on "haircuts from Joe's." At the same price some prefer to get haircuts from Sam, some from Joe.

In these, and in a multitude of other cases, the products are *heterogeneous* rather than homogeneous; hence perfect, and impersonal, competition cannot exist. Second, although heterogeneous, the products are only slightly differentiated. Each is a very close substitute for the other; hence competition exists, but it is a personal competition among rivals who are well aware of each other.

When products are closely related but heterogeneous, one cannot speak of an industry, which is defined as a collection of firms producing a homogeneous good. Nonetheless, it is useful to lump together firms producing very closely related commodities and refer to them as a *product group*. Each producer in the product group has some degree of monopoly power; but not much because other producers market a differentiated but closely related commodity.[2]

9.3   SHORT-RUN EQUILIBRIUM: MONOPOLY ASPECT OF MONOPOLISTIC COMPETITION

The theory of monopolistic competition is essentially a long-run theory. In the short run there is virtually no difference between the analysis of monopoly and of monopolistic competition. Each producer of a differentiated product behaves so as to maximize profit. If he knows his demand

---

[2] At our level of abstraction it is not necessary to specify how closely products must be related in order to be in the same product group.

FIGURE 9.3.1

**Short-Run Equilibrium of the Firm
under Monopolistic Competition**

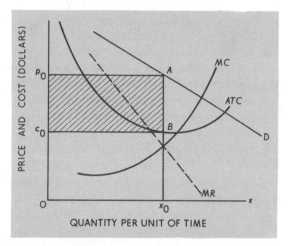

and marginal revenue curves, as in Figure 9.3.1, he equates marginal cost with marginal revenue. In the specific example of the figure, this leads to an output of Ox_0 units per period and a price of Op_0 per unit. In the resulting short-run equilibrium, pure profit is represented by the area of the shaded rectangle p_0ABc_0.

So far as the short run is concerned there appears to be very little *competition* in monopolistic competition. But when a longer view is taken one essential element of monopoly is missing. In particular, a monopoly cannot be maintained if there is free entry. Other firms will enter and produce the homogeneous product; and they will continue to enter until all pure profit is eliminated or until the competitive solution is reached.

In the present case the product is differentiated, not homogeneous, so there is no industry to enter. But other firms are free to produce a closely related product; entrance into the product group is not closed. If one or a few firms are obviously enjoying a highly prosperous situation, other firms will begin to produce a closely related product. They will "enter" the product group, as it were, and their entrance will have market repercussions not greatly different from the entrance of perfectly competitive firms into an industry.

9.4 LONG-RUN EQUILIBRIUM: COMPETITIVE ASPECTS OF MONOPOLISTIC COMPETITION

To follow Chamberlin's development of the theory of monopolistic competition it is necessary to distinguish between two types of demand curves. This is developed in the following subsection, after which we turn to the theory of long-run equilibrium under price and nonprice competition.

9.4.a—Two Demand Curves

In the analysis of perfect competition two demand curves were used: the negatively sloped industry demand curve and the horizontal demand curve confronting each seller. As you will recall, the latter is horizontal because each producer of the *homogeneous product* must accept the going price or sell nothing at all. If he were to raise his price he would

FIGURE 9.4.1

Two Demand Curves

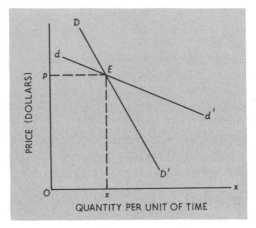

forfeit all sales. If he were to lower it, he would needlessly forfeit some revenue.

The two curves required for the theory of monopolistic competition, shown in Figure 9.4.1, are very similar. Suppose the firm in question attains an instantaneous equilibrium at the point E, with output Ox per period and price Op. Suppose further that the entrepreneur contemplates price maneuvering in order to obtain greater profit.

One of Chamberlin's fundamental assumptions is that a large group of monopolistic competitors exists in each product group. Another is that all firms in the group produce closely related and readily substitutable goods. Hence if the entrepreneur contemplates a price reduction from Op, he will expect a substantial expansion in sales. First, sales to his existing clientele will expand. Second, and more important, if other entrepreneurs do not reduce price he will capture a part of their markets. Thus, he can expect an appreciable expansion of sales.

On the other hand, he can expect a substantial loss in sales if he increases his price. Not only will sales to existing customers decline but some of his customers will switch to other producers who have not raised their prices. Consequently, assuming such a large number of sellers in the market that each expects his actions to go unnoticed by his rivals, every entrepreneur will expect his demand curve to be very elastic. The entrepreneur's expected or anticipated demand curve is shown by the relatively elastic curve *dd'* in Figure 9.4.1.

Anticipating highly elastic demand, each entrepreneur has an incentive to reduce price; and thus *all* entrepreneurs have this incentive. But if all prices are reduced simultaneously, each entrepreneur will gain only that increment in sales attributable to the general price reduction. He will not capture portions of his rivals' markets. Thus if the actions of one entrepreneur are matched by all other entrepreneurs in the product group, demand will in fact be far less elastic, such as the curve *DD'* in Figure 9.4.1. In other words, *DD'* is the curve showing the quantity demanded from any one seller at various prices under the assumption that his competitors' prices are always identical with his.

Relations: The curve *dd'* shows the increased sales any entrepreneur can expect to enjoy by lowering his price, providing all other entrepreneurs maintain their original prices. *DD'*, on the other hand, shows the actual sales to be gained as a general downward movement of prices takes place.

9.4.b—Summary of Assumptions

All Chamberlin's specializing assumptions have been discussed or implied, yet it may be well to recount them now. First, many firms produce a differentiated product. Each commodity within the product group is a close substitute for every other commodity; and such a large number of sellers is in the product group that each expects his competitive maneuvering to go unnoticed by his rivals. Second, for the present, price is the variable entrepreneurs manipulate in an effort to increase profit. Finally, as Chamberlin puts it, there is the "heroic assumption that both demand and cost curves for all the 'products' are uniform throughout the group. . [This only requires] that consumers' preferences be evenly distributed among the different varieties, and that differences between them [the products] be not such as to give rise to differences in cost."[3]

The last assumption merits further comment. In perfect competition all products are homogeneous. Thus it is not unreasonable to assume identical costs of production for all entrepreneurs in the industry—an assumption that greatly facilitates analysis because it permits long-run

---

[3] *Op. cit.*, pp. 82–83.

industry equilibrium to be explained by means of a graph pertaining to only one firm. This is precisely the purpose of the assumption under discussion; but it is clearly more restrictive than in perfect competition. Basically one assumes product differences are not so great as to entail cost differences. Different scents for toilet soaps, slightly different tobacco blends, differences in the color of packaging material, and differences in the collar style of men's shirts are but a few examples of product differences that would give rise to little, if any, difference in cost. Yet the assumption is quite restrictive since *marked* quality differences (Volkswagen vis-à-vis Cadillac) are generally precluded.

9.4.c—Large Group, Long-Run Equilibrium with Price Competition

With these assumptions and analytical tools in hand we can proceed immediately to the analysis of long-run equilibrium in the large group case with price competition. The analysis is first restricted to the situation in which the "proper" or "optimal" number of firms is already in the product group.

In Figure 9.4.2 DD' and dd' (solid) give the two demand curves discussed in section 9.4.a above; LAC is the long-run average cost curve for the "typical" firm in question. We assume an initial (short-run) equilibrium attained at point A, with output Ox_1 and price Op_1; short-run pure profit is represented by the area of the shaded rectangle p_1ABc. Each entrepreneur, regarding dd' as his demand curve, realizes he can increase profit by reducing price and expanding output (according to the elastic

FIGURE 9.4.2

**Long-Run Equilibrium When Optimal Number
of Firms Already Exists**

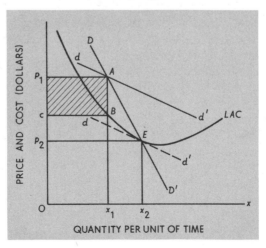

QUANTITY PER UNIT OF TIME

dd'). Hence each reduces price. But instead of expanding along *dd'*, each in fact moves along *DD'*. In Chamberlin's terms, *dd'* slides downward along *DD'*.

Despite the frustration of their initial plans, entrepreneurs hold firm in their belief that *dd'* represents their demand curve. Hence they continue to reduce price in an effort to augment profit; and *dd'* continues to slide downward along *DD'*. Indeed, it must continue its downward movement until it comes to point *E*, where it is shown as the dashed curve. Of course, *dd'* might fall below the dashed line position; all entrepreneurs would then incur a pure loss and price would be raised, shifting *dd'* upward.

The position of long-run equilibrium is *E*, where *dd'* is tangent to *LAC*. Each firm, while having a monopoly of its own "product," is forced to a zero profit position by the competition of rivals producing readily substitutable goods. The reasoning process is as follows:

Proposition: Large group, long-run equilibrium under price competition in a monopolistically competitive product group is attained when the anticipated demand curve (*dd'*) is tangent to the long-run unit cost curve. If *dd'* lies above *LAC*, each entrepreneur believes he can increase profit by reducing price; if *dd'* is below *LAC*, price must be increased to eliminate the pure loss incurred.

Certain questions concerning this equilibrium solution may have been raised in the reader's mind. The first concerns the intersection of anticipated marginal revenue (associated with dashed *dd'*) and marginal cost at the point of tangency between demand and average cost. Would the intersection and the tangency necessarily occur at exactly the same output? If they do not, the profit maximizing entrepreneur would change his output level. This problem can be solved rather easily. As we have shown several times, maximum profit requires $MC = MR$. Since $P = LAC$ at the tangency output, that output gives zero profit. Since *LAC* is concave from above (it lies above its tangent at all neighborhood points), *LAC* is greater than demand at all other points and negative profit results. The zero profit solution is the maximum profit solution; hence *MC* must equal what the entrepreneur *believes* his *MR* to be at the tangency output. Or we might analyze the problem in another way. Since *LAC* lies above anticipated demand at every output other than tangency output Ox_2, total cost lies above total revenue at all outputs except Ox_2, where they are equal. Thus the two total curves must be tangent (their slopes are equal) at Ox_2, and marginal cost must equal marginal revenue at the output corresponding to tangency between demand and average cost.

One might also ask what happens if the anticipated demand curve *dd'* does not have precisely the right slope so as to be tangent to *LAC* at the point where *DD'* cuts *LAC*. Explaining the long-run equilibrium

FIGURE 9.4.3

Long-Run Equilibrium with Entry of Firms

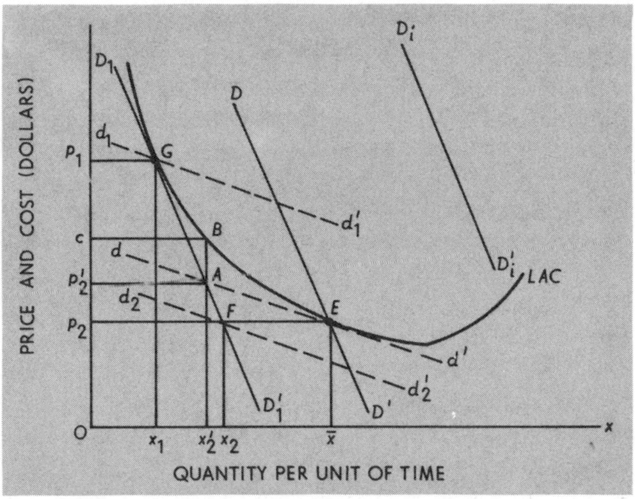

QUANTITY PER UNIT OF TIME

adjustment when there is entry of new firms helps to provide an answer.

Consider Figure 9.4.3, in which D_iD_i' is the initial demand curve and LAC is the long-run average cost curve. The firm in question, and any other in the product group, reaps a very substantial pure profit. Since entry into the product group is open, new firms selling slightly differentiated products are attracted. The greater variety of available products causes the demand for each seller's product to contract. In the process, DD' shifts to the left and probably becomes somewhat more elastic. Simultaneously, if entrepreneurs experiment with price policy, dd' slides down the instantaneously existing DD' and also probably becomes somewhat more elastic.

The transition from the initial D_iD_i' curve to the ultimate long-run equilibrium at point E could come about in a number of ways. One method is illustrated in Figure 9.4.3, where it is assumed that new firms enter the product group until the proportional demand curve shifts from D_iD_i' to D_1D_1'. It might seem that equilibrium is attained at G, with output of Ox_1 and price Op_1 per unit, inasmuch as pure profit is zero at that point. However, each entrepreneur thinks d_1d_1' is his demand curve. A reduction in price would, in his belief, cause an expansion along d_1d_1'; profit would accordingly expand. But each entrepreneur has the same incentive; so as price is reduced by all, dd' slides down D_1D_1' for each.

The only way that G could be a point of long-run equilibrium is for the market *not* to be characterized by active price competition. A "live and let live" outlook on the part of sellers, tacit agreements, open price associations, price maintenance, customary prices, and professional ethics are a few causes of nonagressive price policies. If price competition is, in fact, lacking, individual entrepreneurs will have no regard for the existence of curves such as d_1d_1'. They will be concerned only with the effects of a general price rise or decline, or with the DD' curve. Pure profit is eliminated when enough firms have entered to push demand to D_1D_1'; the firm, ignoring d_1d_1', produces Ox_1 and sells at Op_1, which is a higher price and lower quantity than those forthcoming under active price competition.

Suppose now that price has fallen to Op_2', with output per period Ox_2'. Each firm incurs a pure loss represented by the area of the rectangle $cBAp_2'$. It might seem that each firm could eliminate its pure loss by reducing price to Op_2 and moving to point E. Yet with the number of firms giving rise to D_1D_1', a reduction in price to Op_2 would shift the subjective demand curve further down D_1D_1', to the position d_2d_2'. Temporary equilibrium would be attained at F, with sales of Ox_2 rather than $O\bar{x}$ per firm. The situation is necessarily transitory, however, since each firm incurs a pure loss at F. Ultimately some firms must leave the product group; and there is an incentive to do so. As firms leave the group the proportional demand curve shifts to the right, together with the anticipated demand curve; and both probably become somewhat less elastic. The exit of firms must continue until the proportional curve becomes DD' and the anticipated curve dd'. Long-run equilibrium is attained at E, with the identical long-run conditions detailed above. At this point of long-run equilibrium, as before, dd' must be tangent to LAC; otherwise each entrepreneur would believe that a change in his price-output policy could augment profit; thus an equilibrium could not exist.

9.5 COMPARISONS OF LONG-RUN EQUILIBRIA

A comparison of long-run equilibria is rather difficult inasmuch as it must rest essentially upon statements pertaining to cost curves. Conditions giving rise to monopoly probably lead to noncomparable differences between competitive and monopolistic costs; for similar reasons, noncomparability is also likely between either of these two and monopolistic competition. However, a few generalizations are possible if one bears in mind that the statements are *relative*, not absolute.

9.5.a—Equilibrium in the Firm

For emphasis, it may be well to recount the "competitive" and "monopolistic" aspects of monopolistic competition. A monopolistically competitive firm is like a monopoly in that it faces negatively sloped demand and marginal revenue curves; it therefore determines its price-output policy by equating marginal cost with marginal revenue rather than with price, as in perfect competition. At the same time, the monopolistically competitive firm is like a perfectly competitive one in that it faces impersonal market competition. The long-run result is the absence of pure profit, just as in the competitive case. While all three types may enjoy economic profit in the short run, freedom of entry eliminates it in the long run, except under conditions of pure monopoly. The qualitative nature of rivalry is also different. In perfect competition rivalry is completely impersonal. At the opposite extreme, there is no direct (only indirect and potential) rivalry under monopoly. The case of monopolistic competition is somewhat different, but it lies closer to perfect competition. The monopolistic competitor, at least in abstract, is aware of the slightly differentiated, highly substitutable products of other firms. There would be personal rivalry except for the condition of large numbers—so large that each entrepreneur believes his actions will go unnoticed by his competitors (because they are so numerous that his actions will not have a readily perceptible effect upon any one of them).

9.5.b—Long-Run Equilibria in Industries and Product Groups

In long-run competitive equilibrium, total industry output is produced in a group of plants each of which operates at (long-run) minimum average cost. The product is sold at a price equal to minimum average cost and, it is significant to note, long-run marginal cost equals both price and average cost at this point.

Under monopoly the long-run equilibrium situation is substantially different. The industry output is produced by one firm. The monopolist's plant is unlikely to be of such size as to produce at (long-run) minimum average cost. In any case, price will not equal minimum average cost or marginal cost. Indeed, price will exceed both, so that in long-run equilibrium the marginal social valuation of the commodity exceeds the marginal cost of its production.

In the competitive case, each firm operates a plant to produce the quantity associated with minimum long-run average cost and that size plant and output is called by some "ideal" plant size and "ideal" output. When production of the quantity associated with minimum long-run average cost occurs, the industry's output is sometimes referred to as "ideal." Excess capacity, defined as the difference between actual output and the output associated with minimum long-run average cost, does not exist in long-run equilibrium under perfect competition.

Monopolistic competition is somewhat more difficult to analyze in these terms. In large-group equilibrium with active price competition, price is above marginal cost, although price equals average cost. Since demand is negatively sloped, tangency must occur where average cost is negatively sloped. Therefore, price equals average cost at a point above minimum average cost and at a lower rate of output than that associated with minimum long-run average cost. The difference is excess capacity. In long-run equilibrium under monopolistic competition, each firm has excess capacity.

Some economists, however, argue that the difference is the "cost" society pays for product differentiation and that it is a valid social cost. They then argue that although actual average cost exceeds minimum average cost, when *all* relevant social costs (including the cost of heterogeneity) are included, the firm produces at minimum attainable average cost. Each firm, and the product group as a whole, produces the "sort of ideal" output, and excess capacity does not appear in long-run equilibrium. This argument, however, is *not* universally accepted.

In short, the social welfare aspects of monopolistic competition are ambiguous. From a very microscopic standpoint, each firm produces less than the socially optimal output. On the other hand, if each firm were somehow forced to produce this seemingly desirable level of output at a marginal cost price, private enterprise would no longer represent a viable economic system. Thus the abolition of private enterprise would violate a social welfare criterion (existence of private property rights) that transcends microeconomic considerations, at least in the United States and most industrially advanced western nations. Thus while the theoretical analysis of monopolistic competition is quite clear, the welfare implications of this analysis are not. Micro- and macroeconomic welfare criteria are not consistent or reconcilable. The economist *qua* economist can only indicate the dilemma; establishing definitive social goals and welfare standards is beyond his professional capacity.

9.5.c—Conclusion

During the early stages of its development, the theory of monopolistic competition excited the imaginations of economists, largely because they regarded it as a more *realistic* abstraction from the real world. The anticipated usefulness of the model, however, far exceeded its actual usefulness as an analytical tool or as a framework for developing economic policy

The assumptions may *in part* be more realistic than those of the competitive and monopoly models. For example, it may be more realistic to assume product heterogeneity with close substitutability than to assume either homogeneity or no close substitutability. On the other hand, some of the assumptions of the theory of monopolistic competition are very unrealistic. For example, but also in particular, it is unrealistic to assume that intelligent entrepreneurs believe their price changes go unnoticed when they daily observe that competitors match their price changes.

More important, as stressed in Chapter 1, the relevance of the conclusions—not the realism of the assumptions—is what counts. On this score the competitive and monopoly models are clearly superior. The theory of monopolistic competition is much less useful than the competitive and monopolistic models for analyzing real world markets. But even more can be said. The theory of monopolistic competition does not actually provide a particularly realistic description of real world markets. Therefore, one should not take this theory as a prototype of such markets. It is simply an attempt, although not a particularly successful one, to add more realism to the theory of the firm.

Our reason for devoting so much space to the theory of monopolistic competition is to illustrate the problems involved whenever one attempts to gain realism at the expense of rigorous but simple analysis. It is important to understand the theory of monopolistic competition in order more fully to appreciate the theories of competition and monopoly as analytical devices.

9.6 OLIGOPOLY

Oligopoly, or its limiting form duopoly, is a market situation intermediate between the cases previously studied. In monopoly only one seller is in the market; competition, in either the technical or the popular sense, does not exist. Perfect competition and large-group monopolistic competition represent the opposite. So many firms are in the market that the actions of each are thought to be imperceptible to the others. There is competition in the technical sense, but little or none in the popular sense. The reverse tends to be true in oligopoly; technically, competition is lacking but sometimes there is intense rivalry or competition in the popular sense.

Oligopoly is said to exist when more than one seller is in the market, but when the number is not so large as to render negligible the contribution of each. A market has few enough sellers to be considered oligopolistic if the firms recognize their *mutual interdependence*. In monopoly and competition, firms make decisions and take action without considering how these actions will affect other firms and how, in turn, other firms' reactions will affect them. Oligopolists must take these reactions into account in their decision-making process.

When contemplating a price change, a design innovation, a new advertising campaign, and so on, Ford Motor Company must anticipate how GM and the Chrysler Corporation will react because, without doubt, Ford's actions will affect the demand for Chevrolets and Plymouths.

This, in short, is the oligopoly problem and the central problem in oligopoly analysis. The oligopolistic firm is large enough to recognize (a) the mutual interdependence of the firms in the oligopoly and (b) the fact that its decisions will affect the other firms who in turn will react in a way that affects the initial firm. The great uncertainty is *how one's competitors will react.*

Since so many industries meet the general description of oligopoly, it would at first glance seem that a general theory of oligopoly would have been developed. The problem in developing an oligopoly theory, however, is the same as the oligopoly problem itself. Mutual interdependence and the resulting uncertainty about reaction patterns make it necessary for the economist to make specific assumptions about behavioral patterns, i.e., specific assumptions about how oligopolists *believe* their competitors will react and about how their competitors actually react.

Therefore, as we shall see, the solution to the oligopoly model (i.e., equilibrium price and output) depends critically upon the assumptions the economist makes in regard to the behavioral reaction of rival entrepreneurs. Since many different assumptions can and have been made, many different solutions can and have been reached. Thus there is no "theory of oligopoly" in the sense that there is a theory of perfect competition or of monopoly. There is, that is, no unique, general solution, but merely many different behavioral models, each of which reaches a different solution. Further, none of these models gives a reasonably realistic account of any *one* oligopolistic industry, so no general result can be expected.

A brief discussion of a few of the classical models of oligopoly should highlight some of the problems involved in the attempt to gain realism at the expense of generality. The discussion of these models is intended simply to illustrate the problem of "realism v. generality," not to present a thorough analysis of the models (or, for that matter, to present all the classical models). Except for game-theory models and the Hotelling Case, little credence is today accorded the solutions set forth in this section. Most of the models described were formulated for duopoly (in which there are only two sellers), but they apply to oligopoly as well.

Formal speculation about the duopoly problem is sometimes dated from the work of a French economist, A. A. Cournot, in 1838. He assumed that two duopolists own two mineral springs; they are situated side by side and furnish identical mineral water. There is a cost of sinking the well, but after sinking the well the added cost of selling a cup of water is zero. Therefore, marginal cost is zero at every level of output. Each duopolist believes that the other will not change the *quantity* he sells regardless of what he himself does. Given these assumptions, after many changes in price and output, each duopolist sells one third the output at which marginal cost (zero) equals price (that is, the output at which demand crosses the horizontal axis). Price is lower, total output greater, and profits lower than under monopoly. Price is higher, total output is lower, and profits higher than under perfect competition. This is one solution, but it is based on a rather naïve assumption: each entrepreneur believes his rival will never change his volume of sales, even though he repeatedly observes such changes.

The next solution was developed by an English economist, F. Y. Edgeworth, in 1897. The two firms in the Edgeworth Case are the same as those posited by Cournot; they sell a homogeneous product, are situated side by side, and have zero marginal costs. The only change is that each entrepreneur believes his competitor's *price* will remain constant. Under this assumption an equilibrium price and quantity cannot result. Both fluctuate continually, and so the solution is indeterminant.

The Edgeworth solution improves upon Cournot's analysis because *price* rather than *output* is the relevant decision variable for the entrepreneur. Yet in Edgeworth's model, the result of using price as the decision variable is to introduce indeterminacy. Empirically, duopoly and oligopoly markets tend to be relatively stable. To be sure, occasional price wars occur; but typically prices fluctuate very seldom in these markets. To explain stability in duopoly and oligopoly markets, Harold Hotelling, in 1929, constructed a model that has become famous for its far-reaching significance.

In Hotelling's model two entrepreneurs produce a physically identical product at zero marginal cost. However, the products of the duopolists are differentiated in the eyes of the buyers because of locational differences. Buyers are located uniformly along a straight road. At the same price each buyer purchases from the closer duopolist. Each duopolist is motivated to move as close as possible to the other. They end up locating side by side at the middle of the road. Price and location are stable; and this tends to explain why theaters locate along Broadway and why the Methodists and Baptists are so much alike.

Somewhat later Chamberlin proposed a stable duopoly solution that depends upon mutual recognition of interdependence. Chamberlin's case is exactly that of Cournot except for one assumption and the final result. Chamberlin assumes that the duopolists mutually recognize that the best they can do is to produce the monopoly output and sell it at the monopoly price; they divide the maximum monopoly profit, perhaps each taking half. In Chamberlin's solution, each entrepreneur understands that his actions affect the other and acts accordingly; Chamberlin obtains a stable solution that may not be too far from reality in homogeneous oligopoly situations. However, this is a case of tacit collusion (see following section).

Another model of stable oligopoly price that was at one time popular is the "kinked demand curve hypothesis" of Paul Sweezy. In this model the oligopolist believes that if he raises his price his competitors will not change their prices. He therefore would lose a large volume of sales if he raises price. On the other hand, he believes that if he lowers his price his competitors will lower their prices also. He would therefore gain very little by a price cut. He has little incentive either to raise or to lower price. If all oligopolists believe likewise, a stable price results. The major question in regard to this model is why price happens to be what it is in the first place. The kinked demand theory does not explain how the interaction of demand and cost establishes a unique price-quantity equilibrium; but it rationalizes price ex post. However, the object of price theories is to *explain* how a price gets set, not why it does not change.

The last solution to be examined in this section is the application of game theory to oligopoly behavior developed by John von Neumann and Oskar Morgenstern. Their solution requires oligopolists to behave as though they were participants in some game of chance. Each business strategy is a move in the game. The heart of game theory is the minimax principle; and there is much criticism of application of this principle to decision making in economics and business. Essentially, the minimax principle requires each player with a given set of decision possibilities to maximize his profit under the assumption that his rival always takes the least desirable course of action from the former's standpoint. Slightly less precisely, the minimax principle requires the player (or entrepreneur) to adopt the plan of action that will make the *best* of the *worst* possible situation. But this plan of action will not be the *best* if the *worst* possible situation does not arise. It does not allow the entrepreneur to exploit favorable changes in the market or, in any sense, to be "dynamic."

In the real world, of which this is supposed to be a description, it appears that many entrepreneurs attempt to maximize profit under the assumption that very favorable conditions will prevail. And, of course, they generally expend considerable effort to influence the market so as to make the assumption correct. On a more theoretical level, game theory requires more information than is likely to be available. In theoretical economics it seems that the successful application of game theory must await further refinements if, indeed, it can be achieved at all.[4]

9.7   SOME "MARKET" SOLUTIONS TO THE DUOPOLY PROBLEM

The classical treatments of duopoly, with the exception of Chamberlin's model and a few others, are based upon the assumption that entrepreneurs act independently of one another even though they are interdependent in the market. We turn now to some theories based upon explicit or implicit collusion among firms. We should note that so far we have excluded the possibility of collusive behavior not only in this chapter but in Chapters 7 and 8 as well. The reason is that collusive behavior is illegal

---

[4] For more complete analyses of the models mentioned in this section and the sources of these models see C. E. Ferguson, *Microeconomic Theory* (rev. ed.; Homewood, Ill.: Richard D. Irwin, Inc., 1969).

according to the Sherman Act and other legislation and court decisions. However, antitrust litigation still flourishes; so oligopolists must in fact recognize their mutual interdependence.

9.7.a—Cartels and Profit Maximization

A *cartel* is a combination of firms whose objective is to limit the competitive forces within a market. It may take the form of open collusion, the member firms entering into an enforceable contract pertaining to price and other market variables. This is perhaps best illustrated by the German *Kartelle;* but the NRA codes of our Great Depression years fall into this category as well. On the other hand, a cartel may be formed by secret collusion among sellers; many examples of this exist in American economic history. Most tend to date to the early years of the 20th century; but at the time of this writing the Federal Trade Commission has pending an action against a group of paperboard manufacturers, charging them with collusive price fixing—that is, with forming an illegal cartel. And in academic administrative circles, the American Economic Association is charged with having a cartel that sets exorbitant prices for the services of new Ph.D. recipients.

The cases of open and secret collusion offer the best examples of cartels. However, in a broad sense trade associations, professional organizations, and the like perform many functions usually associated with a cartel. Of the wide variety of services a cartel may perform for its members, two are of central importance: price fixing and market sharing. In this section, we will examine price fixing in an "ideal" cartel.

Suppose a group of firms producing a homogeneous commodity forms a cartel. A central management body is appointed, its function being to determine the uniform cartel price. The task, in theory, is relatively simple, as illustrated by Figure 9.7.1. Market demand for the homogeneous commodity is given by DD', so marginal revenue is given by the dashed line MR. The cartel marginal cost curve must be determined by the management body. If all firms in the cartel purchase all inputs in perfectly competitive markets, the cartel marginal cost curve (MC_c) is simply the horizontal sum of the marginal cost curves of the member firms. Otherwise, allowance must be made for the increase in input price accompanying an increase in input usage; MC_c will stand further to the left than it would if all input markets were perfectly competitive.

In either case the management group determines cartel marginal cost MC_c. The problem is the simple one of determining the price that maximizes cartel profit—the monopoly price. From Figure 9.7.1 marginal cost and marginal revenue intersect at the level $OA;$ thus the market price Op is the one the cartel management will establish. Given the demand curve DD', buyers will purchase Ox units from the members of the cartel. The

FIGURE 9.7.1

Cartel Profit Maximization

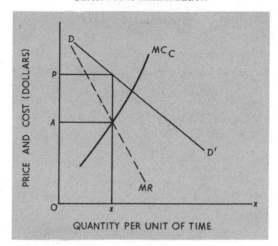

second important problem confronting the cartel management is *how* to distribute the total sales of *Ox* units among the member firms.

9.7.b—Cartels and Market Sharing

Fundamentally there are two methods of sales allocation: nonprice competition and quotas. The former is usually associated with "loose" cartels. A uniform price is fixed and each firm is allowed to sell all it can at that price. The only requirement is that firms do not reduce price below the cartel price. There are many examples of this type of cartel organization in the United States today. For instance, in most localities both medical doctors and lawyers have associations whose code of ethics is frequently the basis of price agreement. All doctors, for example, charge the same rate for office and house calls. The patient market is divided among the various doctors by nonprice competition: each patient selects the doctor of his choice. Similarly, the generally uniform prices of haircuts, major brands of gasoline, and movie tickets do not result from perfect competition within the market. Rather, they result from tacit, and sometimes open, agreement upon a price; the sellers compete with one another but *not* by price variations.

The so-called fair trade laws of many states establish loose, but very legal, cartels. Under these laws the manufacturer of a commodity may set its retail price. The retail sellers of the commodity (the sometimes reluctant members of the cartel) are forbidden by law to charge a lower price. The various retailers compete for sales by advertising, customer credit policies, repair and maintenance services, delivery, and such. But price is not a variable in the market.

The second method of market sharing is the *quota* system, of which there are several variants. Indeed, there is no uniform principle by which quotas can be determined. In practice, the bargaining ability of a firm's representative and the importance of the firm to the cartel are likely to be the most important elements in determining a quota. Beyond this are two popular methods. The first of these has a statistical base, either the relative sales of the firm in some precartel base period or the "productive capacity" of the firm. As a practical matter, the choice of base period or of the measure of capacity is a matter of bargaining among the members. Thus the most skillful bargainer is likely to come out best.

The second popular basis for the quota system is geographical division of the market. Some of the more dramatic illustrations involve international markets. For example, an agreement between Du Pont and Imperial Chemicals divided the market for certain products so that the former had exclusive sales rights in North and Central America (except for British possessions) and the latter had exclusive rights in the British Empire and Egypt. Another example is an agreement between the American company Röhm and Haas and its German counterpart Roehm und Haas. The former was given exclusive rights in North, Central, and South America, and in Australia, New Zealand, and Japan; the latter was given Europe and Asia, except for Japan. These illustrations can be multiplied many times over, but they should serve to indicate the quota by geographical division.

While quota agreement is quite difficult in practice, in theory some guidelines can be laid down. Consider the "ideal" cartel represented by Figure 9.7.1. A reasonable criterion for the management group would be "minimize total cartel cost." Minimum cartel cost is achieved when each firm produces the rate of output for which its marginal cost equals the common cartel marginal cost and marginal revenue. Thus each firm would produce the amount for which its marginal cost is OA (Figure 9.7.1); by the summing process to obtain MC_c, total cartel output will be Ox. The difficulty involved with this method is that the lower cost firms obtain the bulk of the market and the bulk of profits. To make this method of allocation acceptable to all members, a profit sharing system more or less independent of sales quota must be devised.

In certain cases the member firms may be able to agree upon the share of the market each is to have. This is illustrated in Figure 9.7.2 for an "ideal" situation. Suppose only two firms are in the market and they decide to divide the market evenly. The market demand curve is DD', so the half-share curve for each firm is Dd. The curve marginal to Dd is the dashed line MR, the half-share marginal revenue for each firm. Suppose each firm has identical costs, represented by SAC and SMC. Each will

FIGURE 9.7.2

Ideal Market Sharing in a Cartel

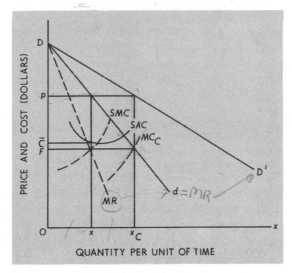

QUANTITY PER UNIT OF TIME

decide to produce Ox units with price Op corresponding to the intersection of MC and MR. A uniform price of Op is established and $Ox_c = 2\,Ox$ units are supplied. This happens, in our special case, to be a tenable solution because the market demand curve is consistent with the sale of Ox_c units at the price Op.

To see this, let us go the other way around. Suppose a cartel management group is formed and given the task of maximizing cartel profit. With the demand curve DD', the management group views Dd as marginal revenue. Next, summing the identical SMC curves, it obtains cartel marginal cost MC_c. The intersection of cartel marginal cost and cartel marginal revenue occurs at the level OF, corresponding to output Ox_o and price Op. The same is true for the individual firms, so the firms' decision to share the market equally is consistent with the objective market conditions. But this is a rare situation; cost differences between the firms would have created a situation inconsistent with market conditions and the voluntary market-sharing agreement would collapse. That, as we shall see, is what is most likely to happen to cartels anyhow.

9.7.c—Short and Turbulent Life of Cartels

Unless backed by strong legal provisions, cartels are very likely to collapse from internal pressure (before being found out by the Federal Trade Commission). A few large, geographically concentrated firms producing a homogeneous commodity may form a very successful cartel

-and maintain it, at least during periods of prosperity. But the greater the number of firms, the greater the scope for product differentiation, and the greater the geographical dispersion of firms the easier it is to "cheat" on the cartel's policy. In times of marked prosperity profit may be so great that there is little incentive to cheat. But when profits are low or negative there is a marked incentive; and when the incentive exists enterprising entrepreneurs will discover what they believe to be ingenious methods of cheating.

The typical cartel is characterized by high (perhaps monopoly) price, relatively low output, and a distribution of sales among firms such that each firm operates at less than minimum unit cost. In this situation any one firm can profit greatly from secret price concessions. Indeed, with homogeneous product, a firm offering price concessions can capture as much of the market as he desires, providing the other members adhere to the cartel's price policy. Thus secret price concessions do not have to be extensive before the obedient members experience a marked decline in sales. Recognizing that one or more members are cheating, the formerly obedient members must themselves reduce price in order to remain viable. The cartel accordingly collapses. Without effective *legal* sanctions, the life of a cartel is likely to be brief, ending whenever a business recession occurs.

9.7.d—Price Leadership in Oligopoly

Another type of market solution of the oligopoly problem is *price leadership* by one or a few firms. This solution does not require open collusion but the firms must tacitly agree to the solution. Price leadership has in fact been quite common in certain industries. For example, Clair Wilcox lists, among others, the following industries as characterized by price leadership: nonferrous alloys, steel, agricultural implements, and newsprint.[5] Similarly, in their interview study Kaplan, Dirlam, and Lanzillotti found that Goodyear Tire and Rubber, National Steel, Gulf Oil, and Kroger Grocery follow the price leadership of other firms in the market.[6]

To introduce the price leadership model, consider the simple illustration in Figure 9.7.3, an extension of the market sharing cartel model of Figure 9.7.2. Two firms produce a homogeneous commodity whose market demand is given by DD'. By either explicit collusion or tacit agreement the firms decide to split the market evenly. Thus each views dd' as his demand curve and MR as his marginal revenue curve. In this case,

---

[5] Clair Wilcox, *Competition and Monopoly in American Industry,* Temporary National Economic Committee, Monograph No. 21 (Washington, D.C.: U.S. Government Printing Office, 1940), pp. 121–32.

[6] A. D. H. Kaplan, Joel B. Dirlam, and Robert F. Lanzillotti, *Pricing in Big Business* (Washington, D.C.: Brookings Institution, 1958), pp. 201–07.

FIGURE 9.7.3

Price Leadership by the Lower Cost Firm

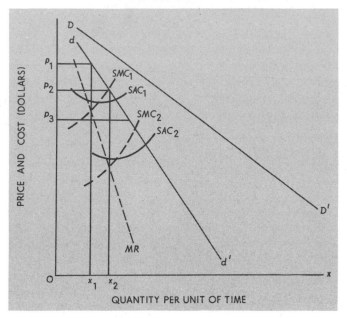

however, the costs of the two producers are different; firm one has substantially higher costs than firm two, as shown by $SAC_1 - SMC_1$ and $SAC_2 - SMC_2$ respectively.

Other things equal, firm one would like to charge Op_1 per unit and sell Ox_1 units. This price-output policy would lead to maximum profit for firm one; but firm two can do much better since its marginal cost is substantially below its marginal revenue at this point. In this situation, firm two has an effective control. Being a lower cost producer, entrepreneur two can set the lower price Op_2 that maximizes his profit. Entrepreneur one has no choice but to follow; if he tries to retain Op_1, his sales will be zero. Hence the higher cost firm must be content to accept the price decision of the lower cost firm.

The particular solution shown here is not a very likely one. If this situation existed in a market, entrepreneur two would hardly agree, tacitly or otherwise, to split the market evenly. But given the antitrust laws in the United States he would not drive entrepreneur one out of the market. He has the power to do so. By setting a price such as Op_3, he can earn a pure profit and ultimately drive firm one out of the market. But then he would face the legal problems of monopoly. A better solution, from the viewpoint of the lower cost firm, is to tolerate a "competitor." Thus while not sharing the market equally, as in this illustration, entrepreneur

FIGURE 9.7.4

Price Leadership by the Dominant Firm

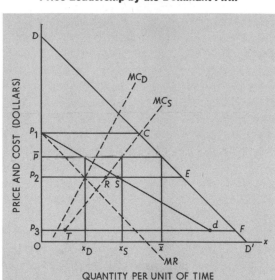

QUANTITY PER UNIT OF TIME

two would nevertheless set a price high enough for entrepreneur one to remain in the market.

A much more typical example of price leadership is illustrated by Figure 9.7.4. The model is a somewhat exaggerated representation of a situation which, some say, exists in several American industries. There is one (or a small number of) dominant firm(s) and numerous small ones. As shown by the marginal cost curves in Figure 9.7.4, the dominant firm is almost as large as all the small firms combined (MC_D is the marginal cost of the dominant firm and MC_S is the horizontal sum of the marginal cost curves of the small firms).

The dominant firm could possibly eliminate all its rivals by a price war. But this would establish a monopoly with its attendant legal problems. A more desirable course of action for the dominant firm is to establish the market price and let the small firms sell all they wish at that price. The small firms, recognizing their position, will behave as perfectly competitive firms do. That is, they will regard their demand curve as a horizontal line at the prevailing price and sell that amount for which marginal cost equals price. Notice that this does not entail the long-run zero profit solution because price may be set far above (minimum) unit cost.

The problem confronting the dominant firm is to determine the price that will maximize its profit while allowing the small firms to sell all they wish at that price. To do this it is necessary to find the demand curve for the dominant firm. Suppose DD' is the market demand curve and MC_S is the horizontal summation of the marginal cost curves of the small firms. Since the small firms equate marginal cost and price, MC_S is also the collective supply curve of the small firms.

First, suppose the dominant firm sets the price Op_1. The small firms would sell p_1C units, exactly the market quantity demanded. Hence sales by the dominant firm would be zero, and p_1 would be a point on its demand curve. If price Op_2 were set by the dominant firm, the small firms would sell p_2R units, and the dominant firm would sell $RE = p_2S$ units; thus S is also a point on its demand curve. Finally, suppose the price were set at Op_3. The small firms would sell p_3T units and the dominant firm $TF = p_3d$ units. For a price below Op_3, only the dominant firm would sell. Hence its demand curve is p_1dFD', and its marginal revenue is given by the dashed line MR.

Equating marginal revenue and marginal cost (MC_D), the dominant firm sets the price $O\bar{p}$ and sells Ox_D units. At this price the small firms sell Ox_S units; and by construction of the demand curve p_1dFD', $Ox_D + Ox_S$ must equal $O\bar{x}$, the total quantity sold at price $O\bar{p}$.

Many variations of this basic price leadership model can be constructed by changing the assumptions. One may allow for two or more dominant firms, for product differentiation, for geographically separated sellers and transportation cost, and so on. Nonetheless, the basic results are much the same; and they may help to explain price-output policies in some oligopoly markets.

9.8 COMPETITION IN OLIGOPOLY MARKETS

Practically speaking, active price competition is seldom if ever observed in oligopolistic markets. To be sure, price wars occasionally erupt; but this really does not indicate price competition. A price war indicates that the (probably implicit) communication channels among firms in the market are temporarily out of repair. In the normal course of events, the preprice-war situation is quickly restored.

Absence of price competition, as we have said, is what one typically observes in the real world. It is also the inference to be drawn from almost every model of oligopoly behavior analyzed so far. With the exception of the Edgeworth model, the normal prediction is stable price with competition for market sales taking some form other than active price competition. The alternative forms of nonprice competition are as diverse as the minds of inventive entrepreneurs can make them. Yet there is one central feature: an entrepreneur attempts to attract customers to himself (and, therefore, away from rivals) by some means other than a price differential. Nonprice competition accordingly involves the differentiation of a product that is fundamentally more or less homogeneous. The ways of differentiating are diverse, but three principal methods deserve mention.

Perhaps the most important technique of nonprice competition is advertising. In the United States, and increasingly in European countries, advertising is the uniformly most accepted method of attracting customers, at least to businessmen if not to economists. The "pros and cons" of advertising expenditure have been argued at length; the argument is likely to continue because the question at stake is a moot one. But for good or not, advertising is an established practice that is presumably considered worthwhile, for otherwise businessmen would not continue to spend billions of dollars annually on this type of nonprice competition.

Another important type of nonprice competition consists of creating bona fide (and sometimes spurious) quality differentials among products. The general effect of quality differentiation is to divide a broad market into a group of submarkets among which there is usually a relatively large price differential. The automobile market offers a good example. There are definite, physically specifiable differences between a Ford Falcon and the Ford Motor Company's Continental. There is also a substantial price difference; no one buyer is likely to be a potential customer in both markets, except perhaps for automobiles to perform two fundamentally different services (family car and business runabout).

Ford is not alone in creating quality differentials, however. General Motors and Chrysler do the same; and they engage in active nonprice competition within each of the submarkets. Further, the automobile market example brings to light a social criticism of quality competition. Quality differentials may be created so that items supposedly in one class overlap with items in another, as do, for example, Pontiac, Oldsmobile, and Buick. Thus within the broad market not only is there competition to create new quality classes and gain the competitive edge of being the first in the market; there is also competition within quality classes.

Finally, a third major technique of nonprice competition is design differences. This type could also be illustrated by the automobile market; but the market for golf clubs serves just as well. MacGregor, Wilson, Spalding, and other producers now change models annually, just as do automobile manufacturers. They also create (possibly spurious) quality differentials as between sporting-goods stores and pro shops. But within, say, the pro-shop market, the competition among companies is strictly a matter of club design.

These three types of nonprice competition far from exhaust the possible methods but they do illustrate the ways in which entrepreneurs can spend resources in an effort to attract customers to their particular "brands."

9.9 WELFARE EFFECTS OF OLIGOPOLY

Since there are many models of oligopoly behavior, each predicting different results, it is impossible to be precise about the welfare effects of oligopolistic market organization. Furthermore, any set of static welfare criteria one applies to the situation may be relatively insignificant in a dynamic context. Nonetheless, a few things may be said.

First, whatever the model, two characteristics common to all oligopoly markets can be isolated. Firms in an oligopoly presumably produce their output at the minimum attainable unit cost. But there is no reason to believe their output uniquely corresponds to minimum long-run average cost. Hence oligopoly requires more units of resources per unit of commodity produced than absolutely necessary. Furthermore, since pure economic profit normally accompanies oligopolistic market organization, price is higher than both average and marginal cost. In whatever equilibrium is reached, the marginal valuation of buyers is greater than the marginal cost of output. If the commodity were priced at either marginal or average cost, buyers would like to purchase more than producers would be willing to sell.

A second consideration is also important. Vast amounts of resources are devoted to advertising and to creating quality and design differentials. The allocation of some resources for these purposes is doubtless justifiable. For example, to the extent that advertising merely reports price and seller location, it helps keep buyers better informed. Similarly, certain quality and design differentials may be socially desirable. Nonetheless, there is a strong presumption (based upon purely empirical grounds) that oligopolists push all forms of nonprice competition beyond the socially desirable limits. In absence of evidence to the contrary, it is reasonable to conclude that buyers in oligopoly markets would be better off if there were more active price competition and less nonprice competition.

As noted, the welfare criteria imposed so far are static; and from the standpoint of these criteria, oligopoly fares rather badly. However, dynamic considerations should not be entirely ignored. Industrial research and development, the now famous R & D, was essential to the development of our modern industrial economy and is essential to its continued viability and growth. Many argue, with considerable persuasiveness, that R & D usually thrives only in oligopolistic markets. Neither perfect competitors nor pure monopolists have the incentive; and perfect competitors are usually not large enough to support research departments. Oligopolistic firms, on the other hand, always have the incentive: improve the product or reduce its cost so as to increase profit. Furthermore, such firms are typically large enough to absorb the short-run cost of R & D in order to reap its long-run payoff. In short, all sorts of static welfare criteria may be violated more or less with impunity if the dynamic rate of growth is sufficiently rapid. Some economists, and all oligopolists, hold that oligopolistic market organization is essential for the dynamic growth of the economy.

9.10 BARRIERS TO COMPETITION

We have studied four theoretical market structures: perfect competition, pure monopoly, monopolistic competition, and oligopoly. We have examined the behavioral characteristics and some welfare implications of each. Before our study of markets is complete one final task remains: a brief examination of why some industries are oligopolies or even approach monopolies and why others are closer to perfect or monopolistic competition. Or, in some industries why do the few largest firms produce a large percentage of total output while in other industries no firm has a substantial share of the total market? Part of the answer to this question lies in the barriers to entry of new firms. If oligopoly or monopoly is to exist for long, something must prevent new firms from entering the industry or prevent those that do enter from growing. Another part of the answer lies in the reasons why some firms are able to attain an oligopoly or monopoly position in the first place. These factors are called the bases of oligopoly or monopoly.

One of the most important bases of monopoly or oligopoly is the control of raw material supplies. If one firm, or perhaps a few firms, control all of the known supply of a necessary ingredient of a particular product, the firm or firms can refuse to sell that ingredient to other firms at a price low enough for them to compete. Since no others can produce the product, a monopoly or oligopoly results. For example, for many years the Aluminum Company of America (Alcoa) owned almost every source of bauxite, a necessary ingredient in the production of aluminum. The control of resource supply, coupled with certain patent rights, provided Alcoa with an absolute monopoly in aluminum production. Indeed, it was only after World War II that the federal courts effectively broke Alcoa's monopoly of the aluminum market. The International Nickel Company has enjoyed much the same position over a relatively long period.

Nonetheless, a firm's control of the source of raw material supply does not guarantee that it will choose to exploit its opportunity to be a monopolist. If diseconomies of scale set in at a low level of output, relative to demand, the firm may find it more profitable to sell the raw material to other firms. The number of firms that may enter the industry depends in large part on economies of scale. If economies of scale are only attainable at a relatively large level of output (but not the entire market output), few firms will enter and oligopoly will result. If all economies of scale are attainable at low levels of output, more firms will enter. However, the sole owner of the raw material remains a monopolist in the raw material market. Only if it is more profitable will he choose to be a monopolist of the product as well.

Another barrier to competition lies in the patent laws of the United States. These laws make it possible for a person to apply for and obtain the exclusive right to produce a certain commodity or to produce a commodity by means of a specified process that gives it an absolute cost advantage. The patent is applicable for 17 years, but it is subject to renewal after that time. Obviously, such exclusive rights can easily lead to monopoly or, if a few firms hold the patents, to oligopoly. Alcoa is an example of a monopoly based upon both resource control and patent rights. E. I. Du Pont de Nemours & Co. has enjoyed patent monopolies over many commodities, cellophane being perhaps the most notable. At one time the Eastman Kodak Company enjoyed a similar position (by lease from a German company); more recently the Minnesota Mining and Manufacturing Company ("Three M") has enjoyed patent monopoly or near-monopoly for products such as their Scotch Tape and Thermofax Copier.

Despite these notable examples, holding a patent on a product or on a production process may not be quite what it seems in many instances. In the first place, like the exclusive owner of some necessary raw material, the holder of a product patent may not choose to exploit his monopoly position. If diseconomies of scale set in at a low level of production, the patent holder may find it more profitable to sell production rights to a few firms (in which case oligopoly results) or to many. Second, the owner of a patented lower cost production process may have a cost advantage over competitors, but he may sell only a small part of the industry's total output at his equilibrium position. The new technique will lead to patent monopoly only if his firm can supply the market and still undersell competition. Third, a patent gives one the exclusive right to produce a particular, meticulously specified commodity or to use a particular meticulously specified process to produce a commodity others can produce. But a patent does not preclude the development of closely related substitute goods or closely allied production processes. International Business Machines has the exclusive right to produce IBM machines; but many other millisecond computers are available and there is keen competition in the computer market. The above-mentioned Du Pont patent on cellophane gave Du Pont a monopoly in that product. According to the U.S. Supreme Court, however, the relevant market is not the cellophane market but the market for flexible packaging material, in which Du Pont had an 18 percent share—obviously not a monopoly position. The same is true of production processes. Thus while patents may sometimes establish pure monopolies, at other times they are merely permits to enter highly—but not perfectly—competitive markets.

A third source of oligopoly or monopoly, clearly related to the two sources just discussed, lies in the cost of establishing an efficient production plant, especially in relation to the size of the market. The situation we are now discussing is frequently called "natural" monopoly or "natural" oligopoly. It comes into existence when the minimum average cost of production occurs at a rate of output so large that one or a few firms can supply the entire market at a price covering full cost. If minimum average cost occurs at a rate of output sufficient, or more than sufficient, for just one firm to supply the entire market and cover full cost, a natural monopoly results.

Suppose there exists a situation in which a few firms supply the entire market, and each enjoys a pure profit. Because of the advantages of large size, cost at smaller rates of output is so high that entry is not profitable for small-scale firms. On the other hand, the entry of another large-scale producer is also discouraged because the added production of this firm would increase supply and drive price below the pure profit level for all firms. Therefore, entry is discouraged.

Suppose a similar situation exists, but now only two firms are in the market. Suppose also that the long-run average cost curve of each is such that splitting the market between the two requires each firm necessarily to produce at a relatively high average cost. Each has an incentive to lower price and increase output because average cost will also decline. But if both act in this fashion, price will surely fall more rapidly than average cost. Economic warfare ensues, and the ultimate result is likely to be the emergence of only one firm in a monopoly position. The term natural monopoly simply designates that the natural result of market forces is the development of a monopoly organization. One may carry the analysis further and describe similar circumstances in which the relations between average cost and market demand can cause an industry to become oligopolistic.

Examples of natural monopoly are not hard to come by. Virtually all public utilities are natural monopolies and vice versa. Municipal waterworks, electrical power companies, sewage disposal systems, telephone companies, and many transportation services are examples of natural monopolies on both local and national levels.

Another frequently cited barrier to competition is the advantages established firms sometime have over new firms. On the cost side the established firms, perhaps because of a history of good earnings, may be able to secure financing at a more favorable rate than new firms. On the demand side, older firms may have built up over the years the allegiance of a group of buyers. New firms might find this difficult to overcome. For durable goods buyer allegiance can be built by establishing a reputation for service. No one knows what the service or repair policy of a new firm may be. Or the preference of buyers can be built by a long, successful advertising campaign; this type of allegiance is also probably more prevalent for durable goods. Although technical economies or diseconomies of scale may be insignificant, new firms might have considerable difficulty establishing a market organization and overcoming buyer preference for older firms.

The role of advertising in fostering oligopoly has, however, been a source of controversy. Some argue that advertising acts as a barrier to entry by strengthening buyer preferences for the products of established firms. On the other hand, consider the great difficulty of entering an established industry without access to advertising. A good way for entrenched oligopolists to discourage entry would be, in fact, to get the government to prohibit advertising. The reputation of the old firms would enable them to continue their dominance. A new firm would have difficulty informing the public about the availability of a new product unless it advertised. Thus advertising may be a way to overcome the advantages of being established. The effect of advertising on oligopoly remains a point of disagreement among economists.

The final source of monopoly and oligopoly to be discussed here is government. Although the United States does enforce antitrust laws with varying degrees of severity, governments at all levels frequently act to further monopoly and erect barriers to competition. One method is the granting of a market franchise. Use of a market franchise is frequently associated with natural monopolies and public utilities, but it need not be. A market franchise is actually a contract entered into by some governmental body (for instance, a city government) and a business concern. The governmental unit gives a business firm the exclusive right to market a good or service within its jurisdiction. The business firm, in turn, agrees to permit the governmental unit to control certain aspects of its market conduct. For example, the governmental unit may limit, or attempt to limit, the firm to a "fair return on fair market value of assets." In other cases the governmental unit may establish the price and permit the firm to earn whatever it can at that price. There are many other ways in which the governmental unit can exercise control over the firm. The essential feature, however, is that a governmental unit establishes the firm as a monopoly in return for various types of control over the price and output policies of the business.

Another way in which the government inhibits competition, some assert, is by purchasing from the larger firms rather than the smaller firms in many industries. Those who hold this position maintain that government contracts give the larger firms an advantage not only over other firms in the industry but also over prospective entrants. Others posit that tariffs hinder entry into oligopolistic industries. While tariffs do not necessarily prevent competition, they do make it easier for firms in an industry to collude. Another governmentally fostered base of oligopoly and monopoly is the federal tax structure. When this tax structure encourages reinvestment in established corporations at the expense of investment in new entrants, even though the new firms would be more efficient, competition is inhibited.[7]

9.11 OLIGOPOLY AND ECONOMIC ANALYSIS

Writing in 1952, Professor Fritz Machlup commented that "Familiarity with the classical models (of oligopoly) has become a kind of hall-mark of the education of an economic theorist, even if it helps him more in the comprehension of the traditional lingo than in the analysis of current economic problems."[8] And again: "Sliding along a smooth curve until it intersects another curve is a healthy mental exercise; and solving a set of simultaneous equations is too; but neither of these will ensure our understanding of the way a man makes up his mind when he ponders a business decision."[9]

Machlup's statements point up the problem. When the number of sellers is very large, each can confidently and properly expect that *his independent* actions will have an imperceptible effect upon the market. A competitive producer does not have to guess how his rivals will react to his policies because he does not have any *rivals*. Neither does a monopolist; so no guesswork is involved. But oligopoly is a matter of close rivalry among firms; and building a *model* of oligopoly behavior is usually a matter of specifying how one oligopolist tries to second-guess his opponents. Therefore, economic analysis based upon such models is almost bound to be unreliable because neither economists nor psychiatrists are likely to guess how businessmen guess when confronted with a business decision.

This indictment may be a bit strong because there is one guess that is frequently good, namely that intelligent oligopolists will collude, openly if possible, surreptitiously or tacitly otherwise. This is the reason for studying the Chamberlin model, the cartel model, and the price leadership model. But note: all of these could as well have been studied in Chapter 8 as in the present chapter. When any kind of collusion is allowed, monopoly or near-monopoly results emerge. In these cases, it is a matter of taste whether one says his analysis is based upon monopoly or oligopoly models.

In general, one is well prepared for economic analysis if he has a thorough understanding of the competitive and monopoly models though,

---

[7] For a more detailed discussion of the bases of monopoly, see George J. Stigler, *The Theory of Price* (New York: Macmillan & Co., 1949), pp. 197–217.

[8] Fritz Machlup, *The Economics of Sellers' Competition* (Baltimore: The Johns Hopkins Press, 1952), p. 369.

[9] *Ibid.*, p. 370.

as Machlup said, he will not know all the jargon of the trade unless he studies oligopoly models as well.

QUESTIONS AND PROBLEMS

1. "The smaller the seller's share in the market, the greater the temptation for him to cut prices in slack time." Discuss.
2. *a*) Draw the necessary curves to show a monopolistic competitor enjoying pure profits.
   b) Show the amount of pure profit.
   c) Now draw demand and marginal revenue curves that, presumably under the influence of newcomers' competition, are so much further downward and to the left that pure profit is zero.
3. Assume that the bituminous coal industry is a competitive industry in long-run equilibrium. Now assume that the firms in the industry form a cartel.
   a) What will happen to the equilibrium output and price of coal and why?
   b) How should the output be distributed among the individual firms?
   c) After the cartel is operating, are there incentives for the individual firm to cheat? Why or why not?
4. Why do we say that there is no general theory of oligopoly?

chapter
10

Theory of Distribution

10.1 INTRODUCTION

We have now developed the modern or neoclassical theory of value—a theory explaining the origin of demand, supply, and market price. A central part of this theory of value is the marginal cost of production and its possible reflection in the supply curve. Costs and supply, in turn, depend upon the technological conditions of production and the cost of productive services. So far we have assumed that both are given; and we will continue to assume that the physical conditions of production are technologically given and do not change over the time period relevant to our analysis. But now we must determine the prices of productive services, the distribution half of "value and distribution," or modern microeconomic theory.

Broadly speaking, the theory of input pricing does not differ from the theory of pricing goods. Both are fundamentally based upon the interaction of demand and supply. In the present case, demand arises from business firms (rather than consumers) and supply, at least the supply of labor services, arises from individuals who are not only sellers of labor time but also consumers. Furthermore, for the more interesting cases of capital and labor, one determines the price of using the resource for a stipulated period of time, not the price of purchasing the resource. In other respects, however, the theory of distribution is the theory of value of productive services.

The previous level of abstraction is maintained throughout. This is certainly to be expected in the first part of the chapter, which presents the marginal productivity theory of distribution in perfectly competitive input and output markets. When imperfections appear in either market, however, the situation changes appreciably. This is especially true when large employers bargain directly with representatives of powerful labor organizations. When there are market imperfections, labor unions tend to arise.

The theoretical discussion in the latter part may seem far removed from the dramatic world of GM v. UAW. Indeed it is, in a certain sense. Yet the theoretical results obtained do set limits within which collective bargaining agreements are likely to occur.

Our point of view is that collective bargaining between management and union representatives constitutes bilateral monopoly, an indeterminate economic situation. Our analysis sets broad limits within which the solution lies. To push further requires one or more *courses*, not chapters. For example, there is a substantial body of theory concerning the collective bargaining process, but an understanding of labor markets also requires an extensive knowledge of the institutional framework within which labor unions and business management operate. This type of knowledge must be acquired in "applied" courses or contexts, just as applied courses supplement other portions of microeconomic theory.

10.2   DEMAND FOR A PRODUCTIVE SERVICE: PERFECT COMPETITION

As indicated in the Introduction, this section is not intended to be a practical man's guide to wage determination. Yet marginal productivity theory constitutes a framework in which practical problems can be analyzed; thus it is a useful tool for economic theorists. The theory developed here is applicable to any productive service, although the most natural application refers to the demand for labor. Thus when we speak of the demand for labor, the demand for a productive service of any type is implied.

10.2.a—Demand of a Firm for One Variable Productive Service

It is intuitively obvious that a firm would increase the amount of labor used if the additional labor contributes more to the firm's income than to its cost. Assume that the wage rate is $10 a day and that the price of the product the firm sells is $1. If increasing its labor force by one more worker adds more than 10 units of output per day, the firm would hire the additional worker. The *value of the marginal product* (more than $10) exceeds the wage rate ($10). If an additional worker adds less than 10 units, he would not be hired. The value of the marginal product would be less than the wage.

Definition: The value of the marginal product of a factor of production is the addition to total revenue attributable to the addition of one more unit of the factor. Thus the value of the marginal product is equal to the marginal product multiplied by commodity price.

Let us consider another numerical example. A perfectly competitive firm sells a product for $5 and employs labor at $20 a day. Table 10.2.1

TABLE 10.2.1
Value of the Marginal Product and
Individual Demand for Labor

Units of Variable Input	Total Product	Marginal Product	Value of Marginal Product
0........................	0	—	—
1........................	10	10	$ 50
2........................	30	20	100
3........................	50	20	100
4........................	65	15	75
5........................	75	10	50
6........................	80	5	25
7........................	83	3	15
8........................	84	1	5
9........................	81	-3	-15

lists the daily total product, marginal product, and value of marginal product (price of the product times marginal product) for zero through nine workers. Under these conditions the firm hires six workers. It would not hire fewer than six since hiring the sixth adds $25 to revenue but costs only $20. The firm increases net revenue by $5. It would not hire seven workers because revenue would increase by $15 while cost would increase by $20, thereby causing a decrease in net revenue of $5. If, however, the wage rate dropped below $15 (say to $14) the work force would increase to seven (an additional $15 revenue can be gained at a cost of $14). If wages rose above $25 but remained below $50, the firm would reduce the labor force to five.

Exercise: In order to ascertain that hiring six workers is profit maximizing at a wage of $20, assume a fixed cost of $100 and compute the profit rates for all units in stage II (recall from Chapter 5 that Stage II is the range from maximum average product to zero marginal product).

To get more directly to the proposition we seek, consider Figure 10.2.1. Suppose the value of the marginal product is given by the curve labeled VMP. The market wage rate is $O\overline{w}$, so the supply of labor to the firm is the horizontal line S_L. First, suppose the firm employed only OL_1 units of labor. At that rate of employment, the value of the marginal product is $L_1C = Ow_1 > O\overline{w}$, the wage rate. At this point of operation an additional unit of labor adds more to total revenue than to total cost (inasmuch as it adds the value of its marginal product to total revenue and its unit wage rate to cost). Hence a profit-maximizing entrepreneur would add additional units of labor; and indeed, he would continue to add units so long as the value of the marginal product exceeds the wage rate.

Next, suppose OL_2 units of labor were employed. At this point the

FIGURE 10.2.1
Proof of $VMP = \bar{w}$ Theorem

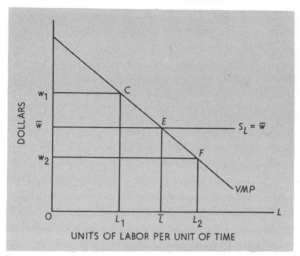

value of the marginal product $L_2F = Ow_2$ is less than the wage rate. Each unit of labor adds more to total cost than to total revenue. Hence a profit-maximizing entrepreneur would not employ OL_2 units, or any number for which the wage rate exceeds the value of the marginal product. These arguments show that neither more nor fewer than $O\bar{L}$ units of labor would be employed and that to employ $O\bar{L}$ units leads to profit maximization. The statements are summarized as follows:

Proposition: A profit-maximizing entrepreneur will employ units of a variable productive service until the point is reached at which the value of the marginal product of the input is exactly equal to the input price.

In other words, given the market wage rate or the supply of labor curve to the firm, a perfectly competitive producer determines the quantity of labor to hire by equating the value of the marginal product to the wage rate. If the wage rate were Ow_1 (Fig. 10.2.1), the firm would employ OL_1 units of labor to equate the value of the marginal product to the given wage rate. Similarly, if the wage rate were Ow_2, the firm would employ OL_2 units of labor. By definition of a demand curve, therefore, the value of the marginal product curve is established as the firm's demand for labor curve.

Definition: The firm's demand curve for a *single* variable productive service is given by the value of the marginal product curve of the productive service in question. This is, of course, limited to production in stage II.

10.2.b—Firm's Demand Curves When Several Variable Inputs Are Used

When a production process involves more than one variable productive service, the value of the marginal product curve of an input is not its demand curve. The reason lies in the fact that the various inputs are interdependent in the production process, so a change in the price of one input leads to changes in the rates of utilization of the others. You will recall from Chapter 5, however, that a factor's marginal product curve is derived under the assumption that the amount of other inputs remains constant. Therefore, changes in the rates of utilization of other inputs shift the marginal product curve of the input whose price initially changes.

Consider Figure 10.2.2. Suppose an equilibrium initially exists at

FIGURE 10.2.2

Individual Input Demand When Several Variable Inputs Are Used

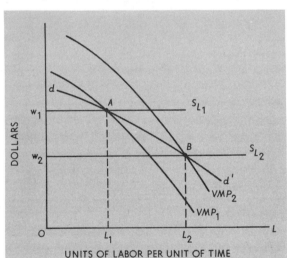

UNITS OF LABOR PER UNIT OF TIME

point A. The market wage rate is Ow_1, the value of the marginal product curve for labor is VMP_1 when labor is the only input varied, and OL_1 units of labor are employed. Now let the equilibrium wage rate fall to Ow_2, so that the perfectly elastic supply curve of labor to the firm is S_{L_2}.

When the wage rate falls from Ow_1 to Ow_2, the usage of labor expands. However, the expansion does not take place along VMP_1. When the quantity of labor used and the level of output change, the usage of other variable inputs changes as well. Under these conditions labor's marginal product curve shifts.[1]

---

[1] Unfortunately this assertion, which is essential for the results of this section, cannot be proved graphically and the mathematical proof is long and tedious. For

Since the value of the marginal product is equal to marginal product multiplied by the constant market price of the commodity, the value of the marginal product of labor curve must shift as well. Suppose it shifts to VMP_2. The new equilibrium is reached at point B. Other points similar to A and B can be generated in the same manner. Thus the demand curve dd' can be determined from successive changes in the market wage rate and the value of the marginal product curve. Thus the input demand curve, while more difficult to derive, is just as determinate in the multiple input case as in the single input situation.

The results of this section may be summarized in the following important

Proposition: An entrepreneur's demand curve for a variable productive agent can be derived when more than one variable input is used. This demand curve must be negatively sloped.[2]

10.2.c—Market Demand for a Variable Productive Service

The market demand for a variable productive service, just as the market demand for a commodity, is the horizontal sum of the constituent individual demands. However, in the case of productive services the process of addition is considerably more complicated, because when all firms expand or contract simultaneously the market price of the commodity changes. Nonetheless, the market demand curve can be obtained, as illustrated in Figure 10.2.3.

A typical employing firm is depicted in panel a. For the going market price of the commodity produced, d_1d_1' is the firm's demand curve for the variable productive service, as derived in Figure 10.2.2. If the market price of the resource is Ow_1, the firm uses Ov_1 units. Aggregating over all employing firms, OV_1 units of the service are used. Thus point A in panel b is one point on the market demand curve for the variable productive service.

Next, suppose the price of the service declines to Ow_2 (because, for example, the supply curve of the variable service shifts to the right). Other things being equal, the firm would move along d_1d_1' to point b', employing Ov_2' units of the service. But other things are not equal. When all firms expand their usage of the input, total output expands. Or stated differently, the market supply curve for the commodity shifts to the right because of the decline in the input's price. For a given commodity de-

---

detailed treatments of the general case, see C. E. Ferguson, "Production, Price, and the Theory of Jointly Derived Input Demand Functions," *Economica*, November, 1966; "'Inferior Factors' and the Theories of Production and Input Demand," *Economica*, May, 1968; *The Neoclassical Theory of Production and Distribution* (London and New York: Cambridge University Press, 1969), chaps. 6 and 9.

[2] This proposition requires a mathematical proof. See the citations in footnote 1.

FIGURE 10.2.3

Derivation of the Market Demand for a Variable Productive Service

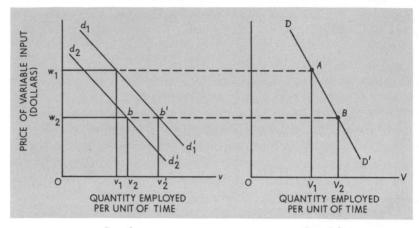

Panel *a*	Panel *b*
The Demand of a Firm for a	Market Demand for a
Variable Productive Service	Variable Productive Service

mand, commodity price must fall; and when it does the individual demand curves for the variable productive service also fall.

In panel *a*, the decline in individual input demand attributable to the decline in commodity price is represented by the shift leftward from d_1d_1' to d_2d_2'. At input price Ow_2, b is the equilibrium point, with Ov_2 units employed. Aggregating for all employers, OV_2 units of the productive service are used and point B is obtained in panel *b*. Any number of points such as A and B can be generated by varying the market price of the productive service. Connecting these points by a line, one obtains DD', the market demand for the variable productive service.

10.3 SUPPLY OF A VARIABLE PRODUCTIVE SERVICE

All variable productive services may be broadly classified into three groups: natural resources, intermediate goods, and labor. Intermediate goods are those produced by one entrepreneur and sold to another, who in turn utilizes them in his productive process. For example, cotton is produced by a farmer and (after middlemen) sold as an intermediate good to a manufacturer of damask; the damask, in turn, becomes an intermediate good in the manufacture of upholstered furniture. The short-run supply curves of intermediate goods are positively sloped because they are the *commodity outputs* of manufacturers, even if they are variable inputs to others; and, as shown in Chapter 7, short-run commodity supply curves are positively sloped.

Natural resources may be regarded as the commodity outputs (usually) of mining operations. As such, they also have positively sloped short-run supply curves. Thus our attention can be restricted to the final category: labor.

10.3.a—General Consideration

As population increases and its age composition changes, as people migrate from one area to another, and as education and reeducation enable people to shift occupations, rather dramatic changes can occur in the supply of various types of labor at various locations throughout the nation. These changes represent *shifts* in the supply curve and are quite independent of its slope. To get at the supply curve for a well-defined market, assume that the following are constants (they are temporarily impounded in *ceteris paribus*): the size of the population, the labor force participation rate, and the occupational and geographic distribution of the labor force. One first asks, what induces a person to forego leisure for work?

10.3.b—Market Supply of Labor

The analytical exercise in Chapter 4 (Section 4.6) shows how an individual supply of labor is derived from indifference curves between leisure and income (the student should review that exercise before going on). In that section we showed that given a wage increase, an individual might choose to work more (sacrifice leisure) or to work less (take more leisure), depending upon the shape of his indifference map. Therefore, an individual's supply of labor curve may be positively sloped over some range and negatively sloped over other ranges of the wage rate. The crucial question, however, is how their *sum* behaves—what is the shape of the market supply curve of any specified type of labor.

In fact, considerably more can be said about the *sum* than about the constituent parts. First, consider the situation in which one industry exclusively uses a specialized type of labor. In the short run nothing can be said about the slope or shape of the labor supply curve. It may be positive, it may be negative, or it may have segments of positive and negative slope. But now let us relax our assumption concerning occupational immobility; and, in the long run, one must. The master baker can become an apprentice candlestick maker if the financial inducement is sufficient. But more to the point, young people planning their education and career must surely be affected by current returns in various professions. Thus in the long run the supply of specialized labor is likely to have a positive slope.

The other case, in which labor is not specialized to one particular industry, is even more clear. In particular, if more than one industry uses a particular type of labor, the labor supply curve to any one industry must be positively sloped. Suppose any one industry increases its employment; the wage rate must rise for two reasons. First, to expand employment workers must be obtained from other industries, thereby increasing the demand price of labor. Second, the industries that lose labor must reduce output; hence commodity prices in these industries will tend to rise, causing an additional upward pressure on the demand price of labor. Thus the industry attempting to expand employment must face a positively sloped supply of labor curve.[3]

In summary, we have the following:

Relation: The short-run supply curves of raw materials and intermediate goods are positively sloped, as are the supply curves of nonspecialized types of labor. In the very short run the supply of specialized labor may take any shape or slope; but in the long run it too tends to be positively sloped.

10.4 MARKET EQUILIBRIUM AND RETURNS TO INPUTS

10.4.a—Equilibrium in the Input Market

The demand for and supply of a variable productive service jointly determine its market equilibrium price; this is precisely marginal productivity theory. In Figure 10.4.1, DD' and SS' are the demand and supply curves. Their intersection at point E determines the market equilibrium price $O\overline{w}$ and quantity demanded and supplied $O\overline{v}$.

If the price of the variable input (say labor) exceeds $O\overline{w}$ more people wish to work in this occupation than employers are willing to hire at that wage. Since there is a surplus of workers, wages are bid down by the workers until the surplus is eliminated (in the absence, of course, of minimum wages). If the wage rate is below $O\overline{w}$, producers want to employ more workers than are willing to work at that wage. Employers, faced with a "shortage" of labor, bid the wage rate up to $O\overline{w}$. The analysis is similar to that in Chapter 2. The only features unique to this analysis are the methods of determining the demand for variable productive services and the supply of labor services. The fact that input demand is based upon

---

[3] There are two possible exceptions, each of which leads to a horizontal industry supply of labor curve. First, if the industry is exceedingly small or if it uses only very small quantities of labor, its effect upon the market may be negligible. That is, the industry may stand to the market as a perfectly competitive firm does to the industry. Second, if there is unemployment of the particular type of labor under consideration, the supply of labor to all industries may be perfectly elastic up to the point of full employment. Thereafter the supply curve would rise. The latter is a disequilibrium situation not encompassed in the analysis here.

FIGURE 10.4.1

**Market Equilibrium Determination of the Price of a Variable
Productive Service**

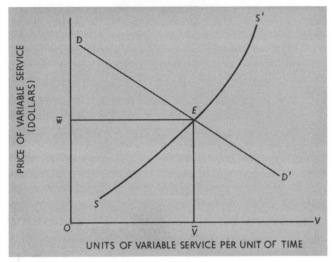

the value of the marginal product of the input gives rise to the label
"marginal productivity theory."

10.4.b—Short Run and Quasi Rents

Since all resources are variable in the long run, marginal productivity
theory covers all resources in the long run. However, in the short run
certain inputs are fixed; they cannot be varied and hence a "marginal
product" cannot readily be generated. The return to short-run fixed
factors, denoted "quasi rent," therefore requires another explanation.

The explanation of quasi rents requires the customary cost curve graph,
illustrated in Figure 10.4.2. In that figure, ATC, AVC, and MC denote
average cost, average variable cost, and marginal cost respectively. Suppose market price is $O\overline{P}$. The profit-maximizing firm produces $O\overline{Q}$ units
of output and incurs variable costs which, on average, amount to $OA =
\overline{Q}D$ dollars per unit of output. Thus the total expenditure required to
sustain the necessary employment of variable productive services is
represented by $OAD\overline{Q}$. Total revenue is $O\overline{P}E\overline{Q}$; thus the difference
between total revenue and total variable cost is $A\overline{P}ED$. Similarly, if
market price were OA per unit, the difference between total revenue and
total variable cost would be $HAFG$.

This difference *is* quasi rent, which must always be nonnegative (if

FIGURE 10.4.2

Determination of Quasi Rent

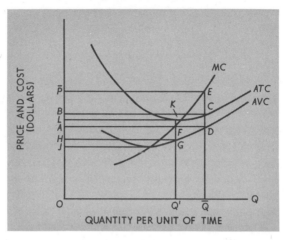

price fell to *OJ*, total revenue and total variable cost would be equal; if price fell below *OJ*, production would cease and total revenue and total variable cost would both equal zero). Notice that quasi rent is the total return ascribable to the fixed inputs. If price is $O\bar{P}$, quasi rent can be divided into two components: the amount *ABCD* representing their opportunity cost, and the amount $B\bar{P}EC$ representing the pure economic profit attributable to their use in this industry rather than in their best alternative use. Similarly, if market price is *OA*, quasi rent (*HAFG*) has two components: the amount *HLKG*, the opportunity cost of using the fixed inputs in this industry; and the (negative) amount *ALKF*, which represents the pure economic loss incurred as a penalty for using the resources in their current employment.

It should be emphasized that quasi rent is strictly a short-run phenomenon. In the long run when all factors are variable, quasi rent is always eliminated.

10.5 MONOPOLY IN THE COMMODITY MARKET

The analytical principles underlying the theory of resource price and employment are the same for perfectly and imperfectly competitive markets. Supply and demand determine market equilibrium resource price and employment; and marginal productivity considerations are the fundamental determinants of demand. However, since commodity price and marginal revenue are different in imperfectly competitive markets, the value of the marginal product of a variable resource is not the relevant guide. Since the principle of employment theory is the same for all types of imperfect competition in the selling market, our attention is restricted to monopoly.

10.5.a—Marginal Revenue Product

When a perfectly competitive seller employs an additional unit of labor, his output is augmented by the marginal product of that unit. In like manner, his total revenue is augmented by the value of its marginal product inasmuch as commodity price remains unchanged. When a monopolist employs an additional unit of labor, his output is also increased by the marginal product of the worker. However, to sell the larger output, commodity price must be reduced; hence total revenue is not augmented by the value of the marginal product of the additional worker.

A numerical example might help to explain. A monopolist must decide whether to hire 10 or 11 workers, all other factors fixed. He is faced with the following set of possibilities.

Units of Labor	Total Product	Marginal Product	Price	Total Revenue
10	100	—	$5.00	$500
11	120	20	4.80	576

Ten units of labor can produce 100 units of output; 11 can produce 120. The marginal product of 11 workers is 20 units. But in order to sell the additional 20 units, the monopolist must reduce commodity price from $5 to $4.80. Total revenue increases by $76 (from $500 to $576). This additional revenue, attributable to the addition of one unit of the variable input, is called the *marginal revenue product.*

Note that the marginal revenue product, $76, is less than the value of marginal product ($4.80 × 20 = $96). Except for the first unit of the input, this is always the case. Marginal revenue product is the *net* addition to total revenue. First, there is the gross additional revenue attributable to hiring one more unit of input and expanding sales. In our example this is 20 × $4.80 = $96 (VMP). The increased output can only be sold when price is reduced from $5 to $4.80. Therefore, a $0.20 price reduction must be taken on the 100 units that could have been sold at $5. This "lost" revenue of $20 must then be deducted from the added gross revenue to get the net change of $76.

Marginal revenue product is simply marginal product multiplied by marginal revenue. In our example, marginal revenue is $3.80 (i.e., the added total revenue of $76 divided by the 20 units increase in sales).

Marginal product is 20, so marginal revenue product equals $76. Again, since a monopolist's price always exceeds his marginal revenue, the value of a variable input's marginal product exceeds its marginal revenue product.

Definition: Marginal revenue product equals marginal revenue multiplied by the marginal physical product of the variable productive service; or, marginal revenue product is the net addition to total revenue attributable to the addition of one unit of the variable productive service.

10.5.b—Monopoly Demand for a Single Variable Input

In the example of Section 10.5.a, the addition of one unit of the variable input adds $76 to total revenue. Clearly if the wage rate (presumably determined in a perfectly competitive market) is more than $76, the monopolist would not increase labor input from 10 to 11 units. Alternatively, if the wage rate were less than $76, the monopolist could gain by adding the 11th worker. As one would probably anticipate, the monopolist adds a variable input, all other inputs fixed, until the price of the variable input equals its marginal revenue product.

To illustrate, consider the marginal revenue product curve in Figure 10.5.1. It must quite obviously slope downward to the right because two forces work to cause marginal revenue product to diminish as the level of employment increases: (*a*) the marginal physical product declines (over the relevant range of production) as additional units of

FIGURE 10.5.1

Monopoly Demand for a Single Variable Service

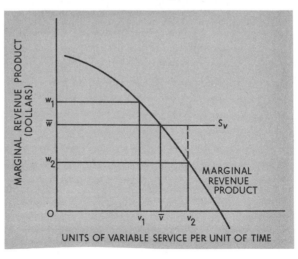

the variable service are added, and (b) marginal revenue declines as output expands and commodity price falls.

By assumption, the monopolist purchases the variable service in a perfectly competitive input market. Hence he views his supply of input curve as a horizontal line at the level of the prevailing market price, $O\overline{w}$.

Our task is to prove the following:

Proposition: An imperfectly competitive producer who purchases a variable productive service in a perfectly competitive input market will employ that amount of the service for which marginal revenue product equals market price. Consequently, the marginal revenue product curve is the monopolist's demand curve for the variable service when only one variable input is used.

Given the market price $O\overline{w}$, our task is to prove that equilibrium employment is $O\overline{v}$. Suppose the contrary, in particular that Ov_1 units of the variable service are used. At the Ov_1 level of utilization the last unit adds Ow_1 to total revenue but only $O\overline{w}$ to total cost. Since $Ow_1 > O\overline{w}$, profit is augmented by employing that unit. Furthermore, profit increases when additional units are employed so long as marginal revenue product exceeds the market equilibrium price of the input. Thus a profit-maximizing monopolist would never employ fewer than $O\overline{v}$ units of the variable service. The opposite argument holds when more than $O\overline{v}$ units are employed, for then an additional unit of the variable service adds more to total cost than to total revenue. Therefore, a profit-maximizing monopolist will adjust employment so that marginal revenue product equals input price. If only one variable productive service is used, the marginal revenue product curve is, therefore, the monopolist's demand curve for the variable service in question.

Analogous to the case of perfect competition, when more than one variable input is used in the production process the marginal revenue product curve is not the demand curve (for the reasons discussed in Section 10.2.b). After a wage decrease the marginal revenue product curve shifts. The input demand curve is generated exactly as in Figure 10.2.2; the only change is the substitution of *MRP* for *VMP*.

10.5.c—Equilibrium Price and Employment

The analysis of market equilibrium price and employment of a variable agent is no different whether the employers are monopolists or perfect competitors. The market demand for the service is simply the sum of the individual demands of the various monopolists.[4] Similarly, if all sorts of

---

[4] This is subject to minor qualification in case of oligopoly and monopolistic competition. In these cases it must be considered that, like perfect competition, when all firms attempt to expand output market price falls.

producers use the variable service, the market demand curve is the sum of the various component *industry* demand curves. Equilibrium price and output are determined where the demand for the input intersects the supply. The important difference between monopoly and perfect competition is that the monopolist's demand is based upon marginal revenue product rather than the value of marginal product. This gives rise to what is sometimes called monopolistic exploitation.[5]

10.5.d—Monopolistic Exploitation

According to Mrs. Robinson's definition, a productive service is exploited if it is employed at a price that is less than the value of its marginal product. As we have seen in the foregoing portion of this chapter, it is to the advantage of any individual producer (whether monopolist or competitor) to hire a variable service until the point is reached at which an additional unit adds precisely the same amount to total cost and total revenue. This is simply the input market implication of profit maximization.

When a perfectly competitive producer follows this rule a variable service receives the value of its marginal product because price and marginal revenue are the same. This is not true, however, when the commodity market is imperfect. Marginal revenue is less than price and marginal revenue product is correspondingly less than the value of the marginal product. Profit-maximizing behavior of imperfectly competitive producers causes the market price of a productive service to be less than the value of its marginal product.

If the market price of the commodity reflects its social value, the productive service receives less than its contribution to social value. Raising the input price is not a remedy, however, because producers would merely reduce the level of employment until marginal revenue product equaled the higher input price. The trouble initially lies in the fact that imperfectly competitive producers do not use as much of the resource as is socially desirable and do not attain the correspondingly desirable level of output. The fundamental difficulty rests in the difference between price (marginal social valuation) and marginal (social) cost at the profit-maximizing output. Thus so long as imperfectly competitive producers exist there must be some "monopolistic exploitation" of productive agents.

The significance of this exploitation can easily be exaggerated. Furthermore, the alternatives to exploitation are not attractive. Either there must be state ownership and operation of all nonperfectly competitive

---

[5] This term is apparently attributable to Joan Robinson. See her *Economics of Imperfect Competition* (London: Macmillan & Co., Ltd., 1933), pp. 381–91.

industries or else there must be rigid price control by the state. For a variety of reasons, either alternative is likely to raise more problems than it solves.

Question: Why would a person work for a monopolist and be exploited, when he could work for a perfect competitor and escape exploitation? Hint: What are workers interested in?

10.6 MONOPSONY: MONOPOLY IN THE INPUT MARKET

Thus far we have assumed that the price of an input is determined by supply and demand in the resource market. The entrepreneur, whether a perfect competitor or a monopolist, believes he can acquire as many units of the input as he wants at the going market price. In other words no firm, acting alone, has a perceptible effect upon the price of the input. This obviously is not the case in all situations. There are sometimes only a few, and in the limit one, purchasers of a productive service. Clearly when only a few firms purchase an input, each will affect input price by changing input usage. We therefore need new tools to analyze the behavior of such firms.

For analytical simplicity we consider only a single buyer of an input, called a monopsonist. However, the analytical principles are the same when there are a few buyers of an input, called oligopsonists.

10.6.a—Marginal Expense of Input

The supply curve for most productive services or productive agents is positively sloped. Since a monopsonist is the sole buyer of a productive service, he faces this positively sloped market supply of input curve. In order to hire more of an input he must raise the price of that input. Each unit of input receives the same price. Therefore, in order to increase his usage of an input the monopsonist must pay *all* units an increased price. Thus he considers not simply the price of an additional unit of input but the *marginal expense* of purchasing additional units.

An example might clarify this point. Assume that a monopsonist can hire 20 units of labor at a wage of $2 an hour and 21 units at $3 an hour. With 20 units the total hourly wage bill is $40, with 21 units it is $63. Hiring the additional unit of labor costs an additional $23 per hour. The added unit costs $3; the increase of $1 per hour for the original 20 units costs $20, for a total of $23. When we consider the addition of one unit of an input, the addition to total cost is the *marginal expense of input*. It includes the price paid to the additional unit *plus* the increase that must be paid to the units already employed. Therefore, for every unit except the first, the marginal expense of input exceeds input price.

The supply curve of a variable input and the marginal expense of input

FIGURE 10.6.1

Marginal Expense of Input

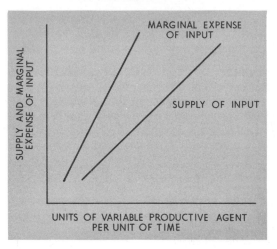

curve are shown graphically in Figure 10.6.1. Since the price per unit rises as employment increases, the marginal expense of input exceeds price at all employment levels; and the marginal expense of input curve is positively sloped, lies to the left of the supply curve, and typically rises more rapidly than the latter.

Definition: The marginal expense of input is the increase in total cost (and in total variable cost and in total cost of input) attributable to the addition of one unit of the variable productive agent.

10.6.b—Price and Employment under Monopsony

The market demand curve for a productive service is the demand curve of the single buyer under monopsony. If only one variable input is used in the production process, the demand curve is the value of the marginal product curve (if the firm is a perfect competitor in the commodity market) or the marginal revenue product curve (if it is a monopolist). Assume that the firm is a monopolist. The firm is confronted with a positively sloped supply of input curve and the higher marginal expense of input curve. The situation is illustrated in Figure 10.6.2. Using this graph we will prove the following:

Proposition: A profit-maximizing monopsonist will employ a variable productive service until the point is reached at which the marginal expense of input equals its marginal revenue product. The price of the input is determined by the corresponding point on its supply curve.

The proof of this proposition follows immediately from the definitions of marginal revenue product and marginal expense of input. Marginal revenue product is the addition to total revenue attributable to the addition of one unit of the variable input; the marginal expense of input is the addition to total cost resulting from the employment of an additional unit. Therefore, so long as marginal revenue product exceeds the marginal expense of input, profit can be augmented by expanding input usage. On the other hand, if the marginal expense of input exceeds its marginal revenue product, profit is less or loss greater than if fewer units of the input were employed. Consequently, profit is maximized by employing that quantity of the variable service for which the marginal expense of input equals marginal revenue product.

FIGURE 10.6.2

Price and Employment under Monopsony

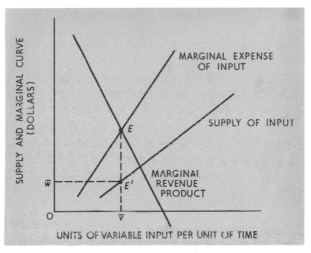

This equality occurs at point E in Figure 10.6.2, and $O\bar{v}$ units of the service are accordingly employed. At this point the supply of input curve becomes particularly relevant. $O\bar{v}$ units of the variable productive agent are associated with point E' on the supply of input curve. Thus $O\bar{v}$ units will be offered at $O\bar{w}$ per unit. Hence $O\bar{w}$ is the market equilibrium input price corresponding to market equilibrium employment $O\bar{v}$. If the monopsonist is a perfect competitor in the commodity market the situation is similar, except that the demand curve is the value of marginal product curve. It employs the variable input until the value of marginal product equals the marginal expense of input.

10.6.c—Monopsonistic Exploitation

In subsection 10.5.d it was shown that monopoly in the commodity market leads to monopolistic exploitation in the input market. Each productive service is paid its marginal revenue product, which is less than the value of its marginal product. Monopsonistic exploitation is something in addition to this, as illustrated by Figure 10.6.3. The monopsonist-monopolist depicted here hires Ov units of the variable input, because at this level $MEI = MRP$, at a price of Ow. Some monopolistic exploita-

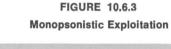

FIGURE 10.6.3

Monopsonistic Exploitation

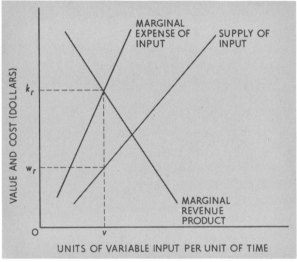

tion is involved since marginal revenue product is less than the value of the marginal product of Ov units. Some additional (monopsonistic) exploitation develops also since the variable input receives even less than its marginal revenue product. It receives Ow, and its marginal revenue product is Or, which in turn is less than the value of its marginal product.

10.7   ANALYTICAL EXERCISE: THE EFFECTS OF LABOR UNIONS

A study of labor unions and of the collective bargaining process, even on a purely theoretical level, is beyond the scope of this work. However, the issue of monopsonistic exploitation allows one briefly to indicate the economic effects of labor unions. Consider any typical labor market with some kind of supply of labor curve; for simplicity, assume that it is positively sloped. If the workers in this market are unionized, the union bargaining representative fundamentally has one power to exert: he can make the effective supply of labor curve a horizontal line at any wage level he wishes, at least until the horizontal line reaches the existing supply curve. Thus the marginal expense of input is the same as the supply price of labor over the horizontal stretch of the union supply curve. That is to say, the union representative can name a wage rate and guarantee the availability of workers at this price.

To introduce this topic, let us suppose the labor market in question is perfectly competitive (large number of purchasers of this type of labor) and unorganized. The situation is depicted in panel *a*, Figure 10.7.1,

FIGURE 10.7.1

Effects of a Labor Union in a Perfectly Competitive Labor Market

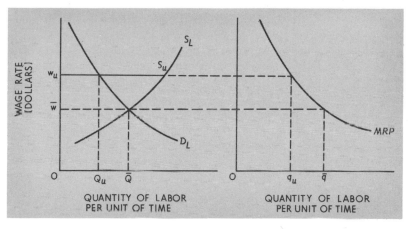

Panel *a*	Panel *b*
The Market	The Firm

where D_L and S_L are the demand for and supply of labor respectively. The market equilibrium wage rate is $O\bar{w}$ and $O\bar{Q}$ units of labor are employed. Each individual firm (panel *b*) accordingly employs $O\bar{q}$ units. Next, suppose the labor market is unionized. If the union does not attempt to raise wages the situation might remain as it is. However, securing wage increases is the *raison d'être* of unions. Thus suppose the bargaining agency sets Ow_u as the wage rate; in other words, the union supply of labor curve $w_u'S_uS_L$ is established. OQ_u units of labor are employed, each firm taking Oq_u units. The result is a rise in wages and a decline in employment. In perfectly competitive input markets this is *all* unions can do.

This does not necessarily mean a union cannot benefit its members. If the demand for labor is inelastic, an increase in the wage rate will result in an increase in total wages paid to the workers, even though the number of workers employed is less. If the union can somehow equitably divide the proceeds of OQ_u employed workers among the $O\overline{Q}$ potential workers, all will benefit. Such a division is easy to achieve. Suppose $OQ_u = \frac{1}{2} O\overline{Q}$ and that a 40-hour week characterizes the market. Then OQ_u units of labor can be furnished by having $O\overline{Q}$ units work a 20-hour week.

The other side of the coin is worth examining, however. If the demand for labor is elastic, total wage receipts will decline and the union cannot compensate the $Q_u\overline{Q}$ workers who are unemployed because of the increase in wage rates. Thus in perfectly competitive labor markets labor unions are not an unmitigated blessing.

In monopsonistic or oligopsonistic markets, however, unions may easily benefit their members if they employ rational policies. Consider the monopsony labor market represented by Figure 10.7.2. If the labor force is not organized, equilibrium is attained at point c, where marginal revenue product equals the marginal expense of input (based upon the positively sloped supply of input curve S_L). The equilibrium wage is $O\overline{w}$, and equilibrium employment is $O\overline{L}$. Now suppose the workers establish a union that bargains collectively with the monopsonist.

At one extreme the union may attempt to achieve maximum employment for its members. To this end, it establishes the supply of labor curve

FIGURE 10.7.2

Economic Effects of a Labor Union in a Monopsonistic Labor Market

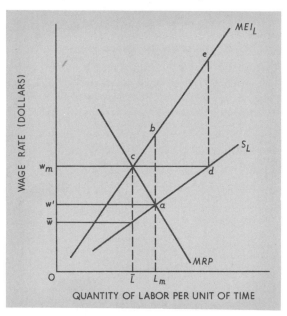

$w'aS_L$. The associated marginal expense of input curve accordingly becomes $w'abMEI_L$. Marginal revenue product equals the marginal expense of input at point a; OL_m units of labor are therefore employed at the wage Ow'. Consequently, as one alternative, the union can achieve a small increase in wages accompanied by an increase in the number of workers employed. Each unit of labor receives its contribution to the firm's total receipts; the exploitation uniquely attributable to monopsony is eliminated.

At another extreme, suppose the union decides to maintain the initial level of employment OL. It accordingly establishes the supply curve $w_m dS_L$. Marginal revenue product equals the marginal expense of input at point c; hence equilibrium employment is $\overline{OL}$ and the associated equilibrium wage is Ow_m. This wage rate is the maximum attainable without a reduction in employment below the preunion level. At the wage Ow_m, however, the union can achieve a substantial wage increase without affecting employment. Again, the unique portion of monopsonistic exploitation is removed.

We have considered only two extremes. The union can, in fact, select intermediate policies, scoring increases in both employment and the wage rate. The union can harm its members only if the demand for labor is elastic and it sets the supply of labor curve so that the equilibrium wage exceeds Ow_m. But even then the unique portion of monopsonistic exploitation would be eliminated. Thus we have a general principle that broadly describes the economic effects of labor unions: labor unions can eliminate the portion of total monopsonistic exploitation that is uniquely attributable to monopsony in the labor market; however, the portion attributable to monopoly can in no way be eliminated by trade union activity.

Question: Why would northern textile workers favor a minimum wage of $1.60 per hour when they are making more than $1.60 already? Why might some rational southern textile workers making less oppose this? (Hint: Northern textiles compete with southern textiles.)

QUESTIONS AND PROBLEMS

1. "A payment system based upon marginal productivity is a just system since everyone gets what he deserves." Comment.
2. Analyze some effects of a federal minimum wage. Do they differ from the effects of a state or local minimum wage?
3. From the point of view of a whole industry, the supply of a certain type of skilled labor may be scarce and, at the same time, of infinite elasticity from the point of view of each single firm within the industry. Explain.
4. You are attempting to get a labor union started in a firm. What conditions would make your job easier? What conditions would make it harder?

chapter 11

Welfare and Competition

11.1 INTRODUCTION

In Chapter 1 we emphasized two points that should be reiterated now. First, social welfare is the *dominate quiesitum* of economic theory. Second, the theory of general economic equilibrium is too mathematical to be treated at this level of study. Unfortunately, most of "welfare economics" depends upon general equilibrium theory and is, therefore, too mathematical as well.

Let us go another way around. We now have many pieces of something like a jigsaw puzzle. We have the principles of consumer behavior; we have the technological conditions determined by production functions, and we know how these conditions determine cost; we know how producers equate marginal cost with marginal revenue; and finally, we know how all this affects the factor markets. The question is: can all these pieces be fitted together to form a coherent picture?

The answer is yes if there is competition in all markets. Adam Smith explained this in a very heuristic manner when he talked about his doctrine of the "invisible hand." Each person, acting in his own self-interest, is led by the price system to act in a way that benefits the whole society. If we get much more rigorous than this, we are in the midst of the full mathematical complexities of general equilibrium theory.

In this chapter we cannot try to put the pieces together in a logical order. It can be done, but it can only be done in a more advanced course. But what we can try to do is to indicate why perfect competition can lead to maximum social welfare, and why it sometimes does not.

11.2 GENERAL EQUILIBRIUM

Before turning to welfare economics, a few words on general equilibrium are in order. We do this by means of a fanciful example, below, but first we must recount what *general* equilibrium means.

Given a set of commodity prices, consumers determine their demands by equating marginal rates of substitution with the corresponding commodity price ratios. Given a set of input prices, producers determine supply by equating the marginal rates of technical substitution with the corresponding input price ratios. Finally, workers determine the supply of labor by equating the marginal rate of substitution of income for leisure with the wage rate.[1] *The problem* of general equilibrium is as follows: can we find a set of prices at which the demands of consumers are voluntarily fulfilled by the supplies of producers who use all productive resources that are voluntarily supplied at the going set of prices? If so, a general equilibrium may exist.

Now to our fanciful example—a highly stylized account of the way in which a general equilibrium might in fact be obtained in a competitive economy. First, suppose that all commodities are, for all practical purposes, instantaneously producible. Next suppose that each morning, all consumers, producers, and resource suppliers in the economy meet in a large forum or marketplace. The society employs an auctioneer, who begins the business by shouting out a set of resource and commodity prices.

Given these prices, each consumer equates his *MRS's* with the price ratios and gives the auctioneer a list of his quantities demanded. Similarly, each producer equates his *MRTS's* with the input-price ratios, determines his cost, and consequently determines the profit-maximizing quantities he is willing to supply. These lists of quantities supplied also go to the auctioneer. Finally, resource suppliers determine the number of hours they are willing to work by equating the *MRS* of income for leisure with the announced wage rate. Each worker also notifies the auctioneer of his decision.

The auctioneer must now do four things: (*a*) he aggregates all consumers' lists of quantities demanded to determine the aggregate quantity demanded of each commodity at the announced set of prices; (*b*) he aggregates all producers' lists of quantities supplied to determine the aggregate quantity supplied of each commodity at the announced set of prices; (*c*) by reference to each firm's production function and then by aggregation, he determines the aggregate quantity of labor demanded at the announced set of prices; and (*d*) he aggregates the resource suppliers' lists of quantities of labor offered to determine the aggregate quantity of labor supplied at the announced set of prices.[2]

---

[1] Notice that all resources supplied except labor—which includes entrepreneurship, janitorial work, the services of a neurosurgeon, and so on—are *produced* resources and therefore fall in the second category. Agricultural land is an exception. It can easily be accommodated within the theory; but at this level of abstraction, it hardly seems necessary to do so.

[2] There is a fine point that we should mention, but upon which we need not dwell. Consumers are also resource suppliers. Thus their labor supply decision determines their expected income, which in turn helps to determine their demand for commodities.

The auctioneer now knows the aggregate quantities demanded and supplied of both commodities and resources. A general equilibrium will exist if, and only if, quantity demanded equals quantity supplied in *every* market, commodity and resource alike. Otherwise there will be an excess demand for some commodities and an excess supply of others; and there will either be an excess demand for or supply of labor resources. Thus, unless *every market* is in equilibrium (i.e., quantity demanded equals quantity supplied), every economic agent cannot be in equilibrium. Finally, there cannot be a general equilibrium unless each economic agent is in equilibrium, for otherwise some individual would take market action to change things.

At the first set of prices announced by the auctioneer, quantities demanded and supplied will doubtless not be equal in. all markets. The auctioneer must then announce a new set of prices, raising prices in those markets in which there is excess demand, lowering them when there is excess supply. After the second set of tentative prices becomes available, each consumer, producer, and resource supplier again gives the auctioneer a list of his quantities demanded or supplied. And again, market quantities demanded and supplied probably will not balance.

A third set of prices will be required, and this set also will probably not establish a general equilibrium. However, so long as bidding is competitive, the auctioneer can "zero in" on the general equilibrium set of prices because he has one sure guide to follow: raise price when there is excess demand, lower it when there is excess supply.[3]

As stated initially, this is a fanciful account of the process of attaining a general economic equilibrium—it is not even approximately descriptive of any real world market except the New York stock exchanges. However the account is indicative of the way in which competitive bids and counterbids in all markets push the economy *toward* a general equilibrium. Needless to say, it is never in fact attained. But there is a tendency toward it; and at times we can profitably analyze the situation that would exist if the general equilibrium existed. This is true for many problems; but it is perhaps most important in analyzing the social welfare results of various forms of market and economic organization.

11.3　SOCIAL WELFARE

11.3.a—The Difficult Concept of Social Welfare

The concept of social welfare is difficult either to define or to describe. This is largely because it encompasses so many conflicting interests. In

---

[3] Technically, the procedure just described is called a Walrasian *tatonnement* process.

a full-employment economy, with which we are exclusively concerned,[4] if one person gets more of some good or service, someone else must get less. What benefits one must hurt someone else if things are properly organized (more on this later). When one transfers this idea of conflicting interest to the aggregate level, there is the familiar trade-off between guns and butter, between potatoes and stereo tapes, and so forth. Some people prefer potatoes, some stereo tapes. When more of one of these commodities is produced, it is necessary to produce less of the other. Thus if more potatoes are produced, potato-lovers benefit and stereo-lovers suffer.

There is a similar type of consideration on the individual level. As a *consumer*, I benefit when I get more and you or someone else gets less. But as a *citizen*, the same may not be true. That is, overall I may feel better off if I give up some of my income or consumption so that others may consume somewhat more. Thus, for example, childless couples may vote in favor of school bond taxes; people contribute to the Salvation Army, the United Fund, and other agencies that redistribute income from better to less well-off families. This is just to say that each household is confronted with a choice that involves two different roles: as consumers, the more they have the better off they are; but as citizens, they may elect to forego some consumption in order to help others.

This too may be aggregated, as it were, to yield the national counterpart. As a nation of consumers, the more we consume the better off we are. Yet each year we give billions of dollars (and therefore consumption goods) in foreign aid to underdeveloped countries. Again we have two roles: a nation of consumers and a nation that is conscious of the wants of those who are less well off.

11.3.b—Pareto Optimality

For the reasons just given, and for related ones as well, it is virtually impossible accurately to define social welfare; and in particular, it is impossible to define *maximum* social welfare. Yet almost daily, a society must make decisions that affect its welfare: *should* we give foreign aid to underdeveloped countries? *should* we tax the consumption of tobacco, alcohol, gasoline, jewelry, and so on? *should* we give income to those households who cannot earn income? There are many such questions that confront a society. Most of them involve economic considerations, so surely economists must be able to say *something* about them.

Actually they can say very little. Economists cannot establish the goals of a society nor can they say what is "good" for one person or for a

---

[4] The effects of unemployment and the resulting underemployment equilibrium are usually treated in courses in macroeconomic theory.

collection of people. In general, economists can only determine the most efficient way by which to achieve a stipulated goal. Nonetheless, economists can make one prescriptive statement: if a change can be made such that one or more people are better off and *none* worse off, the society's welfare will be increased if the change is made. We must first define "better off":

Definition: A person is said to be better off in organization A than in organization B if he gets as much of every good and service and more of at least one good or service in A than he gets in B.

We can now turn to the concept introduced above, which is called "Pareto optimality," in honor of the Italian-Swiss economist Vilfredo Pareto. We may formulate it as a

Definition: A social organization is said to be Pareto optimal if there is no change that will benefit some people without making some others worse off.

Definition: A person is said to be worse off in organization A than in organization B if he has less of some good or service and no more of any good or service in A than he has in B.

This is admittedly a very weak concept of social welfare. To illustrate this, suppose a new transcontinental highway is to be constructed. This will benefit millions of travelers. But it also forces the government to condemn (under the right of eminent domain) the homesteads of a few families. These families, of course, are paid a "fair market price" for their property. However, some of the families may be unwilling to sell for a fair market price; yet they must by law, and they are made worse off. Millions may benefit and one be harmed. Economists qua economists cannot say that the new highway increases or decreases social welfare.

To summarize the implications of the concept of Pareto optimality:

Principles: (a) if there is a change that will benefit one or more people without making *anyone* worse off, the change is socially desirable; (b) if a change helps some and hurts others—the *numbers* are immaterial—no conclusion can be reached by an economist.

11.3.c—Perfect Competition and Pareto Optimality

While the concept of Pareto optimality is a weak one, it does establish some useful boundaries for the concept of social welfare and for the role of economists in making welfare recommendations. In this section we want to indicate why the following important proposition concerning Pareto optimality is true:

Proposition: Assume that there is perfect competition in every market. The set of input and output prices that establishes a general economic equilibrium will also establish a Pareto optimal organization of society.

Let us first consider consumers. If there is perfect competition, all consumers face the same set of commodity prices. Since each consuming unit sets *MRS* equal to the price ratio, the *MRS* of any one consumer is equal to the *MRS* of *any other* consuming unit. Since all consumers are just willing to exchange commodities in the same ratio, it is impossible to make one better off without making another worse off (i.e., suppose the *common MRS* of X for Y is 3:1. If someone is allowed to trade 2:1, someone else must be *forced* to trade at a ratio at which he would not voluntarily trade). Thus, a Pareto optimum is established.

Next consider producers. In maximizing profit, entrepreneurs necessarily arrange the combination of inputs so as to minimize the unit cost of production. Under perfect competition, the factor-price ratios are the same to all producers. Since each producer equates his *MRTS* to the common factor-price ratio, the *MRTS* is the same for all. Consequently, there is no reallocation of inputs that would increase one producer's output without reducing another's. Again we have a Pareto optimal organization.

Finally, in this competitive general equilibrium, the number of hours of work voluntarily offered is exactly equal to the number of hours voluntarily demanded. An increase in wages would help some, but some others would be unemployed. That is, an increase in wages would make some better off, some worse off. A decrease in wages would cause an excess demand. Thus a change in wages from the general equilibrium level will upset both Pareto optimality and general equilibrium.

11.4 PERFECT COMPETITION AND SOCIAL WELFARE: A FINAL VIEW

So far we have said that perfect competition will lead to a Pareto optimum, and this is the best economists can recommend. In certain cases, this is not even true. Either perfect competition may break down or the results of perfect competition are not the socially desirable ones. In concluding this book we shall treat these cases briefly, with one tremendous caveat. What we have to say is only an introductory statement. It requires one or more *courses* to treat this problem adequately.

11.4.a—Social Benefits and Social Cost

Let us suppose that commodity prices are given.[5] Each consumer, in order to maximize the satisfaction obtainable from a given money income,

---

[5] In the general equilibrium model, prices are variables whose optimizing values are determined within the model. For simplicity, but not of *necessity,* we assume prices are parameters.

sets his marginal rate of substitution between two goods equal to their price ratio. This process—as explained in Chapter 4—generates each consumer's demand curve for each commodity. Summing the individual commodity demand curves horizontally gives the market demand curve for each commodity.

An individual demand curve shows the *marginal valuation* the consumer attaches to the commodity in question. That is, the demand curve shows, at each point, just how much the consumer is willing to give up in order to obtain an additional unit of a good. Thus when summed to obtain market demand, the latter shows just how much the society is willing to give up to obtain one more unit of the commodity. Now since we are discussing demand curves, the amount society is willing to give up is expressed as a price in terms of money. But money represents a general command over all resources and, hence, over all other commodities. Consequently, at each point the market demand curve shows society's marginal valuation of the commodity in question in terms of the available resource base. This marginal valuation is called, at each point on the demand curve, the *marginal social benefit* of the commodity.

Our attention has so far been directed toward the consumer; let us now turn to the *perfectly competitive producer*. Given commodity price, the producer sets marginal cost equal to price in order to maximize profit. That is, the producer's *marginal private cost* (or supply price) is set equal to demand price, or marginal social benefit.

The implications should be clear. The resources society *is willing to sacrifice* in order to obtain an additional unit of the good precisely equal the amount of resources the producer must, by the given technology, use to produce an additional unit. Other things equal, resources are allocated optimally and society's well-being is maximized.[6]

Now we must deal with this "other things equal" business. We have just said that in competitive equilibrium, the additional resources a producer must use to produce an additional unit of a commodity is marginal cost. But the calculation involves *marginal private cost*. Let us now define

---

[6] This assumes that demand represents marginal social benefit, which in turn assumes that income is distributed in the way society wants it distributed. This may or may not be the case. In an economy characterized by perfect competition, each person receives the value of his marginal product, i.e., he receives what he contributes to the total social output. For various reasons, some people are much more productive than others; they consequently receive much more and contribute much more to the formation of market demand. Further, there are "inheritances" or "endowments" of resources that some people receive through no effort of their own. These people also help form demand.

If the ethic of a society is such that the competitive distribution of income is regarded as desirable, demand does represent marginal social benefit. It would certainly not in a *pure* communist society in which the ethic is "from each according to his abilities, to each according to his needs."

marginal social cost as the minimum resource sacrifice that society as a whole must make in order to obtain an extra unit of a commodity. Then if marginal private cost equals marginal social cost, resources are indeed allocated optimally.

In this case the competitive pricing mechanism is Adam Smith's "invisible hand." Each consumer simply tries to maximize his satisfaction without regard to the entire society. Similarly, each producer attempts to maximize profit, taking no account of the way in which his actions affect the economy. But the competitive price system leads each person, acting in his own self-interest, to a course of action that benefits society as a whole. Social welfare is maximized (subject to the qualification in footnote 6), and no change can improve the society's well-being.

11.4.b—External Economies and the Market Mechanism

In many cases, perhaps in most, there is no reason to expect a divergence between marginal private cost and marginal social cost. In his own self-interest, the producer uses the *minimum* amount of resources technologically required for his output. So, it would seem, marginal private cost is always equal to marginal social cost. There are three situations, however, in which the competitive market mechanism breaks down.

11.4.c—Technological Difficulties

The first way in which the competitive market mechanism may break down is by a breakdown in competition itself. Let us suppose there exists a commodity whose production function shows continuously increasing returns to scale. Further suppose that factor prices are constant or that they do not rise fast enough to offset increasing returns to scale. In this situation, the long-run average cost curve is not U-shaped—it is a continuously declining curve.

Suppose such a market is initially organized competitively and has somehow attained a temporary equilibrium. Each firm has an incentive to expand output because: (*a*) average cost declines as output expands, and (*b*) each perfect competitor expects his actions to go unnoticed by his rivals. Thus *each* competitor expects to reduce average cost and expand output tremendously (believing all other producers will continue their previous price-output policy).

But what one producer has an incentive to do, all have an incentive to do, and as industry output expands, the industry "slides down" the negatively sloped market demand curve. As this sliding down continues, a point will be reached at which price is less than average cost. Then all firms make losses, and some firms will leave the industry. But so long as the entrepreneur believes *his* demand curve is a horizontal line he has an incentive to expand output so as to reduce average cost; and of course he believes that if he expands enough, he will eliminate his losses.

Again, however, *all* entrepreneurs have the same incentive; and as industry output expands, losses increase. More firms leave the industry. This must continue until the number of firms is so small that each recognizes that its actions *do affect* market price.

The ultimate organization of the market is uncertain. According to Zeuthen, "economic warfare" may result, with all but one firm finally eliminated from the market. In this case, monopoly emerges. On the other hand, the last few entrepreneurs left in the market may decide upon the quiet life of collusive oligopoly. As in the Chamberlin model, they decide to "live and let live" and divide the monopoly profit among themselves. In either case, perfect competition breaks down. Marginal cost is set equal to marginal revenue rather than price.

Thus even if marginal private cost equals marginal social cost, the latter is less than marginal social benefit. At the price where marginal revenue equals marginal cost, society is willing to sacrifice more resources to gain an additional unit of the good than is socially necessary (price is greater than marginal social cost). The monopolist or oligopolist, however, will not use these resources because to do so would reduce their profit.

This is the result that always comes about under monopoly or oligopoly. There is an "underproduction" of the commodity in the sense that society is willing to give up more resources than necessary to expand output. But output is restricted to preserve the monopoly profit.

Principle: If there are constantly increasing returns to scale, competition will break down; and the market price mechanism will not allocate resources optimally (i.e., the price mechanism will not allocate enough resources to the monopolized sectors).

11.4.d—Ownership Externalities

The second reason why perfect competition may not lead to optimal resource allocation is called ownership externaltities. To get at this we must begin with two definitions. An *external economy* is said to exist when marginal social cost is less than marginal private cost. Thus when marginal private cost equals marginal social benefit, marginal social cost is less than marginal social benefit. More resources *should* be allocated to producing the commodity in question, but they are not. On the other hand, an *external diseconomy* exists when marginal social cost exceeds marginal private cost. At such a point, marginal social benefit is less than marginal social cost. An undesirably large amount of resources is allocated to producing the commodity in question.

Definitions: An external economy (diseconomy) exists where marginal social cost is less than (greater than) marginal private cost.

At this stage it is quite reasonable to ask *how* marginal private cost and marginal social cost can diverge. One of the chief answers is "by the existence of ownership externalities." Briefly, this means that there is some scarce resource owned by a person but for some reason, the owner cannot charge a price for the use of this resource. And when prices cannot be charged, misallocation of resources results.

Our discussion to this point must seem murky indeed. From here on we proceed by use of examples, the first of which is the classic example of an ownership externality. Suppose an apple orchardist and a beekeeper are situated side by side. The production of apples, we shall assume, requires labor only. The production of honey, on the other hand, requires the labor of the beekeeper *and* apple blossoms to provide the bees with the nectar used to make honey.[7]

Now put yourself in the position of the apple orchardist. Suppose apple production is perfectly competitive; you determine output so as to make your marginal private cost (labor cost, in this case) equal to price. Apple blossoms are a by-product you own; but you cannot keep the bees out of your orchard and you cannot charge the beekeeper for the nectar taken from the blossoms. Thus, the marginal private cost of expanding apple production is the cost of the additional labor necessary to expand production.

Let us now reverse our position and look at the problem from the point of view of society as a whole. Expanding apple production does indeed cost some labor resources that could be used elsewhere. But expanding apple production also means increased apple blossoms and the nectar they contain. Thus an expansion of apple production is accompanied by an expansion of honey production; and honey is a "good" in the sense that it has a positive price.

Let us recapitulate. To the apple orchardist, expanding production entails the marginal cost of the labor involved. To society it does so as well; but society, without further use of resources, gets more honey as a result. Thus the marginal social cost of expanding apple production is the marginal private cost *minus* the value of the additional honey produced. Clearly, society would be better off if more resources were allocated to apple production. But the apple orchardist, looking at competitive prices and his marginal private cost, would never expand production to the socially optimal point.

In this case of ownership externality there is a simple solution, if it can be brought about. Let the apple orchardist buy the beekeeper's business.

---

[7] In this example, we abstract from the cross-pollenization service provided by the bees.

This "internalizes" the externality in the sense that the orchardist-bee-keeper makes the same cost calculation as society does. The owner of this joint enterprise recognizes that an increase in apple production means more blossoms, more nectar, and more honey that *he* can sell in the market. That is, the internal cost accounting of the combined orchardist-beekeeper alerts him to the fact that the marginal cost to his joint enterprise of additional apple production is less than the direct cost attributed to the apple part of his business. Thus a solution to this type of externality problem can be achieved by integrating the firms involved.

Unfortunately, other types of ownership externalities are not so easily resolved; and more unfortunately still, these types are by far the most important. We begin with a rather trivial example and then consider some of the most important problems confronting the American economy today.

Suppose there is a woman who supports herself and her children by doing hand laundry. Being poor she cannot afford an automatic dryer. Consequently, she must hang the clothes in her yard to dry. But a factory is situated alongside; and its smokestack belches forth soot that dirties the freshly washed clothes. The woman must wash again.

This problem is almost insoluble. The factory creates an external dis-economy because the marginal social cost of smoke disposal exceeds the marginal private cost. The factory owner has no interest in buying the hand laundry because he would be confronted with the smoke problem. The trouble lies in the fact that the air space above the woman's yard is a scarce resource; but she cannot build the equivalent of the Astrodome and charge admission to each bit of soot. She owns a scarce resource, but she cannot charge for its use; hence the factory uses it to her deteriment.

The simple example above suggests some situations of much more far-reaching importance. The marginal private cost of dumping industrial waste into a river is very small. The marginal social cost is much greater because of the resources required to eliminate the consequent water pollution. No one "owns" rivers, only the land adjacent to them. Thus in the absence of government action, there is no one to set a price on this scarce resource. With a zero price attached to using rivers and lakes for waste disposal, we face an ever increasing problem of water pollution.

Exactly the same reasoning applies to air pollution. The marginal private cost of disposing of industrial smoke and automobile exhausts is negligible. But when there are many factories and many cars in the same location, the result is smog and air pollution. Again, the cost to society far exceeds the marginal private cost of smoke disposal; and there is no automatic corrective device built into the competitive market mechanism. Some type of external control is necessary if the externality problem is to be solved.

As a final example of this type of externality, let us consider the problem of airport congestion and the ensuing delays in passenger traffic. To an airport authority, the marginal private cost of landing a private plane is much less than the marginal private cost of landing a commercial jet. The control tower time is less, the instrument usage is less, and the impact stress on the concrete is much less. As a consequence, airport authorities charge a landing fee for private planes that is only a fraction of the landing fee paid by commercial aircraft. In a small airport that has but few commercial flights per day, this is a reasonable practice. It is merely price discrimination based upon different price elasticities. With few commercial flights, there is no reason to believe that private aircraft traffic will delay commercial passenger service. Hence marginal private and marginal social cost probably do not diverge.

In large, busy airports—such as Chicago, Atlanta, Washington, and New York—the situation is entirely different. Handling private air traffic causes a significant delay in commercial flights. This does not cost the airport authority or the owners of private aircraft. But it does cost the commercial airlines and the passengers. It costs the airlines mainly in fuel burned in holding patterns and in waiting on runways. It costs the passengers in the inconvenience of delay and the money value of the time wasted. Marginal social cost accordingly exceeds marginal private cost. From society's point of view, too much air space is used by private airplanes because air space is a scarce commodity (resource) that bears a zero price.

11.4.e—Public Good Externalities

The final case to be discussed here is that of public good externalities. This is much more complicated than the other two situations in which there is a breakdown of the market machanism. One of the main reasons for this is that the experts in the areas of public goods and public choice cannot decide upon the exact definition of a public good. We provide a brief discussion only for the purpose of indicating that a problem exists. Any further analysis must be left to courses in public finance.[8]

For our purposes, we shall define a *public good* as one whose consumption by individual A does not preclude its consumption by individuals B, C, D, and so on. An apple is a private good. If I consume an apple, you cannot consume the same one. Good examples of public goods are open-air concerts and pyrotechnic displays. Within very broad limits, as many people as desire can "consume" the concert or the fireworks. Up to a very limited point, the same applies to public schools, libraries, and

---

[8] There is a good justification for this slight treatment. This is a course in market decision making, i.e., how consumers, producers and resource owners react to the signals given by market-determined prices. The case of public goods typically involves nonmarket decision making, as do some other problems treated by economists.

so on. In the latter cases a "capacity ceiling" is reached much more quickly.

The problems presented by this situation can only be sketched in a heuristic manner. A minor problem first: In many cases of public goods, it is difficult, if not impossible, to *exclude* people who are unwilling to pay a positive price for the good. In this case, private enterprise would never supply the good. Thus let us suppose that the production of a true public good is organized by a perfectly competitive industry and that exclusion of people unwilling to pay a positive price *is* possible.

If the industry is organized competitively, factor prices and the production function will determine marginal cost for each firm. These marginal cost curves establish the industry supply curve. There is a demand curve for the public good; and the intersection of supply and demand determines a competitive market price. Each firm then equates marginal cost with market price to maximize profit.

Consumers take this price as given and adjust their purchases accordingly. Let *a* be the *public* good *privately* supplied, and let *b*, *c*, *d*, and so on be private goods privately supplied. Each consumer arranges his purchases so that the marginal utility per dollar spent on each commodity is the same. Let MU_i be the marginal utility of commodity i and p_i be its price. Using this notation, each consumer arranges his budget so that

$$\frac{MU_a}{p_a} = \frac{MU_b}{p_b} = \frac{MU_i}{p_i} = \frac{MU_d}{p_d}, \text{ etc.}$$

Now for every consumer, the marginal utility of a dollar's worth of various other commodities is so low that he does not elect to purchase them.

This presents no problem so far as private goods are concerned. If a consumer decides not to purchase a private good, less of the good is produced and fewer of society's resources are used to produce it. The same, however, does not apply to public goods.

For many consumers the marginal utility of a dollar's worth of *a*, the public good, will be so low that he will not purchase it at a competitively determined price. That is,

$$\frac{MU_a}{p_a} < \frac{MU_b}{p_b} = \frac{MU_c}{p_c}, \text{ etc.}$$

The consumer does not choose to purchase the public good at the competitive price, even though he would at lower prices (in the limit, a zero price). In this case, however, when a consumer elects not to consume the good, *none of society's resources are saved* because, by definition, a public good is one that may be consumed in the same amount by all consumers.

Herein lies the problem. Regardless of the total consumption of the public good, the same amount of society's resources must be used to produce it.[9] Now it is reasonable to assume that for consumers who elect not to purchase the public good, the marginal utility of the good is not zero. That is, even though

$$\frac{MU_a}{p_a} < \frac{MU_b}{p_b} = \frac{MU_c}{p_c} \text{, etc.}$$

$MU_a \neq 0$. Thus if a zero price were charged these consumers, they would consume the public good. They would be better off, and no one would be worse off because no more of society's resources are used when they consume it.

Principle: If the production of a public good is in the hands of private enterprise, social welfare is less than it would otherwise be because some consumers are excluded from the market when price is greater than zero. Since their consumption of the good is "free" to society in the sense that it entails no further resource sacrifice, society as a whole would be better off if these people were allowed to consume the good at zero price; but under free enterprise, they are not.

This is not an indictment of the free enterprise system. It is merely a recognition of the fact that there are some goods that are not optimally consumed when price is set by the competitive market mechanism.

11.5   CONCLUSION

In most cases perfect competition, by means of the price mechanism or Smith's "invisible hand," leads to the optimal allocation of resources. In a few instances it does not; and in this section we have merely listed these "perverse" cases. It is impossible to determine empirically how important they are. About the best one can say is that in any economic society there is some role for governmental economic controls; *but* the government's role should be limited to markets where the price mechanism does not allocate resources efficiently. In particular, it should not extend to arbitrary controls over markets where demand and supply is an efficient allocative device. This may seem to be a weak conclusion for an entire textbook. In fact, it is not. The function of microeconomic theory is to determine the relative efficiency of various types of market organization. The chief conclusion is that perfect competition is, in general, optimal. The purpose of this last section is simply to show that there are some situations, whose importance cannot be determined, in which this conclusion may not hold. Generally, however, competitively determined prices in competitive markets allocate resources in something like an optimal way.

---

[9] By this we mean that if a public good is produced in a competitive market, demand and supply will determine the equilibrium output. But that output could be consumed by many more people without sacrificing more resources.

Index

*This book has been set in 10 and 9 point Cale-
donia, leaded 2 points. Chapter numbers are
in 18 and 24 point Helvetica and chapter
titles are in 18 point Helvetica Medium. The
size of the type page is 27 by 46 picas.*